THEOLOGY FOR THE

CENTER OF THE

Theology for the 21st Century is a series sponsored by the Center of Theological Inquiry (CTI), an institute, located in Princeton, New Jersey, dedicated to the advanced study of theology. This series is one of its many initiatives and projects.

The goal of the series is to publish inquiries of contemporary scholars into the nature of the Christian faith and its witness and practice in church, society, and culture. The series will include investigations into the uniqueness of the Christian faith. But it will also offer studies that relate the Christian faith to the major cultural, social, and practical issues of our time.

Monographs and symposia will result from research by scholars in residence at the Center of Theological Inquiry or otherwise associated with it. In some cases, publications will come from group research projects sponsored by CTI. It is our intention that the books selected for this series will constitute a major contribution to renewing theology in its service to church and society.

WILLIAM E. STORRAR
DIRECTOR, CENTER OF THEOLOGICAL INQUIRY

WALLACE M. ALSTON, JR., ROBERT JENSON,
AND DON S. BROWNING
SERIES EDITORS

What Dare We Hope?
By Gerhard Sauter

The End of the World and the Ends of God
Edited by John Polkinghorne and Michael Welker

In Search of the Common Good
Edited by Patrick Miller and Dennis McCann

God and Globalization, 4 vols.
By Max L. Stackhouse et al.

GOD AND GLOBALIZATION:
THEOLOGICAL ETHICS AND THE SPHERES OF LIFE

MAX L. STACKHOUSE, GENERAL EDITOR
WITH PETER J. PARIS, DON S. BROWNING,
AND DIANE B. OBENCHAIN

Sponsored by
The Center of Theological Inquiry
Princeton, N.J.
1999–2001

The world is presently going through a monumental social, political, and economic shift that has implications for faith, ethics, human understanding and social well -being. It is clear that the categories of analysis by which most of us have understood the social worlds around us are at least partially obsolete. How are we to understand the new, complex global civilization toward which we are being thrust? What are the ways that religion, theology and ethics, in close interaction with our social, political, and economic situation can help guide globalization?

The contributors to the first three volumes have sorted the "powers," those "principalities," "authorities" and "dominions" that are shaping the multiple spheres of life in our world and have proposed creative new perspectives on the massive range of pertinent issues that lie at the intersection of religion and globalization. They provide insight into ethics, religion, economics, and culture that will interest not only theologians, ethicists, and clergy of many traditions but also academics, social scientists, professionals, and those engaged in business and technology who seek to understand the move toward a global civilization from a social and ethical point of view. This last interpretive volume, written by the general editor of the previous contributions, argues for a view of Christian theology that, in critical dialogue with other world religions and philosophies, is able to engage the new world situation, play a critical role in reforming the "powers" that are becoming more diverse and autonomous, and generate a social ethic for the twenty-first century.

GOD AND GLOBALIZATION:
THEOLOGICAL ETHICS AND THE SPHERES OF LIFE

Vol. 1: *Religion and the Powers of the Common Life*
Edited by Max L. Stackhouse with Peter J. Paris

Vol. 2: *The Spirit and the Modern Authorities*
Edited by Max L. Stackhouse with Don S. Browning

Vol. 3: *Christ and the Dominions of Civilization*
Edited by Max L. Stackhouse with Diane B. Obenchain

Vol. 4: *Globalization and Grace:*
A Christian Public Theology for a Global Future
By Max L. Stackhouse with a Foreword by Justo González

God *and* Globalization

VOLUME 4

GLOBALIZATION
AND
GRACE

Max L. Stackhouse

with a Foreword by
Justo González

continuum

NEW YORK • LONDON

2007

The Continuum International Publishing Group Inc
80 Maiden Lane, New York, NY 10038

The Continuum International Publishing Group Ltd
The Tower Building, 11 York Road, London SE1 7NX

www.continuumbooks.com

Printed in the United States of America

Continuum is a member of Green Press Initiative, a nonprofit program dedicated
to supporting publishers in their efforts to reduce their use of fiber obtained from
endangered forests. We have elected to print this title on 50% postconsumer waste
recycled paper. For more information, go to www.greenpressinitiative.org.

Library of Congress Cataloging-in-Publication Data

God and globalization : religion and the powers of the common life / edited by
    Max L. Stackhouse with Peter Paris.
        p.   cm. - (Theology for the twenty-first century)
    Includes bibliographical references and index.
    ISBN 1-56338-311-X
    1. Christian ethics. 2. Globalization – Moral and ethical aspects.
3. Globalization – Religious aspects – Christianity. I. Stackhouse, Max L.
II. Paris, Peter J., 1933. III. Series.

BJ1275.G63 2000
261.8 – dc21
                                                                          00-020203

Volume 4: Globalization and Grace – ISBN 978-0-8264-2885-1

Dedicated to my students
at Princeton Theological Seminary during the last dozen years —
a wonderfully wide-seeing, wide-reaching collection
of talented commitment and dedication,
studying to serve the churches of Christ
and the peoples of the world —
they tolerated my explorations
into globalization with grace.

CONTENTS

Acknowledgments

My thanks to:

The United Theological College, Bangalore, India; The Divinity School, Silliman University, the Philippines; The Pacific Theological College, Fiji; The Atlantic School of Theology, Canada; The Smithsonian Institution, Washington, DC; The Philosophical Faculty, Peking University, Beijing; The Presbyterian College and Seminary and Ewah University, Korea; The Theological Faculty, University of Melbourne, Australia; the University of the Western Cape, South Africa; Madras Christian College, India; The Theological Faculty, University of Heidelberg, Germany; The Theological Faculty, University of Edinburgh; Eastern Theological College, Jorhat, Assam, India; The Center for the Study of Christianity, Zhejiang University, Hangzhou, China; Hong Kong Baptist University; Charles University, Prague, The Czech Republic; Debrecen University, Hungary; Stellenbosch University, South Africa; Trinity College University, Dublin; and the Taiwan Theological College and Seminary. These institutions and innumerable personal friends and generous scholars hosted me, informed me of the dominant views in their contexts, and invited me to lecture, debate and try out new perspectives as I developed this project and my theological approach to globalization. And special thanks to Renemsongla Ozukum of Northeast India, who helped me bring my draft manuscript into readable form, and to Frank Oveis, senior editor, and John Eagleson, copyeditor for Continuum, for bringing the draft into publishable form. None of my hosts and conversation partners are responsible for any misleading interpretations I may have given their insights and contributions.

MLS
November 2006

FOREWORD

It is now eight and a half years since a group of twenty scholars met at Princeton's Center of Theological Inquiry for the first of a series of conversations on "God and Globalization." The group included noted specialists in such fields as economics, anthropology, missiology, psychology, philosophy, world religions, and Christian theology. As we met, I wondered why I had been invited into the conversation. As a historian, I have worked mostly on the events that were shaping the Graeco-Roman world eighteen centuries ago, and on their aftermath in succeeding centuries. This group was analyzing what is taking place in our time, and trying to discern what it may mean for the future of humankind and of religion. They were discussing the complex issues of economic development as they play out in today's world; they were experts on the various cultures and religious traditions mingling and clashing today; they were wondering about the church's mission in the new global society of the twenty-first century. I listened to the conversation as an interested human being whose lot it is to live in this global society, but I wondered what my contribution could be to the conversation we were launching.

We were dealing with the radically new phenomenon of globalization. Certainly, history does not repeat itself, and we would err were we to believe that what took place in the first centuries of the Common Era will tell us what will happen in its twenty-first century. We must certainly avoid the common error of thinking that the first centuries of church history were an idyllic time, and that were we simply to repeat what was done then all would be well. The church of the New Testament and of the patristic age was as divided in its views about the world and society as we are. They had personality, institutional, and theological conflicts just as we do. Any guidance they could give us would be as dubious and ambivalent as there are different responses today to the challenges confronting us. Thus, a simplistic look at the history of the church would not be of much use for us today.

On the other hand, I have long been convinced that history is not merely about the past. There are patterns in history — otherwise, we would have no means whereby to discern the future, or the consequences of our present actions. What reason would I have to expect the sun to rise in the east tomorrow morning, except that it has a long history of doing so? Every sunrise is different. I cannot and should not expect tomorrow's sunrise to be exactly like today's. But today's and yesterday's sunrises do give me a glimpse as to what to expect tomorrow and how to prepare for it.

History is not just a matter of antiquarian curiosity — of collecting data for the sake of the collection itself. History is read and written from the present, and out of the future for which one hopes or which one fears. And history is also read and written as an attempt to bring the past to bear on the present and on the future. Thus, the field itself of church history as it is written today shows the impact of the globalization our group was discussing. The books on general church history that I studied half a century ago were written from a perspective in which the North Atlantic represented the final and best form of Christianity. Now church history must be written differently, not because the past has changed, but because we are looking at it from the perspective of a church whose centers of strength and vitality are no longer confined to the North Atlantic.

As we ask different questions of history, it provides different answers. When in the nineteenth century it became fashionable for European aristocrats to conduct archaeological digs in Egypt, they excavated palaces, royal tombs, and magnificent temples. They were trying to discover what life in ancient Egypt was like, but what they were actually studying was the lives of those who in that ancient society held positions similar to theirs. Thus they carted away sand and rubble from ancient palaces, and dumped it on the most convenient place. Today, archaeologists seeking to understand the daily life of ancient Egyptians often have to begin by carting away all the debris that earlier archaeologists piled on the remains of the villages where the people lived who built the palaces and temples. Ancient Egypt itself has not changed. What has changed is the sort of question posed to its remains. And that change reflects a change among the archaeologists themselves — their social class, their understanding of society, etc.

Thus, for me as a historian our conversation about today's globalization has implied an ongoing circle of interpretation that leads from today's globalization to a reinterpretation of the history of the church, then from that reinterpretation of the past to a reinterpretation of the future, then back to the present, and so on in an endless but fruitful circulation.

As I now reflect on our conversation of the past eight years, I am ever more convinced that no other time in Western history illustrates processes similar to today's globalization better than the founding of Greco-Roman civilization in the four centuries immediately before, and the four centuries immediately after, the advent of Christianity. Clearly, what was happening then was not exactly the same as today's globalization. For one thing, it was not truly "global," for it involved only a relatively small area of the world around the Mediterranean basin. Nor did it involve the means of communication of today's globalization — means that are unprecedented both in their scope, as mass media, and in their speed, as through the Internet. And it did not involve the ecological perils of the present process — perils that make today's globalization a matter of enormous consequences not only for human life, but for all life on the planet. Yet, even while acknowledging those differences, there is a sense in which one may interpret first the Hellenization, then the Romanization, and finally the Christianization of the Mediterranean basin as a sort of globalization. It is in this sense that the history of those times may illumine some aspects of our present history.

To review that earlier history in a few words, it suffices to remember that late in the fourth century B.C.E., Alexander the Great had launched his vast campaign of military conquest. As is the case with every imperialist enterprise, his had an ideological justification: to bring the advancements and the benefits of Greek culture to the rest of the world. In this he succeeded to an amazing degree. Three centuries after his death, Greek was still spoken over vast reaches of his former empire. Even in Egypt, with its millennial civilization, those who spoke Greek and who followed Greek social customs were considered superior to those who spoke Coptic and followed the ancient Egyptian traditions. This process of "globalization" did not stop as the various Hellenistic kingdoms founded by Alexander's successors disappeared. Rome came to take their place, building an empire largely on the remains of the Hellenistic kingdoms, and on the foundation of the measure of cultural unity brought about by Alexander's conquests.

Thus, to reflect on that earlier "globalization," on the way it was seen by various participants, and on the role of Christianity within it may help us understand more clearly some of the issues facing us as we enter the global world of the third millennium. How is this process to be evaluated? How does it affect people's lives and allegiances? How are we to look at the development of Christianity within our own historical context?

The first three volumes in this series on "God and Globalization," as well as the volume with which Dr. Stackhouse now brings the project to completion, make it clear first of all that globalization is not a simple matter. In those volumes, and particularly in this one to which I am now honored to write a foreword, it is clear that there are different and contrasting ways to define, to explain, and to evaluate globalization. Indeed, Dr. Stackhouse and our other colleagues have given us a carefully nuanced view of the present globalization, avoiding oversimplifications that would reduce globalization, for instance, to an economic or a political phenomenon, or that would simply condemn it outright as a process of worldwide impoverishment, or would bless it as humankind's greatest hope.

In the early centuries of the Christian era, evaluations of the globalization that was then taking place were similarly complex and contradictory. Some were quite positive. One of many that could be mentioned dates from the year 143 C.E. — or the year 896, counting from the foundation of Rome. The great capital city of the world was celebrating the anniversary of its founding. At the Atheneum, a young man from Smyrna — Aelius Aristides was his name — spoke of the glories and benefits of Roman rule:

> Praise of your city all men sing and will continue to sing. Yet their words accomplish less than if they had never been spoken. Their silence would not have magnified or diminished her in the least, nor changed your knowledge of her. But their encomiums accomplish quite the opposite of what they intend, for their words do not show precisely what is truly admirable....
>
> You have everywhere appointed to your citizenship, or even to kinship with you, the better part of the world's talent, courage, and leadership, while the rest you recognized as a league under your hegemony.... And as the sea, which

receives from its gulfs many rivers,...so actually this city
receives those who flow in from all the earth....

Thus like an ever-burning sacred fire the celebration never
ends, but moves around from time to time and people to
people, always somewhere, a demonstration justified by the
way all men have fared. Thus it is right to pity those outside
your hegemony, if indeed there are any, because they lose such
blessings.[1]

In this judgment, Aelius Aristides was not alone. Indeed, later
historians such as the noted Edward Gibbon have wholeheartedly
agreed with him:

If a man were called to fix the period in the history of the
world, during which the condition of the human race was
most happy and prosperous, he would, without hesitation,
name that which elapsed from the death of Domitian to the
accession of Commodus. The vast extent of the Roman Empire was governed by absolute power, under the guidance of
virtue and wisdom.[2]

Yet, not all whose lot it was to live in those supposedly blessed
times had the same positive feelings toward Rome and her rule.
Toward the end of the reign of Domitian, just as Gibbon's "happy
times" were being inaugurated, an exile on the isle of Patmos of
whom little is known — except that his name was John, and that he
was a Christian — depicted Rome as a harlot seated on seven hills
and drunk on the blood of the martyrs. To John, the Roman legions
were like a "beast from the sea," and those who served Roman rule
in his native Asia Minor were the "beast from the land," serving the
beast from the sea. (One may well imagine that John would have
said that Aelius Aristides, a man hailing from Smyrna and rejoicing
that Rome had included among its collaborators in its way to empire, represented precisely what John meant by the "beast from the
land.") And, lest we think that this was the case during the reign of
Domitian, but conditions eased thereafter, we should be reminded
that Eusebius tells repeated stories of persecution during the reign

---

1. *Roman oration*, 4.6, 59, 62, 99. Translated by J. H. Oliver, *The Ruling Power:
A Study of the Roman Empire in the Second Century Thorugh the Roman Oration of
Aelius Aristides* (Philadelphia: The American Philosophical Society, 1953), 895–907.

2. *The History of the Decline and Fall of the Roman Empire*, 2nd ed. (New
York: Harper & Brothers, 1850), 1:95.

of the same Antonines whose government Gibbon so praises — in particular, Marcus Aurelius, in many other ways one of the wisest of ancient Roman emperors.

No matter how widespread were the benefits of a common civilization, there were those who were excluded from them. Some, like the Christians whom Domitian and others persecuted, were excluded because the globalizing powers saw them as subversive. In the particular case of Christians, their staunch monotheism stood in the way of Rome's policy of bringing people together by intermingling their gods and religions. The resistance of Jews is well known — first, resistance against Hellenism in the Maccabean rebellion, then resistance against Rome in a long sequence of revolts leading to hundreds of crucifixions in Galilee, to the revolt of 66 C.E. that Titus crushed in 70 C.E., and finally to the rebellion of Bar Kochba. In Egypt, there were similar rebellions in 152 and 172–73 C.E.

Others were excluded simply because they lived in areas that the new cosmopolitan civilization considered marginal. The very word, to "civilize," meant to "citify." Both Rome and its Hellenistic forerunners were convinced that the greatest of human inventions was the city, and set out to build and improve cities throughout the Mediterranean basin, thus bringing the benefits of city life to countless thousands — much as many today seek to take the benefits of democracy and capitalism to countless millions. In North Africa, the Berbers were never quite assimilated into the Roman Empire, mostly because they refused to give up their traditional ways of live. The very ideology of "citification" marginalized rural areas and those who lived in them. The produce of land formerly devoted mostly to feeding the local small farmers was now diverted to cities. In an ever increasing degree, what was to be planted was not determined by the needs of those living on the land, but rather by the needs and the interests of those living in cities. In Asia Minor, for instance, land formerly devoted to cereals was now diverted to producing wine and olive oil, with the result that the price of wheat rose by 1,200 percent, and the price of barley by 800 percent. When Emperor Domitian sought to put a stop to the process by limiting the acreage used in vineyards and olive groves, the protest of rich landowners was such that his edict was rescinded. It is as a protest against such conditions that a voice in the book of Revelation cries out: "A quart of wheat for a day's pay, and three quarts of barley for a day's pay, but do not damage the oil and the wine!" (Rev. 6:6). Something similar was happening in Egypt, where entire rural villages disappeared as their inhabitants either moved to the cities — even though this was repeatedly forbidden by law — or fled to uninhabited areas, there to live as small farmers, as brigands, or as monks — for in the early years of Egyptian monasticism there was little difference between a fugitive and a monk.

Yet negative feelings about the process that today we would call "globalization" did not come only from those who were marginalized, but also from many who were at the very centers of power and influence. In this regard, the life and opinions of Tacitus are illustrative. Apparently, his family was not of Roman origin, but had come from Cisalpine Gaul, and had received Roman citizenship as part of the process whereby Rome progressively expanded such citizenship to people from neighboring areas. Nevertheless, Tacitus became a man of wealth and influence, to the point that by the year 97 C.E. he attained the consulship. Thus, he had profited from Rome's "globalizing" influences both by being allowed to become part of the Roman aristocracy and by then receiving much of the wealth that flowed from the provinces to the capital. Yet, when he later wrote his memoirs he complained about the manner in which that globalization itself was having an impact on Rome, which to him was a "cesspool for all that is sordid and degrading from all over the world."[3] Tacitus could rejoice in the manner in which Roman power had expanded throughout the world, but he bemoaned the impact that this was having on Rome itself, as the rest of the world came to the capital city. (At this point it would be interesting to draw comparisons with today's anti-immigrant stance among many who have profited and still profit from the economic consequences of globalization, but resent others invading their cultural space and, so to speak, "globalizing" the traditional centers of colonial and neocolonial power.)

Similar views were expressed regarding the transformation of agriculture. In ancient Rome, the land had been held by citizens who were also small farmers. However, as it became necessary to have a standing army, and then as city life took preponderance over the rural, Roman citizens ceased cultivating the land, employing slave labor in ever larger farms. Pliny the Elder — a friend, or at least an

3. *Annals,* 15.44.

acquaintance, of Tacitus' uncle — sees a sign of decadence in the
abandonment of agricultural labor on the part of Roman citizens,
who are turning soft by the ease of city life[4] — though Pliny himself
does not seem to have ever had a hand on a plow. And Columella
decries the growth of latifundia and the use of slave labor[5] — even
though his own lands were managed by a slave overseer, while he
lived in the city. Clearly, thinking Romans were concerned over the
concentration of land in a few hands, which was one of the many
results of growing Roman power. (Are there parallelisms here with
some of the reports one reads about the farm crisis in the United
States, Japan, and elsewhere?)

In brief, it is clear that the evaluations of the "globalizing" process in the centuries around the advent of Christianity were no less
contrasting and even ambivalent than are similar evaluations of today's globalization. Aelius Aristides believed that Rome was a gift to
the world; John of Patmos was convinced that Rome was an oppres-
sive harlot. Tacitus was proud that Rome had become an imperial
power, but resented the presence in Rome of those whom he considered sordid and degrading aliens. Pliny and Columella yearned
for times past when the land was held by small farmers, yet profited from the benefits of emerging latifundia. Furthermore, one can
look beyond these various evaluations and see further ambiguities
in them. John of Patmos complained about the power of Rome, yet
it was thanks to that power that pirates had practically disappeared
from the Mediterranean, and that the means of communication ex-
isted that allowed Christianity to spread. Aelius Aristides rejoiced
in the new life that Rome had brought to cities such as his native
Smyrna, but he had to come to Rome to prove his worth as an ora-
tor. Tacitus complained about the foreign "scum" invading Rome,
but his own family was not Roman in origin. (And here again one is
reminded of today's ambiguities, as when I use a computer to write
essays warning the rest of the world about the dangers of runaway
technology.)

How did all of this affect common people in their daily lives?
It is difficult to tell, for common people left few records. Yet, it is
possible to glean some information from what records there are —
Christian and other writings, Egyptian ostraca and papyri, tombs

---

4. *Natural history*, 1.18.13.
5. *De re rustica*, 1.7.

and funerary remains. From these records, it would appear first of all that the material life of most people was not much altered. In spite of all that we hear about Greek becoming the lingua franca of the Eastern Mediterranean basin, there is ample evidence that once one left the centers of urban life the ancient languages survived. In rural Egypt people continued speaking Coptic, and most of the surviving written materials from that area are in Coptic. In the book of Acts (14:11–18) we are told that the people in Lystra spoke only Lycaonean, and that this led to a serious misunderstanding as to who Paul and Barnabas were. In Judea and much of Syria Aramaic was still the most common language — and it was also the language used for trade further east.

In those centuries long ago, the globalizing tendencies of Hellenism were powerful — probably as powerful in the Mediterranean basin then as the current globalization if powerful throughout the world. Yet, this did not do away with cultural differences, and certainly did not lead to the imposition of Hellenistic — or later, Roman — culture as a universal culture. In his excellent study of early Gnosticism, Hans Jonas offers an enlightening summary of the process of globalization as it took place in the Hellenistic world and in the centuries that followed. He proposes

> ...a division of the Hellenistic age into two distinct periods: the period of manifest Greek dominance and oriental submersion, and the period of reaction of a renascent East, which in turn advanced victoriously in a kind of spiritual counterattack into the West and reshaped the universal culture. We are speaking of course in terms of intellectual and not political events. In this sense, Hellenization of the East prevails in the first period, orientalization of the West in the second period, the latter process coming to an end by about 300 A.D. The result of both is a synthesis which carried over into the Middle Ages.[6]

Then, as one looks at the Mediterranean basin at the time of Hellenization and Romanization, one is struck by two seemingly contradictory characteristics. On the one hand, there is the obvious fact of cosmopolitanism. While an Athenian in Socrates' time

---

6. Hans Jonas, *The Gnostic Religion: The Message of the Alien God and the Beginnings of Christianity* (Boston: Beacon Press, 1958), 18.

experienced a "world" that was generally limited to Athens and its surroundings, that person's descendants two generations later would experience the world as extending as far east as the Ganges; and still two centuries later Athens would be no more than one among the many medium-sized cities in the Roman Empire. To be "cosmo-politan" means to be a citizen of the universe, and it was thus that people were increasingly understanding themselves at the dawn of the Christian era.

On the other hand, cosmopolitanism was accompanied by individualism. The world had become so wide as to be beyond one's grasp. In the title of one of his novels Latin American author Ciro Alegría described the experience of native peoples coming to grips with the reality of other cultures and powers by saying that *El mundo es ancho y ajeno* — The World is Wide and Alien. People in the centuries of Hellenization and Romanization had to live in a wide and alien world, and they responded by creating their own smaller worlds, their own definitions of reality, their own value systems, and even their own religions.

It is in the field of religion that one can see some of the most profound changes as a result of Hellenistic and Roman expansion. Before such expansion, religion was closely associated with nation and with place. The Athenians had their gods, as did the Romans, the Egyptians, and the Syrians. These gods were quite distinct, reflecting different cultural and social values and traditions. People were their devotees by the mere fact of having been born in a particular land or city. An Egyptian's religion centered on gods such as Isis, Osiris, and Horus. A Roman's religion focused on Saturn, Jupiter, and Neptune. An Athenian would be devoted to Athena, and a Jew to Yahweh. This changed radically with the advent, first of Hellenism, and then of the Roman Empire. People traveled from one area to another. They settled in cities far away from their own. It was difficult to worship the ancient gods, often closely connected with particular sites and regions, in far away lands. Even in their own native areas, people encountered and interacted others who worshiped other gods. The very process of "globalization" led to a sort of globalization of the gods, creating equivalencies that overshadowed the former differences among local gods. Thus Neptune was equated with Poseidon, Mars with Ares, Venus with Aphrodite, and so on. Who was, for instance, the goddess worshiped in the famous temple in Ephesus? Was she the ancient mother goddess worshiped by Lydians and others long before Alexander's conquests? Was she a meteorite fallen from heaven (see Acts 19:35)? Was she the Artemis that was often represented as a woman with many breasts? Was she the Roman Diana? She was all of these and many more. She was actually the combination of a number of ancient goddesses now joined in one — and thus in Acts 19:27 Demetrius is stating no more than the truth when he claims that she is worshiped "by all of Asia and by the entire world."

This intermingling of religions also led to the possibility of people collecting religions and religious insights from a number of different sources, and even creating their own personal religion out of bits and pieces from a number of traditions.

A letter attributed to Emperor Hadrian — but probably from an unknown author of the period — describes the religious atmosphere of Alexandria as follows:

There those who worship Serapis are Christians; and those who call themselves Christian bishops are devotees of Serapis. There is not a chief of the Jewish synagogue, not a Christian elder, nor a Samaritan, who is not also a mathematician, a diviner, and a masseur for athletes.[7]

A classical work depicting this situation is the eleven books of *Metamorphoses,* of Lucius Apuleius, also known as *The Golden Ass.* There, in a long and convoluted narrative that is in part a philosophical treatise, in part a picaresque novel, and in part a satire, the protagonist goes through a series of religious and magical experiences, eventually becoming a devotee and a servant of Isis and Osiris, although still retaining many of his earlier religious beliefs and practices. Even while enwrapped in fantastic stories, in the *Metamorphoses* we have a true indication of the attitude of many toward religion. The ancient religion — whatever it may have been — no longer sufficed. It was up to individuals not only to choose their own religion, but even to create it out of various religious traditions. As a result, the greatest threat to nascent Christianity did not come from physical and legal persecution, but rather from those who simply incorporated Christianity into their own systems of belief, quite often setting aside the centrality of Jesus.

---

7. Latin text in Daniel Ruiz Bueno, ed., *Actas de los mártires* (Madrid: Biblioteca de Autores Cristianos, 1968), 252.

Thus, while today we speak of "Gnosticism" as if it were indeed a formal religion, it was in fact an amorphous group of beliefs and practices, with dozens of different schools and a myriad different shapes, combining occultism with ancient myths, as well as with what was then the best scientific view of the universe.

Here again one can draw parallelisms with our time. Globalization has brought about not only an encounter of religions, but also the tendency for people to create their own religions out of bits and pieces from others, often combining elements from world religions with materials derived from mysterious and supposedly ancient practices and wisdom. The revival of "Gnosticism" — which is in fact quite different from ancient Gnosticism — is only one aspect of this phenomenon. The same phenomenon is behind the huge gatherings that take place at the Mayan ruins of Chichen-Itza on the vernal equinox. People from all over Europe and North America travel there to see the shadow of a serpent climb up the steps of the great temple. They consider this a mystical experience. Yet, were one to ask them about their beliefs, one would find that they hold to a wide variety of religious and semi-religious positions, and that what stands at the very core of their religiosity is a nebulous openness to mystery, and the insistence on being able to define one's own particular and private religion.

While what takes place at Chichen-Itza may reflect some of the fringes of contemporary global religiosity, it points to the one great common denominator in the globalization of religion: people feel free — and perhaps even obliged — to choose from each religion, modern and ancient, what they like, and to employ that material to create a religion of their own. When I was growing up in Latin America, a sign of the loss of authority on the part of the Catholic Church was the common phrase, *soy católico a mi manera* — I am a Catholic after my own fashion. Today, the "after my own fashion" is true in most major world religions. Methodists and Presbyterians are such after their own fashion. Many Hindus are Hindus after their own fashion. Even among Muslims, an increasing number are Muslims after their own fashion. In all these traditions, so-called fundamentalism — although often quite vociferous in claiming that it is the true form of the religion — is in fact a reaction against the changes that are taking place as a result of globalization.

In this context, it is important to realize that it is possible to see Christianity and its eventual success precisely as a response to the new global conditions. In those conditions, ancient regional and national religions took a more global dimension in which birth and nationality were no longer as important as personal decision and initiation. The ancient Egyptian religion of Isis and Osiris, originally limited to Egyptians — and even to a certain social class among Egyptians — became the mystery cult of Isis and Osiris, to which one belonged, not through physical birth, but rather through a process of initiation. The ancient religion survived among more traditional Egyptians, but its more universal counterpart soon surpassed it. Can one then look at Christianity and see it as emerging out of Judaism, and eventually surpassing Judaism in the number of its followers, precisely because it was a religion that made the ancient worship of Yahweh, and many of the ethical demands and promises of Yahweh, available to others, no longer by Jewish birth, but now by conversion and the initiatory rite of baptism? In this regard, Christianity was one of many religions emerging at about the same time, and seeking to respond to the new global situation that was emerging.

Thus, as it was taking shape Christianity had much in common with the general religious tendencies of the time. It emphasized personal decision, and did not limit its scope to those who could claim a particular land of origin or a particular cultural or religious tradition. In this regard, it was not too different from Mithraism, the mysteries of Isis and Osiris, or the cult of the Great-Mother. If it was available to Romans, Egyptians, Greeks and others, so were all those other religions. If it sought to explain the most profound mysteries of life and death, so did they. What made it different was its Jewish origin, and its consequent emphasis on a radical and ethical monotheism. If there is only one God, one cannot simply collect religions à la Lucius Apuleius. If this is an ethically demanding God, one cannot condone all that society accepts; one's behavior must reflect the character of one's God. Radical monotheism admits of no other gods — no matter how attractive they may be.

But then, radical monotheism requires a global perspective. The Judeo-Christian doctrine of creation means that nothing exists beyond the scope and reach of the one God. A radically monotheistic religion must be global precisely because it admits of no other gods. This led early Christianity to respond to the challenges of its time in three apparently contradictory, but actually complementary fashions. First, it rejected the syncretism then in vogue. It would not allow Gnostics and others to turn Christianity into a source for tidbits of religious wisdom which could then be incorporated into whatever polytheistic religion one wished. Second, it embraced within itself a wide variety of views and expressions. When the time came to make a list of authoritative books, it surprisingly decided to include in that list four books — the Gospels — that disagreed on many points, but all agreed on their central message. This made it possible to develop a church which considered itself to be one, even though Alexandrine Christianity, for instance, was very different from Roman and from Antiochene Christianity. Thirdly, by making use of the doctrine of the logos it showed itself ready to accept whatever truth could be found anywhere, and thus avoided the perils of what today we call fundamentalism. All of this allowed Christianity to become a truly global religion, expressing at once both the unity of the world in which it was formed and the diversity within that world.

Thus emerged a religion with a truly global vocation — a religion so global that when Constantine correctly diagnosed the Roman Empire as falling apart thought its inner tensions, he expressed the hope that Christianity would be the "cement" holding the Empire together. In this, he did not succeed, for soon the church itself was divided, and scarcely fifty years after Constantine's death the ancient Roman Empire was being dismembered. But at another level he was right, for as the Empire collapsed it was Christianity that was able to provide both continuity with the past and whatever measure of unity did survive. But that is a story best told elsewhere.

In a way, the challenge before Christianity today is similar to the challenges it faced during its early centuries. It is an attractive quarry from which to draw stones for the building of one's own "personalized" and "designer" religion. There are also within Christianity those who would make it a narrow religion, as if God had created only Christians. But, during the last hundred years Christianity has shown itself to be more than the religion of a particular civilization or a particular people. Today the centers of vitality for much of Christianity are no longer in the North Atlantic, but in places such as Africa, Asia, and Latin America. In each of these areas, Christianity has taken on much of the surrounding culture. It has seen such culture as one of the many gifts of the God who is the creator of all. From the point of view of some within the church itself, much of this is a betrayal and a denial of Christianity as they knew it before becoming incarnate in this our global age. Yet, as one looks at the entire worldwide picture of Christianity, it is apparent that it is well placed to offer a genuine and valuable response to the challenges of today's radical globalization.

These challenges, however, are not limited to the question that so often worries Christians, about the competition from other religions, and whether Christianity will emerge victorious over them. They also involve the possibility of Christianity developing what this volume calls a "public theology" for the present global age. Thus, Dr. Stackhouse's exploration in the pages that follow of the shape of such a public theology is crucial to our response to the issues of globalization. At the same time, such public theology is itself a witness to the global nature of Christianity today. It is no longer a theology that the West offers the rest of the church for its guidance and instruction. It is a theology shaped by many Christians in many parts of the world, reflecting many cultures and traditions, responding to many different situations, in dialogue with many different worldviews and religions, with many different interpretations of many fundamental aspect of the faith, and thus truly global — or, to use a more traditional term, truly catholic! It is to that theology that this book witnesses, and it is as a witness to that theology that I commend it to the church at large.

Justo L. González
Decatur, Georgia
January 2007

GLOBALIZATION

AND

GRACE

Introduction

FAITH AND GLOBALIZATION

I am delighted to be able to bring this fourth and final volume to the light of day, and I apologize to any reader who wondered at the delay between the first three volumes and this one. A troubling and draining, although non-life threatening, medical problem and a series of writing and speaking obligations due to generous interest in the approach of this project prevented a rapid completion of this volume. Also, the number of new publications on the topics that pertain to this series has grown more rapidly than I can read — although I have sought to consult the main works.

The issue is globalization and the place of religion, ethics and theology in it, and the question is whether God is, in any respect, prompting, inviting, allowing or involved in the shaping of this phenomenon. My reflections on the contributions of my colleagues, on what I have observed in numerous trips and consultations in South Asia, Southeast Asia, and East Asia, Eastern Europe and Southern Africa, and some modest exposure to Latin America over the years have brought me to the firm conclusion that there is no greater public issue before humankind than the fact that a new wider public is being created by the complex dynamics of globalization that are essentially social and ethical as these are driven by or legitimated by the often unintended implications of religious convictions, particularly those of Christianity. There are, to be sure, major issues such as ecological peril, nuclear threat, cultural clashes, temptations to imperialism, militant conflicts, and continued poverty. But these all take place within the comprehending dynamics of globalization, sometimes exacerbated by and sometimes mitigated by globalization.

Many, of course, tend to believe that globalization is, essentially, driven by economic interests. That economic interests are powerful I have no doubt. But this is by no means new, while modern globalization is. The inquiry into why globalization is taking its

1

present shape, and organizing the economic forces the way it does convinces me that an economistic view is too limited — so limited, in fact, that to treat it as such is to obscure the scope, structure, force and meaning of the phenomenon.

Globalization, I believe, is a potential civilizational shift that involves the growth of a worldwide infrastructure that bears the prospect of a new form of civil society, one that may well comprehend all previous national, ethnic, political, economic or cultural contexts. It portends a cosmopolitan possibility that modernity promised but could not deliver, and thus can be considered as the most profound postmodernism. The spread, for instance, of the ideals of democracy and human rights, of musical styles and scientific education, of international law and mass media, of technological skills and vast missionary efforts, of medical care and management techniques and both of new ethnic consciousness and a wider acceptance of inter-racial marriage are all parts of globalization. Together these make certain economic changes possible and others necessary. As we shall see, many peoples who were long desperately poor are finding their way out of poverty by efforts to develop complex cultural and social patterns that enable global participation, nearly always by adopting the religious or worldview presuppositions that formed or legitimated them. This is true in spite of the fact that many people and traditions resist such developments or have not yet found out how to become a part of them.

Because of the significance of religious and worldview transformations for globalization, any substantive critique or embrace of these developments will demand attention to religious analysis and to a theology able to form or reform the inner moral fabric driving the globalization process. The previous three volumes of the series already strongly suggest that a major part of the impetus for the globalizing developments derive from the ways in which Christian thought has shaped cultural and social institutions and given rise to transforming patterns of life.[1] The question now is not only whether religions have shaped the formation of civilizations, in concert with other forces, but which ones, if any, can and should guide our thinking and action in regard to globalization. That is a normative question.

---

1. See the essays by scholars of various backgrounds and expertise, as found in the *God and Globalization* series, 3 vols. (Harrisburg, PA: Trinity Press International [now New York: Continuum International]), 2000, 2001, and 2002.

Three Worrisome Developments

I begin, however, with a set of worries. I am worried about the ability of today's Christians to address globalization wisely and effectively. I am worried for three reasons. One is due to what I see as the confused arguments and policies of the present U.S. administration, which has been more identified with the Christian faith by supporters and opponents than most recent U.S. administrations. The policies suggest to many around the world that globalization is little more than an Americanist agenda guiding imperialist and neocolonial policies while hiding raw interests with a thin pious veneer. These policies suggest to others that Christianity is itself not only transformative but fundamentally aggressive and colonial.

It is among the duties of the leaders of any nation to defend the people's interests, but how this is done in relationship to others, and whether the methods and policies have moral and spiritual integrity, are more important issues. The fact that the current administration believes that religion makes a decisive difference in real life makes them alert in response to terrorism. We shall say more of this matter later, but for now it can be said that those who view history through religious lenses are more likely than those for whom religion is an entirely private matter to recognize its power in others. For instance, the present U.S. administration recognizes that all Muslims are not terrorists or militants, but most terrorists are from militant wings of Islam. It is not right, from a theological point of view, for a government to declare war on a religion, but no responsible administration can avoid dealing with them. The question is how!

Moreover, the administration is surely right that the spread of a constitutionally ordered democratic polity that guarantees human rights and supports the flourishing of an open economy is today the moral mandate of any government claiming to be influenced by basic ethical and distinctly Christian-influenced principles. But the persistent reports about the torture of prisoners fuel Islamist militance, and unwarranted violations of the civil liberties of citizens by this administration seem to subvert the very constitutional democracy and human rights that are advocated and, more dangerously, to discredit the moral and spiritual bases on which they were historically developed. Also, the convictions for fraud of managers of major corporations who share the faith of these political leaders and who supported their election cast a shadow over the world's perception of the legitimacy of the political-economic system dominant in globalization and in parts of the U.S. policy.

The reason for the failures of these current political and economic leaders, I believe, is that the form of piety dominant in this overtly "Christian" administration and its corporate allies is not of a sort that breeds a theological ethic able to guide them in discerning the multiple tasks necessary to build up the wider civil society promised in globalization. Their faith could not even lead them to anticipate what had to be done to rebuild a viable society after the defeat of Saddam Hussein. Their faith may be quite profound at the personal level; it may keep them from debilitating addiction and may prompt a desire to defend the nation's values as they perceive them; but the thin public vision has a too slender view of the emerging global dynamics. Therefore they are tempted to national self-righteousness and self-idolatry.[2]

I am also worried about a second trend with global manifestations. This one is reflected in a number of neoliberal economists who have developed a new subdiscipline that interprets religion in reductionist terms. Unlike the Marxist reductionism that sees religion as the sigh of the oppressed and an illusory hope for a better world, and thus an opiate of the masses, and unlike the Weberian interpreters of the impact of religions on economic ethics and social development, this school of thought is represented by the "Chicago School" of "rational choice" theory as it is rooted in the Neo-classical version of economics, now frequently defended on the basis of "evolutionary psychology" — humans are genetically programmed to seek advantage in sex, food and territory. This school does not treat religion as a manifestation of class interests, or as basis for an ethic that could shape or guide political or

---

2. See Ronald Sider et al., *Toward an Evangelical Public Policy* (Grand Rapids: Baker Books, 2005), for an attempt by U.S. Evangelical scholars to overcome this deficit. See also the following essays that seek to chart the major contours of and the distinctions between divergent approaches to public theology: "Public Theology and Civil Society in a Globalizing Era," *Bangalore Theological Forum* 32, no. 1 (June 2000): 46–72; "Public Theology and Political Economy in a Globalizing Era," *Studies in Christian Ethics* 14, no. 3 (2001): 63–86; "Civil Religion, Political Theology, and Public Theology: What's the Difference?" *Journal of Political Theology* (July 2004): 275–93. Condensed as "What Is Public Theology," *Journal for the Study of Christian Culture*, no. 11 (Beijing, 2004): 3–12; full version trans. Xie Zhibin, forthcoming in Chinese.

economic policy or social and corporate practice. Instead, it sees religion as a subjective want that functions by market forces and that can best be understood as a consumer commodity. The research of this school was recently summarized by Lawrence Iannaccone, who is sharply opposed to Marxist and Weberian understandings of economic development and yet wants to defend the integrity of religion by appealing to one of Adam Smith's reflections on religion's personal appeal.[3] He does not treat the populist "Prosperity Gospel" of current T.V. preachers or the healing ministries of house-churches around the world, or the piety of the administration; but there are obvious similarities to the appeals made by them. My objection is not that religion cannot have powerful personal uses, but that its claims to provide a normative guide for structuring the forms of social life are entirely neglected.

My third worry concerns neither the slender public theology of the U.S. administration and its business supporters, nor the narrow utilitarian views of religion by Neo-liberal economists, but the ideological perspective of those who are most visibly against them. I am worried about the caustic interpretations of the faith by those anti-globalization ecumenical voices who have theologically absolutized certain models of liberationist thought and Marxist social analysis. Of particular concern is the movement against globalization within the World Council of Churches, the World Reformed Alliance, and the Lutheran World Federation. Some voices have sought to declare globalization a matter of *status confessionis* — that is, if one believes that globalization bears within it any divinely blessed or grace-filled possibilities, one is a heretic and should be kept out or thrown out of the community of believers. In this view, globalization is a totally immoral economic phenomenon, driven by an ideology of capitalist greed, by which the rich systematically increase their own wealth while further impoverishing the poor. Against this, they assert that "Another World Is Possible."[4] This baptism of class analysis as the guiding mode for interpreting globalization is, I think, a substantive

---

3. See Lawrence R. Iannaccone, "Introduction to the Economics of Religion," *Journal of Economic Literature* 36 (September 1998): 1465–96. Other related, supporting articles are available on his website.
4. See "Alternative to Globalization: Addressing Peoples and Earth" (Geneva: World Council of Churches, 2005), and its less strident companion, *A Caring Economy: A Feminist Contribution to Alternatives to Globalization,* written by Athena K. Peralta (Geneva: WCC, 2005).

theological mistake, a misreading of history and an inaccurate social analysis as faulty on its terms as the previous two are on theirs.
It does not understand how and why the contemporary dynamics
were generated and have such power, and it fails to foresee the devastating consequences for the faith and for the world's poor if their
views are heeded.[5]

What these three influential perspectives share — right, center
and left — is a failure to grasp the way in which religion shapes
the public ethos of civilizations, including the social and economic
spheres of life through its influence on culture, child-rearing, education, technology and law, and the ways in which the Christian faith,
and Protestantism particularly until quite recently, have generated
those forces that are now driving globalization in its several social,
political, cultural and professional dimensions. Thus, it could, in
principle, shape it further. My argument with these three views, in
short, is theological in the first place, and sociopolitical in the second, and economic in the third. Each objection involves a judgement
that these positions have an inadequate view of faith that leads to a
misperception of how religion works in the common life, and how
it could create a new, more inclusive possibility for the common
life. In short, I agree with Peter L. Berger's comment that "Those
who neglect religion (as a cause) in their analysis of contemporary
affairs do so at great peril."[6]

To give voice to my worries about these three developments does
not mean that there is nothing valid about them. The United States,
as the dominant contemporary superpower, at least for the next few
generations in all probability, needs a faith-based ethic guiding its
policies if it is to advocate constitutional democracy, human rights
and an open civil society with a functional economy. No such society
has ever long endured without one, although only a few scholars
have advanced these social ethical possibilities. But the faith has
to be deep, its ethics universalistic and persuasive. The faith has
to be carried out by meeting the felt needs of ordinary people, but
any faith worth having must also make warranted claims about the

---

5. For a discerning critique of this position from within an empathetic reading
of the Marxist tradition and the anti-globalization movement, see Stefan Skrimshire,
"Another *What* Is Possible?: Ideology and Utopian Imagination in Anti-Capitalist
Resistance," *Political Theology* 7, no. 2 (April 2006): 201–19.

6. Peter L. Berger, *The Desecularization of the World* (Grand Rapids: Eerdmans,
2000), 18.

truth of its convictions and the justice of its ethic. The policies of the present administration have not convinced the public on these points, the new discipline of the economics of religion does not attempt to do so, and the presuppositions of the anti-globalists do not appear to be capable of doing so. The latter, however, know that current global dynamics disrupt traditional cultures and cause hardship for those caught in social changes that they did not choose and cannot control. But they do not see the consequences of failure to face these changes and provide the resources to reshape or adapt to them.

Of course, we must recognize that there are competing definitions of faith and of globalization, but these three current developments seem to me to be particularly perilous to the faith and to the global future in part because they have a partial validity that gives them partial credibility. In this regard, I should outline my basic understandings of faith and globalization and why I think they are pertinent to our situation and can help correct these dangers.

Defining the Terms

I am using the word "faith" here as: a confidence in a comprehensive worldview or "metaphysical-moral vision" that is accepted as binding because it is held to be, in itself, basically true and just, even if all dimensions of it cannot be either finally confirmed or refuted. Further, every worldview or comprehending "vision" worth worrying about is functional: it provides a framework for interpreting the realities of life in the world, it guides the basic beliefs and behaviors of persons and it empowers believers to seek to transform the world in accordance with a normative ethic of what should be. This normative view implies that something real and important transcends the mechanics and organics of the physical world as it is and offers a standard and direction for the world as it can be, ought to be and ultimately shall be.

I am persuaded that the Christian faith is the most valid worldview or metaphysical moral vision available to humanity, but I recognize that others have other views that we have to encounter and heed, and that we may gain from other faiths in a globalizing world. A faith, in this broad sense, may be essentially theistic or more humanist or naturalist, and it generally organizes itself into a creed, a code and a cult (in the specific, classical sense of liturgical forms or practices) that together form a religion. Further, I think the evidence is clear that where a religion becomes widely shared, it shapes an ethos that gives identity to a particular culture and tends to promote a social ethic that fosters distinctive public institutions. It molds civilizations. By this definition, worldviews such as a philosophical-ethical Confucianism, an atheistic spirituality such as Buddhism, or a secular-humanist ideology such as Marxism, whenever they form a creed, a code and a cult, and are used to interpret and guide the formation of an ethos, can properly be seen as faiths. They function as "religions," shaping an ethos, even if they are opposed to theistic traditions or do not recognize themselves as religious. They are also subject to theological analysis, for they inevitably contain a "metaphysical-moral vision" — an ontology, a theory of history and ethic — that involves some view of transcendence.

I also need to indicate what I think globalization is. As already suggested and as the systematic treatment of the powers and spheres of life in the first three volumes of this series have indicated, globalization is best understood as a worldwide set of social, political, cultural, technological and ethical dynamics, influenced and legitimated by certain theological, ethical and ideological motifs, that are creating a worldwide civil society that stands beyond the capacity of any nation-state to control. It is influencing every local context, all peoples, all social institutions and the ecology of the earth itself. It is forming an alternative postmodernism, one that has elements of the fragmentation and the relativization of all previous securities, but that also is demanding the rediscovery of universalistic principles of anthropology, spirituality, morality and law, refining distinctive purposes and forming new institutions that require common recognition. Thereby it is creating a newly contentious, comprehending public, one that modulates every regional and local context and yet is adapted into them and adopted by them in novel ways.[7] In that way, it breaks down old barriers between people and creates new ways of interpreting and defining identities as it converts the world in unexpected directions.

Specialists in various fields treat the changes in terms of their disciplines and often tend to attribute the dynamics to the factors

---

7. Peter L. Berger et al., *Many Globalizations: Cultural Diversity in the Contemporary World* (New York: Oxford University Press, 2002).

that most interest them as we also saw in the first three volumes of this series. Further, we have already mentioned the economists (and both business leaders and critics suspicious of business) who treat globalization as an economic dynamic. They see capitalist practices and institutions that can leap over the borders of nations to escape legal limitations, establish new markets and find cheap labor, which simultaneously makes the economy more inclusive and productive.[8] Political scientists (and both politicians and public policy critics) treat globalization as the emerging realignment of power relations in a "new world order" as the Soviet Union began to collapse and the United States became the only remaining superpower facing a militant religio-political movement. Notable among these, for example, is Samuel P. Huntington, who as we shall later see argues that "civilizations," not states, are the units of world organization now, although military and diplomatic policy remains in the hands of those states who are at the center of civilizational clusters, and at the root of what they can do remains the possibility of "applying organized violence...[w]hich Westerners often forget...; non-Westerners never do."[9] Still, Huntington and others agree that various policies are praised for preserving cultural character or blamed for disrupting it, while contrasting partisans point out the need for temporary conflict to establish the long-range prospects for peace beyond cultural particularity. At the margins of political opinion are advocates of benevolent imperialism and opponents of any hegemony.

Meanwhile, communication specialists speak of the spread of information technology and media availability that allows the peoples of the world to discover both unique or distinctive local happenings and customs, and to identify and celebrate old but unrecognized and emerging new commonalities, while cultural critics speak of the collapse of meaning as earlier dominant cultural assumptions are shattered by their exposures to a host of alternatives. Others quote demographers who speak of massive migration flows as those from the south and east migrate to the north

---

8. For a nonreligious, very positive view, see, e.g., Martin Wolf, *Why Globalization Works* (New Haven: Yale University Press, 2004).

9. Samuel P. Huntington, *The Clash of Civilizations and the Remaking of the World Order* (New York: Simon and Schuster, 1998). A more extensive analysis of this work in the context of his other writings will appear in volume 4 of this series, chapter 2.

and west, while anthropological romantics celebrate the values of traditional cultures and mourn the global forces that disrupt indigenous societies.

The problem is that such particular definitions by the advocates of particular disciplines are all correct, although they are partial. More general definitions seek to comprehend these partial perspectives, and these could well be often more accurate even if abstract because they try to grasp the scope of the multiple and complex-causal character of the plural dynamics. They see all the factors mentioned above, and some not mentioned, as contributing to the formation of a religio-cultural and technological public infrastructure in the ethos that, while still fragile, could well lead to a new worldwide society of societies. Such definitions require an orthodox and not merely an Eastern, a catholic and not merely a Roman, an ecumenical and not merely a Protestant, and an evangelical and not merely a Liberal missiological vision. They signal a potential change like the shifts from hunting and gathering societies to agricultural, then urban societies, and then to industrialized nation states. Each shift involved crises and conflicts. Each shift was also made possible by both material and political factors as reshaped by dominant religious and ethical transformations, although some religions seem to have the theological and ethical resources to induce some of the transformations of the shift and to correct, modulate or restrain other aspects of it, and some seem to block or inhibit it. The most successful are able to borrow from other cultures or to generate new doctrines from old sources tested by new experiences that enhanced certain possibilities in material and sociopolitical life which gave legitimation to more promising possibilities. Such developments are now forming the infrastructure of what, thus, could become a new, worldwide federated civil society — not yet, if ever, fully developed as the skeleton of a global civilization.[10] Such things take centuries to mature. It is a decidedly dynamic, incredibly complex phenomenon that requires a comprehensive contextual analysis, a general theology of history and a realistic social ethic to give it viable direction. Further, more and more people foresee material, social and ethical promise or even

---

10. See the remarkable collection of essays by leading international scholars collected by Michael Walzer, ed., *Toward a Global Civil Society* (Providence, RI: Berghahn Books, 1995).

religious benefits than see liabilities, a fact that continues to drive the globalizing forces even as many resist them.

Notably, this partially formed global civil society, as messy, pluralistic, conflictual and contentious as it is, is developing without being under the control of any state — although more developed lands, especially the USA, Great Britain and the EU plus Japan and increasingly China and India, are rapidly generating new possibilities, adapting to the changes demanded, taking advantage of the opportunities afforded and viewing them as basically (with some ambiguity) spiritually and ethically valid. Thus, they reinforce the developments and the new international legal arrangements that have begun to regularize them.

China is a particularly important example in this area.[11] A "new cultural revolution" is adopting international standards in many areas of thought and life, including (essentially Evangelical) Christian ethics, traditions and theologies, stamping them with Chinese characteristics drawn from Tao, Confucianism, Buddhism and Maoism. It is pulling millions out of poverty while the young see hope in the new developments. This is obvious to all who have followed its recent history, even if very large numbers of people seem still caught in stagnation, if the fuller realization of democracy and human rights stands only in the future, and if political crises hover in the background.[12] Still, the prospect of another superpower shaping world history is already on the horizon.

Similarly, India, the second most populous country in the world, is globalizing at an amazing rate. As viewed by Thomas L. Friedman, perhaps the premier reporter on things global, India is seen as the next great cultural, political and economic superpower that may eventually surpass China because of its more democratic traditions, its increasingly world-class educational system, and the growing willingness among the burgeoning middle classes to adapt foreign

---

11. The journalists Nicholas Kristof and Sheryk Wudun, *Thunder in the East* (New York: Vintage, 2001); and David Aikman, *Jesus in Beijing* (New York: Regnery, 2004) are particularly reliable reporters on socioreligious developments of China in my view — I have consulted with Chinese scholars in China every year but one since 1997.

12. See, e.g., George Zhibin Gu, *China's Global Reach* (Victoria, Canada: Trafford Publishers, 2005); David Sheff, *China Dawn: The Story of a Technological and Business Revolution* (New York: Harper Collins, 2002); and James Kynge, *China Shakes the World: The Rise of a Hungry Nation* (London: Weidenfeld & Nicolson, 2006), which accents the fact that 400 million Chinese have been pulled out of poverty by globalization in little more than a decade.

influences into their cultural patterns of life — in spite of persistent patterns of caste discrimination, the rise of a militant Hindu nationalism, and a huge underclass of "Dalit" populations whose vocal leaders debate or oppose globalization.[13] Further, many smaller countries of Asia and many peoples in Latin America and Africa are adopting the worldviews and values that foment development, especially as Evangelical and Pentecostal movements bring them to people long marginalized.

The Temptation to Imperialism

Still, in this context, the USA is the only world-dominant superpower, and is tempted to become imperial. In a world without a universal political order, that dominance is both resented and, ironically, expected to use its power in the trouble spots of the world, from Haiti to Darfur, from Bosnia to Rwanda, from the drug trade in Latin America to the HIV/AIDS crises of Sub-Sahara Africa, to disputes over who should have nuclear capabilities from North Korea to Iran. As the only major north Atlantic nation that was born in a revolution against a colonial empire and the only one that had no colonies in Latin America, Africa or Asia, most Americans do not see the United States as an imperial power; and accusations of neocolonialism, often identified with the imperialism, do not ring true to the U.S.A.'s sense of identity.

Yet, it is surely the case that the United States already functions as a hegemonic power, influencing political, cultural and economic, as well as educational, technological and family patterns around the globe while leaving space for other centers of authority and governance to operate largely on their own terms. This view is in contrast to the argument of the British scholar, Niall Ferguson, that "America is heir to the [British] Empire in both senses: offspring in the colonial era, successor today. Perhaps the most burning contemporary question of American politics is, Should the United States seek to shed or to shoulder the imperial load it has inherited?" Ferguson

---

13. Thomas L. Friedman, *The World Is Flat* (New York: Farrar, Straus & Giroux, 2005); and Gurcharan Das, *India Unbound: The Social and Economic Revolution from Independence to the Global Information Age* (New York: Anchor Books,2002). Here too many are pulled out of poverty although there is also more ideological and populist resistance. See I. John Mohan Razu et al., *Dialogue on Globalization* (Bangalore, India: SCM Press, 2000), and *Globalization as Hydra* (Delhi, India: ISPCK, 2006).

argues that the world needs an imperial center. But at the end of his study, he concludes that the USA is an "empire in denial.... [I]t is an empire that lacks the drive to export its capital, its people and its culture to those ... regions which need them most urgently and which, if they are neglected, will breed the greatest threats to its security. It is an empire, in short, that dare not speak its name."[14]

It could be. But a particular form of hegemonic influence is probably a better description than imperialism or neocolonialism, as Michael Mandelbaum recently argued.[15] He uses the biblical story that tells of David's boyhood defeat of the giant Goliath as the source of his title, and he knows that generations have been raised on the heroism of the little guy against the big one. But Mandelbaum also knows that the same tradition celebrates the development, compared to other real options, of a relatively peaceful and a more just administration under the mature David who tolerated prophetic criticism in the face of internal and external temptations. After all, there is a certain duty of power when the strong is seen from that point of view. And Mandelbaum further argues that in fact the United States has played the background role of providing certain governmental services to the nations of the world for more than half a century. It provides security in many troubled spots and in the face of failing states, it provides a degree of economic stability in an otherwise volatile world economy, and it set ideals of democracy and human rights which, even if it fails to support them in all cases, almost all countries imitate. Yet, it does not seek to exploit or permanently occupy the nations it serves, although many resent its power and often dispute and seek to modify (with considerable success) its policies when they are overreaching or poorly designed.

Mandelbaum's arguments force us to ask to whom the world should turn if no effective world government exists and if local disputes threaten ethnic genocide or wider violence within or beyond any existing regime. Should we tolerate or even foster an international anarchy of totally sovereign states, no matter how they treat their citizens or neighbors? Should we instead turn to Germany, Russia, China, India, Brazil or South Africa, all of which

---

14. Niall Ferguson, *Empire: The Rise and Demise of the British World Order and the Lessons for Global Power* (New York: Basic Books, 2004), xii, 370.

15. Michael Mandelbaum, *The Case for Goliath: How America Acts as the World's Government in the Twenty-First Century* (Washington, DC: World Affairs, 2005).

are now regional powers? Should we advocate efforts to make the United Nations into a centralized world government? Of course, the scope of U.S. influence and its power to intervene directly or indirectly through international agencies is resented by many, for the simple reasons that the way its power has sometimes displaced the authority of other powers and has been used dysfunctionally in far too many cases. But it is not a desire to colonize or control other territories and their resources that guides policy. Rather, it is a sense of moral duty to establish and preserve a network of cooperating polities that can openly interact with one another exchanging resources, capital, goods and services, and jointly constrain whatever totalitarian powers that close down those metaphysical-moral visions, worldviews or religions and their social forms that preserve the possibilities of the rule of law, pluralism, human rights and economic opportunity.[16]

Many observers take a cynical view of such motivations. They say it is oil that is the central concern of U.S. foreign policy. There is no doubt about the fact that oil plays a role. The question of who controls the vast reserves of the Middle East is a weighty one for all in the West and increasingly in the East as well as for those in the Mid-East. If the price of oil were to double or triple again at the hands of some regional autocrat, the entire world economy, and not just the United States, would suffer and it is possible that millions of those who are already living in marginal conditions would be plunged into worse suffering. A new depression given the wider interdependence of the world is not an attractive prospect. Thus, it is a fateful issue as to who will be the stewards of this natural resource and whether the custodians are among those willing to work openly with those who want to advance current economic patterns of progress and aid the causes of democracy, human rights and increased international interaction or wish to use it as a tool to stop current global developments. But to see the current battles in the Middle East as solely about oil and not about the ways in which

---

16. Compare this with Josef Joffe, *Überpower: The Imperial Temptation of America* (New York: W. W. Norton: 1996), which makes similar arguments while recognizing the greater suspicion of European powers of this tendency. On the relationship of these issues to religion see Daniel Philpott, *Revolutions in Sovereignty: How Ideas Shaped Modern International Relations* (Princeton, NJ: Princeton University Press, 2001); and John Carlson and Eric Owens, eds., *The Sacred and the Sovereign: Religion and International Politics* (Washington, DC: Georgetown University Press, 2003).

Islam, Judaism and Christianity differently shape society in general, and the kinds of civilizations they tend to foster in the wider world, is to fail to see what kind of a conflict is presently at hand.

At another level, the power of U.S. popular culture is also a globalizing force, spread by tape, disc, video, movie and satellite TV; and it is seen by many as an homogenizing, immoral influence. Its scope is rooted in the ideals of freedom of expression, and is seen by many people around the world as something to be desired for the sake of freedom — or to be controlled to protect traditional culture or to prevent a turn to "libertine" ethics. This influence grows less because it is imposed, even if it *is* advertised, than because it is invited, pirated and imitated. The police power needed to stop it would be enormous and intrusive, even if some constraints are necessary for the protection of intellectual property and the protection of young people.

More vexing to many is the increased power of the trans-national and multi-national corporations — an old institutional form that was once under the control of leading families, religious authorities, states or royal discretion. Gradually, monasteries and other church-related institutions fought for and won the rights to form artifactual, economically independent institutions beyond the control of familial patriarchy and political authority, and "corporations" became substantially disembeded from these constraints and gained increased relative autonomy in economic behavior — although obviously constrained by market conditions and competition. Thus, while some firms in every country and most firms in Latin America, in Africa, in the Islamic world, and in parts of Asia are familial or state owned and are dominated by patriarchal and political authority, the modern trans-national or multi-national conglomerates are incorporated limited liability holding companies that are formed in one place with many owners from around the globe. They are able, like the explorers of earlier centuries, to roam the world, setting up subsidiaries or branches, linking up to suppliers customers and local populations and making them also "stakeholders" in the corporations. They are in fact much sought after by coalitions of economic and political leaders in developing regions where their plants, factories or outlets are sorely wanted.

These corporations are often said to be totally uncontrolled, but that is not quite right. They are controlled in part by the laws of the host countries, although some of these are quite weak. They are also

increasingly controlled by the growing bodies of international law
and by a host of international treaties, such as the European Union,
NAFTA or other regional trade groupings, and indirectly by the regulative agencies to which the member nations subscribe such as the
World Bank, the International Monetary Fund, and the World Trade
Organization which have negotiated legal agreements with procedures for enforcement and the revision of unjust provisions. Still, the
nature and character of these new actors on the world scene which
I have called "the regencies" in volume 2 ("thrones" on which representative authorities sit, although they are not the power behind
the thrones) are under constant scrutiny by both party countries and
Non-Governmental Organizations and advocacy groups. Revision
and reform are frequent and will be continuous, although further
legal regulation will likely require expanded forms of cooperation
between these trans-national regulatory agencies, the consent of
the world's more powerful nations and the acquiescence of the
corporations themselves.

Another possibility for naming and responding to these "regencies" is imaginatively proposed by Michael Hardt and Antonio
Negri in their postmodern, neo-Marxist work, *Empire*.[17] They
argue that the question of imperialism is passè. Indeed, they suggestively offer an alternative definition of "Empire" as the rise of a
worldwide class of technological and economic managers — a definition which can be extended to refine the issues. While the new
global institutions are sometimes said to be a renewed imperialistic
effort by the West to dominate the rest of the world, historically
"imperialism" refers to a political-military occupation and governance of a territory and its peoples by a foreign power. Further, the
term "colonialism," often associated with imperialism, refers either
to the establishment of a satellite settlement in an imperially dominated territory or, in its "neocolonialism" form, to the economic
domination of a territory by exploiting its resources and marketing
its value-added goods in a way that makes the people dependent on
the foreign power. These categories were used by previous generations when many spoke of the "first, second and third worlds" or —
after the "second" world collapsed — of "the West and the Rest"
or of "The North and the South." Hardt and Negri argue that these

---

17. M. Hardt and A. Negri, *Empire* (Cambridge, MA: Harvard University Press, 2001).

categories no longer apply. Instead, today's "Empire" is a pervasive network of technological, legal, cultural, economic and corporate forces, no longer centered in or controlled by any political or military order, but now coming to dominance all over the world. The title "the multitude" is given to all not a part of that new dominant reality. The authors call on this new proletariat, the multitude, to begin to think and act globally as a mass movement of protest and resistance. "Globalization must be met with a counter-globalization, Empire with a counter-Empire."[18] The turning point of their book, as they move from analysis to prescription is revealing, suggestive but, sadly, finally pathetic:

> In this regard we might take inspiration from Saint Augustine's vision of a project to contest the decadent Roman Empire. No limited community could succeed and provide an alternative to imperial rule; only a universal, catholic community bringing together all populations and all languages in a common journey could accomplish this. The divine city is a universal city of aliens, coming together, cooperating communicating. Our pilgrimage on earth, however, in contrast to Augustine's, has no transcendent *telos* beyond; it is and remains absolutely immanent.... From this perspective the Industrial Workers of the World is the great Augustinian project of modern times.... [19]

With this model in mind, they call upon the Trotskyist proletarian multitude to oppose the new bourgeois dominant patterns of life. How they might do so is not at all clear, and the hints they make are likely to bring about more failed states, suffering, starvation and chaos. Yet, I think they are right that the current political, cultural and economic hegemony of the leading classes of the United States like those that can be found now also in what was once called the "Third World" is at least partly identical with globalization, more than it is with imperialism, colonialism or neocolonialism. The structures and dynamics that they guide can more accurately be seen as a new bourgeois (urbanized) trans-national set of institutions that are progressively pointing toward a new order in the making and the result of key forms of a Christian worldview and interpretations of

18. Ibid., 207.
19. Ibid.

social history, as they almost recognize. But the metaphysical-moral vision behind these has become separated from its deeper roots and from its wider ethical contours at least in the consciousness of many concerned thinkers, such as Hardt and Negri. Thus all we have left, as many see it, is a socially disembodied utopianism that wants to be transformative without being guided by a transcendental vision or a universal moral law.

It is an open question as to whether or not deeper and wider principles and purposes than they consider can be transplanted or rediscovered and reactivated in the new wider public they have helped create. But, insofar as most analyses of that emerging global public are no longer attentive to any theological perspective, the principalities, thrones, authorities, and dominions behind and residually in them tempt scholars to cynical analysis, and the multitude follows their arrogance, idolatry and injustice in the name of simple living, realism, and justice. They have no fundamental basis for a reconstructive vision. Without one, no renewal is possible and a society that hosts these powers without a transcendent base and turns them over to mass rule is likely to become more dangerous. If they dismiss the ultimate ground of normative visions, they will have no basis for altering what is the historical case. Sooner or later such efforts join the rubble of dead, but once thought to be vital civilizations and lost faiths, and great is ever the fall of it. Or they are simply surpassed. But if the theological convictions embedded in them can be nurtured into a transformed and transforming guidance system, the promise of globalization could become more actualized.

Some Historical Precedents

Today's globalization, fostering technological transformation, communication revolution and cultural, social and political realignments as well, are carried largely by institutional arrangements that have deep roots. However, they may turn out to be merely another trans-national exercise in power and greed that is now reaching the whole known world. Something like this has happened before, and perhaps we can learn from those experiences. After humanity spread to most parts of the earth, adapted to the various ecological niches and developed distinctive local religions and societies, some began to find ways to develop links among them. Driven by desires to share their worldviews, cultural curiosity, hopes to learn from others, a quest for profit, a desire for adventure, a lust for control, a chance to get away from unhappy local situations and a love for the exotic, people created routes of travel and institutions of connection and exchange between West and East, North and South.

Combinations of material and ideal interests drove merchants and adventurers, monks and literati to develop and use a variety of treks for caravans, collectively called the Silk Road. It joined Turkey with China, with connecting routes in the West to European and Slavic lands, in the East to Korea and Japan and in between to India, Arabia and Africa.[20] Buddhist, Christian and later Islamic believers, driven by their universalistic religions, took their faiths to others on these routes. For centuries, goods, ideas, weaponry, musical instruments, slaves, spices and pieties were exchanged. Thus, civilizations were enriched. Many died en route while some gained great wealth even if imperial conquerors and local war lords used these roads to their own advantage, sometimes raiding trading posts and demolishing monasteries in search of gold or to punish those disloyal to this or that emperor or "false" god. Such developments can be seen as the first signs of the wider and deeper globalization to come.

Centuries later, new technologies were fostered by the faith-driven view that nature is viewed as fallen and in need of repair, that progress on that front is possible in history, and that social transformations could more nearly approximate the promised New Jerusalem, imaginatively portrayed at the end of the New Testament. Caravans were replaced by clipper ships and then steam ships. These accelerated the exploration of the continents, the colonization of portions of the globe that were less populated and developed, and the spread of Christianity and technology. It also enabled the expansion of slavery, already widely practiced in most of the world, but more importantly it also invited missionary activity in unprecedented numbers. Priests and preachers, educators and doctors, traders and adventurers, soldiers and administrators brought faith-shaped perspectives on God and humanity, new interpretations of the universe and the earth, new means of nurturing the young and curing the sick, new modes of organizing the common

---

20. Comparable routes of trade and cultural exchange (and of conflict) were developed at various times across the Sahara, through the jungles of central and south America, and, by long boat, across the northern Atlantic and between the islands of the south Pacific — as well as along the great rivers of the world.

life to peoples around the world. The colonizers and the missionaries cooperated in much and brought much with them from their
home culture. However, at times it obscured their intended message and almost overwhelmed indigenous societies. But the receiving
peoples adopted only portions of what was offered, and only selectively modulated their preexisting faiths, practices and social
patterns of life. They brought their older views with them into their
new religious and cultural fields of vision and this made wider visions of humanity more common.[21] New synthetic worldviews were
created: over time it became more possible to speak of a worldwide
aspiration for human rights, democratic polities and the modernization of education and social life — most often in indigenous but
partially Christianized cultural terms.[22]

Today's globalization is another such wave of development, a
Joachite moment marked not only by the displacement of older
closed national systems and the formation of new religious and
cultural syntheses, but also by the technological artifacts of communication, from jumbo jets and the Internet to new modes of genetic
and urban ecological engineering. The increased ability to control
the bio-physical world is matched by newly created channels of
access to information and opinion that is different from what is
approved or expected in our communities of origin. Such developments disoriented several established views of what is natural, of
how we think of time and space, and what the normative guidelines for life are and should be.[23] Thus, they force all those who do
not see the world caught up in a nihilistic break-down to ask what
values, principles and purposes should drive our responses to globalization's promises and perils. This involves the reexamination of
classic resources and the selective reaffirmation of neglected truths
and norms. Many are aware, for example, that some are still left
out of the process and that special attention must be paid to those
who are victimized by it — the peasants and ethnic groups of Western China, the Dalits and Tribals of India, the primal peoples and

---

21. See Andrew F. Walls, *The Missionary Movement in Christian History* (Edinburgh: T & T Clark, 1996); and *The Cross-Cultural Process in Christian History*
(Edinburgh: T & T Clark, 2002).

22. These are among the major themes in *News of Boundless Riches: Interrogating
Missions in a Global Era*, ed. by M. L. Stackhouse and Lalsangkima Pachuau, 2 vols.
(New Delhi: ISPCK, 2007), 6.

23. These changes are discussed extensively by Ron Cole-Turner and Jürgen
Moltmann in vol. 2 of the *God and Globalization* series.

regional empires of Central Africa, and the subsistence farmers and hunter-gatherers of Latin America — a fact that suggests a residual ethic of love for the neighbor and justice for all. The disagreements are about the causes of their distress and its remedy.

Equally striking, however, is the dramatic resurgence of old world religions and new prophecies, with some wanting to determine the destiny of globalization. Particularly obvious, of course, is the militant Islam spreading from the Mid-East to Indonesia in the Far East and into North Africa and Europe in the West, as already suggested. It has structural parallels to some Jewish and Christian forms of fundamentalism, but it has its own dynamics that also apply to the resurgence of Buddhism in East Asia, which is probably growing as fast in the East as is Evangelical Christianity, and as fast as several "New Age" spiritualities (which are mostly old paganism) now common among some post-theistic intellectuals in the West. Such developments suggest a widespread quest for a guiding, ethical and spiritual worldview, one that can render a comprehensive vision of morals and meaning for souls and civilization, one that is simultaneously complex enough to take account of the incredible myriad of cultures and beliefs while being simple enough to shape the loyalties of the peoples.

This matter of loyalties, of a quest for a normative worldview, a metaphysical moral vision, in which to place confidence, leads us back to the question of faith. If it is true that globalization has been formed substantially by the mix of religion with social developments in many spheres of life, even if the consciousness of that mix is now thin, it is also true that globalization forces the question again of faith. Globalization is not the result of the naked play of impersonal or amoral or anti-religious forces and purely material interests. What then is, what has been, what can be and what should be the relation of faith to this global formation of a new worldwide civil society and to the powers that have historically generated it and now sustain it incognito? If this view of the nature of globalization is valid, it is then a major mistake to see globalization only as essentially capitalism unleashed, as some pro-globalists and many anti-globalists do. At most that is a confused understanding of one effect as if it were an all-powerful cause. At least it is a truncated view of how history works. Thus, we must take another look to see what the basic failures of dominant interpretations of globalization are.

On Capitalism and Socialism

For most of the twentieth century, the debate over global matters was conducted between a model of political economy that accented capitalism supported by a pluralistic, republican form of democracy, and a model that accented socialism supported by a centralized, proletarian democracy. In historical terms it has been seen in the West as a struggle between two theories of capitalism — one as in accord with human nature and morality by Adam Smith and his disciples and the other as dehumanizing and self annihilating by Karl Marx and his partisans. There is a third view, equally debated, which derives from a century of debate over the work of Max Weber. When we take into account this stream of work, particularly as represented by the Weberian revisionist Peter Berger and others, and some of the definitions of faith and globalization I have sketched, we can return to some of my initial worries on the economic front and offer a more refined view.

What is clear is that Adam Smith's *Inquiry into the Wealth of Nations* is the intellectual and symbolic godfather of "neoliberal" and "rational choice" theories. Smith observed that some countries were more "opulent" (his term) than others and posed this question: Why and how, if humans are pretty much the same around the world and tend to look toward their own interests, if scarcity is ever a problem, and if most are poor (except kings and feudal rulers who get rich by living off the poor), did more and more of the poor begin to create and distribute wealth more widely? His answer was the "division of labor" in which free labor is so organized that each has a different role to play in the production process and thus takes care to improve the techniques used. This allowed greater productivity and encouraged more extensive patterns of exchange; all could gain more by specializing and trading what they could readily produce for what they could not. No more was economics a zero-sum game. The sum could be expanded and the zero become at least some. The producer and system of exchange facilitated by the trader generated quality production, greater efficiency and the increased interaction of people near and far. Together these created a system that allowed both "opulence" and the "moral sentiments" to flourish.

People participate in this system because all are interested in their own well-being, an inclination that cannot be changed in history, one that prompts them to make economic decisions on a cost/benefit basis and that can easily become sinfully self-centered. However, it may also trigger a calculation of mutual benefit and form community. If trade is to flourish, everyone has to produce what others want or need, and this means that one must have a due regard for the sentiments and morals of the other. This, as Smith argues, reveals a kind of "hidden hand" that providentially guides the social process of voluntary exchange in which all parties gain and society is served. If this is allowed to function worldwide, it brings an increase of world well-being, although some may gain more than others — a variable explained by talent, attentiveness and training — if the system has a relative freedom from artificial controls that inhibit or eat up the gains of others. From this basic standpoint, Smith began to explain the dynamics of international trade in what we can now also see as a forecast of today's global development.

Regarding faith, Smith sees religion as a part of human nature, a part that properly has to be cultivated by the clergy, who are the conveyors of spiritual instruction and the providers of consolation in life's tragedies. Also, he argues in ways that opened up horizons of research by contemporary economists. Robert Nelson and Anthony Waterman, in rather different ways, see the development of modern economics as a function of theology that seeks to save humanity from scarcity and want as a parallel of the effort to save the soul from meaninglessness and sin.[24]

The neoliberal "Chicago school" has refined Smith's views in another direction. As mentioned earlier, Lawrence Iannaccone has surveyed this new trend in the economic analysis of religion.[25] Iannaccone interprets religion as a commodity and summarizes studies of how people go religion- or church-shopping and rationally calculate how much to spend in time or money to "consume" religion. Further, he argues that many seek benefits in the life to come, but most also seek benefits in this life, that there are data to show the benefits of religion. Religious people live longer, have happier marriages, lower rates of cancer, stroke or heart disease, do less drinking or drug abuse and have fewer divorces or reports of wife

---

24. R. H. Nelson, *Reaching for Heaven on Earth: The Theological Meaning of Economics* (New York: Rowman and Littlefield, 1993) and *Economics as Religion: From Samuelson to Chicago and Beyond* (State College: Pennsylvania State University Press, 2003); and Anthony Waterman et al., eds., *Economics and Religion: Are They Distinct?* (Ottawa: Springer Publishers, 1994).

25. See note 2 above.

abuse. Others speak of benefits to society — the formation of groups that generate social capital and trust, thus supporting greater social confidence and competence.

If this research holds up in further studies beyond the Western and Christian experience, we can see part of the reason why religion has had a resurgence and has not declined or disappeared under conditions of modernization and globalization.[26] After all, people do make cost/benefit analyses in religion, and Rodney Stark has argued that just such decisions made a big difference in the growth of Christianity in the history of the West[27] — a study with possible implications for why Christianity is growing so fast in Africa and China, and why Islam is growing also in Africa, and Buddhism in East Asia. People do find healthier habits, social and material gains as well as comfort and solace for their souls in these faiths. But people also make their decisions with regard to what they think is true or false, just or unjust and reasonable or unreasonable, and they decide which traditions to draw their criteria from according to which portrayal of ultimate reality is the most comprehensive and coherent. These latter dimensions, Iannaccone does not fully treat, although Stark does, particularly in his most recent work.[28] In the dynamics of global change such matters are indispensable for persons, communities and for the trajectory of civilizations. Thus, we have to ask which religions promote what kinds of habits and cultures, which leave people in poverty, ignorance, powerlessness and unable to face the challenges of change, and which ones lead to "opulence," fulfillment and hope. In this matter, Stark comes closer than Iannaccone, for beyond the tendency to see religion as

26. See intensive local studies, such as Chen Cunfu, *Chinese Christianity in Transformation: A Case Study of Christian Development in Zhejiang Province* (Shanghai: Scholars Press, 2005), especially 135–202. See also the comparative studies, such as Jagdish Bhagwati, *In Defense of Globalization* (New York: Cambridge University Press, 2004); Benjamin Friedman, *The Moral Consequences of Economic Growth* (New York: Alfred Knopf, 2005); and theoretical studies such as Douglass F. North, *Understanding of the Process of Economic Change* (Princeton, NJ: Princeton University Press, 2005) all suggest that they do apply more widely. The work in economic history by Robert W. Fogel substantiates the point diachronically. See his *The Fourth Great Awakening and the Future of Egalitarianism* (Chicago: Chicago University Press, 2000); and newer *The Escape from Hunger and Premature Death 1700–2100: Europe, America and the Third World* (Cambridge: Cambridge University Press, 2004). I shall refer to these works again shortly.

27. See his *The Rise of Christianity: A Sociologist Reconsiders History* (Princeton, NJ: Princeton University Press, 1996).

28. *The Victory of Reason: How Christianity Led to Freedom, Capitalism and Western Success* (New York: Random House, 2005).

a consumer good that fits private preferences, he sees how theology shapes public life and social history.

Besides Adam Smith and these derivative neoliberal/rational choice models, the second great interpretation is Karl Marx's classic analysis which does have a philosophy of history based, he says, on a "scientific socialism." Smith sees capitalism as a stage of economic development after feudalism that bears within the seeds both of a new bourgeois order and, beyond that, of its own eventual destruction, for it leads to a monopoly of power potentially and a polarization of the classes. Economically, the propertied, metropolitan elites increasingly exploit the propertyless workers until they rise up and seize the apparatus of governance and use it to regain control of the means of production. This process can be accelerated by revolutionary action which disposes with those political-military forces who manipulate and protect those with special privilege. Marx, of course, holds that religion is a manifestation of false consciousness that is fomented by these "power elites"; it reflects alienated man's sigh of oppression and it projects his hope for a better life into the clouds. Unlike Smith, Marx sees no providence in capitalism, even if he sees an agonistic historical dialectic and an inevitable, if temporary, triumph before a recommunalization of humanity (to be speeded by revolution).

There is a "doctrine of sin" in Marx: the rise of an individuated, bourgeois class out of the original primary community due to the invention of private property, an exploitive event that leads to series of dominations that can be abolished only if bourgeois property is ended. Further, Marx foresees a kind of salvation: the development of a new extended community of solidarity in the promised industrialized communism with a collective ownership of industrialized means of production, still in the eschatological future that will bring a perfected classless society. This view was thought to die with the demise of Soviet Union, and the turn of Communist China and Socialist India to forms of capitalism and the collapse of the liberation movements after the overthrow of colonialism. In fact, it lives on among those who most militantly supported liberation theology. There is no denying the usefulness of the Marxist criticism of colonial rule. It helped deconstruct colonial oppression, but it has not shown that it could build a viable social, economic or legal order. Its view of history is badly flawed; it cannot imagine

that religiously shaped values generated modernity. Still, a truncated Marxism seemed to be alive in several academics and in the
presuppositions of many ecumenical church leaders, for instance, in
documents such as "Alternative Globalization: Addressing Peoples
and Earth" (A.G.A.P.E.), and in *A Caring Economy: A Feminist
Contribution to Alternatives to Globalization,* both cited above.[29]
Here is no hard communism, but instead a soft socialism governed
by a quasi-Marxist analysis. It says the "WCC has made a clear distinction between globalization as a multi-faceted historical process
and the present form of a pernicious economic and political project
of global capitalism...based on an ideology...[of] neoliberalism"
(1). It is quasi-Marxist because it in fact interprets the multi-faceted
dynamic of globalization entirely in terms of economics, and views
economics as driven by the polarization of classes as caused by capitalism — without saying that the governing faith of the analysis is in
fact Marxist. It sees the material interests of the propertied classes
as the primary cause of all social evils, supported by imperial elites
who control "economic, cultural, political, and military powers that
constitute a global system of domination..." (2). Thus, while the
authors say they want to make a distinction between globalization
as a multi-faceted historical process and economic globalization, in
fact it presents only a reductionist political-economic analysis, the
opposite side of Iannaccone. The report intends to "confront the
suffering, enormous economic and social disparity, abject poverty
and the destruction of life, which result from the neoliberal model of
economic globalization" (5). It intends to call believers into "transformative communities [which] practice an economy of solidarity
and sharing" (5). It calls for an "economy of life" as against the
ruling "economy of death" (10).[30]

I am worried about this document for I find many of my colleagues, clergy and students who hold these views and have had
no existential exposure to socialism or communism which will lead
the church down an incoherent ideological path that will not help

---

29. See note 3 above. Parallel statements have been passed by the World Reformed
Alliance and the Lutheran World Federation.

30. The numbers in parentheses refer to pages in the web site document. The root
concepts can be found in F. J. Hinkelammert, *The Ideological Weapons of Death: A
Theological Critique of Capitalism* (Maryknoll, NY: Orbis Books, 1986); and Ulrich
Duchrow, *Alternatives to Global Capitalism* (Utrecht: International Books, 1994).
See their *Property for People, Not for Profit* (London: Zed Books, 2004).

the poor with whom they self-righteously say they are in solidarity. This view, in my perspective, is in danger of repeating the error that the Roman Catholic Church made when it condemned Galileo for publishing a heliocentric understanding of the universe rather than a geocentric one as the church at that time taught as right doctrine and valid science. Thus, the church failed to see that a mythic view, treated as science, was being displaced by a new paradigm, and it condemned as heretical the new view. In regard to globalization, a new paradigm is in the making that not only displaces the quasi-Marxist view on which this document depends, but compromises the sovereignty of every national government and its ability to control a national economy — in part because technological, scientific, social, cultural, communication, legal, ethical and religious standards have already superceded that prospect, and because the previous period of human history with its proletarian and national socialism shows what disasters happen when the state is given ever wider command over social, cultural, economic and religious life, ostensibly to make everyone more equal.

The Better Evidence

Further, in this case, no major economist of any stripe is cited. If they did consult those who have written explicitly about globalization and summarized the best evidence, such as the Indian economist and Nobel Prize recipient, now at Columbia University, Jagdish Bhagwati's *In Defense of Globalization*, the Nobel Prize recipient from Washington University Douglass C. North's *Understanding the Process of Economic Change*, the Harvard economist Benjamin Friedman's *The Moral Consequences of Economic Growth*, and the Nobel Prize recipient Robert W. Fogel's *Escape from Hunger and Premature Death*,[31] they would find the following:

- Globalization is not impoverishing the poor; it is raising millions who were poor for centuries into new middle classes in the most rapid gains in history, although there are populations that globalization has not reached, especially in cultures that are predisposed to resist exchange with outsiders and change in global directions.

---

31. See note 26 above.

- Inequality has temporarily increased, as is usual in history when new social values, plus new methods of production and modes of organization are introduced, and vast numbers of people are drawn into urbanizing and industrializing economies and have to form new patterns of life. Traditional conventions are disrupted, bringing crisis especially to tribal and peasant populations; but if they are not disrupted, or resist change, they will fall further and further behind. Thus, governments and faith-based organizations must make the resources required by the new modes of life available to all.

- The most desperate people are found in economies that are the most centrally planned, and those most exploited are the victims of local despots or rogue warlords in failed or failing states. The poverty of China and India until recently, and of North Korea and the Islamic world today, plus the tragedies of Haiti, Zimbabwe and Darfur and the crises of Latin American, Russian or Central African mercantilism are not due to globalization.

- Confidence in state managed economies has also been shattered by feudal, colonial, Fascist, Peronist and Communist experience; and even the elaborate welfare state policies of European democratic socialism is being challenged in Holland, Germany, England and the Scandinavian countries, and by the EU itself.

- The migration patterns of those seeking to flee an "economy of death" and to find an "economy of life" flow into areas where democratic capitalist systems are dominant.

- In most parts of the world, more and more people are adopting globalized patterns of life, but are doing so selectively and wedding the resources to features of their own cultures so that they can work on international and cross-cultural bases while preserving what is distinctive to their own values.

- New techniques of measuring comparative results which include not only income and calorie intake, but nutrition levels, height, weight, health, life span, leisure time, overt concern for social, ethical and religious values indicate that the poor in globalizing and modernizing lands have especially gained in comparison with most of previous history. In fact during the development of capitalism on a global scale, the life-span of the people has increased by an average of thirty years. It does not seem to be an "economy of death."

The evidence once assembled is quite overwhelming. This is not to say that the economic systems enjoying the fruits of globalization are without fault, and the analyses which I invoke are not uncritical of realities and policies in the "developed" countries.[32] They criticize:

• Structural inequalities at home and incoherent policies abroad that speak of freedom when many are not free and human rights yet practice or condone torture are scandalous.

• Arguments for more "free trade" while passing protectionist laws on agricultural products or manufactured goods means that some are speaking with forked tongues.

• Policies to expand democracy, but then trying to manipulate the outcomes if elections produce the "wrong" result, discredit democracy and its advocates.

• Substantial revisions of policies by the new international regulatory agencies — IMF, World Bank, WTO, and several branches of the UN — are being made and more need to be made. So also with the regional bodies — NAFTA, EU, OAS, etc.

• The positive developments are not yet reaching all peoples equally, even if it is reaching more and more people more quickly than at any point in history. This is so in spite of factors that inhibit the capacity of people to receive global benefits: family practices and the spread of HIV/AIDS; corruption in politics, business and education in poorer lands; cultural attitudes and religious beliefs that resist the transformation of ways of life that inhibit rapid development, etc.

Again, so on one could go. The biggest problem with both many neoliberal "economics of religion" and the quasi-Marxist church leaders (and even some main-line economists here cited, who in

---

32. Bhagwati, *In Defense of Globalization*; North, *Understanding the Process of Economic Change*; Friedman, *The Moral Consequences of Economic Growth*; Fogel, *The Fourth Great Awakening*.

fact have their data straighter than the other two) is that they all tend to neglect the real power and influence of faith in societies and in globalization. Exceptions can be found in Peter L. Berger et al., *Many Globalizations,* and its sister volume, *Culture Matters,* by Lawrence E. Harrison et al. Both Berger and Harrison sees religious influences as defining for cultures and thus influential in the society and its economic life.[33] This stream of scholarship is not rigorously hostile to capitalism but it shares with the Marxist tradition a recognition that the structural organization of society influences the kind of economy that develops. But beyond Marxism, they see the social order as deeply influenced by dominant religious, worldview or ideological presuppositions. This stream of thought about globalization is generally more identified with Max Weber than with Smith or Marx, and what differentiates this perspective from them is precisely that it sees religion as an independent variable that shapes culture, and recognizes that cultural factors and interests interact with material interests to shape economies. Neither of the other positions treats religion as a decisive cause in the formation of the social forces that engendered modern globalization.

Weber's arguments, to be sure, have been subject to debate and dispute for a century; and he was surely wrong in some of them. Capitalist forms of production and trade were more fully developed in some monastic centers and in both Italian and Germanic cities before the Protestant Ethic than he acknowledges. Weber of course, mentions these, but does not think they reflect or formed a new common ethos as the Puritans did. Further, his volumes on the comparative sociology of religion pose the issue: What kind of religion shapes what kinds of culture and what is the impact of a culture generated by a distinctive religion on social and economic life? This issue remains among the most promising lines of inquiry in a day in which the idea that secularization is the inevitable correlation or result of modernization seems quite senile.

Of course the "economics of religion" view of the Chicago School has a place for religion in personal life, and it does shape

---

33. Berger and Huntington, eds., *Many Globalizations*; and Lawrence E. Harrison and Samuel P. Huntington, eds., *Cultural Matters: How Values Shape Human Progress* (New York: Basic Books, 2000). It is also the case that Bhagwati, North, and Friedman, all cited in note 26, are alert to the role of culture and, especially in North and Friedman's cases, to the religious and theological influences in political and economic life. These will be discussed further in chapter 2.

ethical opinions in such areas as abortion, gay marriage, pornography, etc. But they miss the profound view of Providence which allows that model to flourish. And the pro-Marxist theological types in the World Council have a place for religion as an active force to resist globalization and to create enclaves of "people's movements" that will form anti-capitalist alternative base communities. However, what that alternative looks like is unclear, except that they express solidarity with those who are marginal to global dynamics. That, of course, is a very pastoral thing to do, and one of the functions of the church; but it is not in the least prophetic. It neither specifies the nature of justice for the actual contexts in which people live in a globalizing world, nor invites them to repent for their myopic loyalties, nor prepares them to face the future into which they are being plunged. Moreover, it systematically fails to see the kind of thing that Weber identified, now explored in a variety of ways beyond his work: that in the dominant structures of social, political and economic life, religious themes that were worked out over centuries have been plowed into the very fabric of the common life:

- a this-worldly asceticism that appears in a work ethic that identifies one's calling with professional excellence and a rationalization of economic production and consumption;

- the kind of political life which we call democratic, as it was worked out first in church life and used to legitimate the constitutional polities being advanced around the world;

- the ideas of human rights, based in the idea that each person is made in the image of God, and that each is endowed by our Creator with certain inalienable rights;

- the idea of a corporation independent of family or tribe, and of regime or empire, but operating under just laws by and under the supervision of accountable "trustees";

- the idea that the world, while created good by God, is not holy in itself, and is subject to radical distortion or "fall" and thus properly may come under dominion of a stewardly humanity — an idea that made modern scientific technology and the cybernetic revolutions possible; and

- the idea that there is an ultimate end for humanity beyond death, and that the vision of that end is the New Jerusalem,

a cosmopolitan and complex urban civilization into which all
the peoples of the earth can bring their gifts. This is the key to a
theology of history and thus to the dynamics of globalization.

All these notions and more are among the background beliefs
that have shaped human behavior in the most developed lands for
centuries, and I submit that we cannot understand the globalizing
forces if we do not grasp the ways in which these ideas are derived
directly from biblical and Christian religious resources, and how
they have substantively shaped our history. Such faith-based ideas
may not have been held by all branches of the Christian tradition
in the same measure, but these are the ones that became pregnant
in many of the patterns of life that sustain globalization. Such ideas
are today not at the front of the minds of today's business, political,
scientific, technological, legal or ministerial leaders; but they are so
woven into the cultural presuppositions of those in the West who are
generating the forces of globalization that these forces are enhanced
by a preconscious faith in them. Many, of course, see the results of
these developments as simply secular, and they seem to many like
simply the rational thing to do. In addition, many seek to adopt,
or to resist, the forms of capitalism, technology, democracy and
human rights without attending to the fundamental presuppositions
on which they rest.

What Then Do We Need?

I doubt that we can accurately grasp, reform, correct, or redirect
globalization without wrestling with these theological themes and
their presuppositions. Nor can we get an accurate read on the principles by which we need to evaluate the consequences of present
trends, if we do not see whence they came and where they have been
going. The systemic amnesia about these motifs, which today besets
many university faculties, nearly all journalism and media mavens,
most political and business leaders, scientists and technologists and
no small numbers of theological seminaries means that we are driving with flawed mental maps as to where we came from, where we
are going and how we might best get to where we want to be.[34]

34. Two very suggestive new studies reveal that those with theological positions
other than my own are also raising these points. See David Hollenbach, S.J., *The
Global Face of Public Faith* (Washington, DC: Georgetown University Press, 2003);

Clearly none of these ideas came from primal, Taoist, Confucian, Hindu, Buddhist, or Islamic cultures, although some parallels exist. Moreover, each of these traditions has other ideas about how the world should be organized. As Christianity has spread around the world, new religious developments are appearing — some rather wan and fragile; others, such as the Pentecostal movement, quite robust and promising, often forming syntheses with the cultural presuppositions shaped by other religions. It is dynamics at this level that have shaped complex civilizations in the past, and it is at least some of these options that must be examined as we inevitably encounter these traditions under conditions of globalization. In short, the really existing dynamics of globalization cannot be grasped or guided without studying the relationship of faith to culture, culture to societies, and societies to the formation of a new public: a worldwide civil society and possibly a new civilization, from which economic developments cannot be isolated! We need a theology wide and deep enough to interpret and guide this new public.

The following chapters are designed to provide at least one basis for that new public theology, one that is faithful to biblical and classical theological resources.

---

and William Schweiker, *Theological Ethics and Global Dynamics* (Oxford: Blackwell Publishers, 2004).

– Chapter 1 –

THE QUESTION
A REVIEW AND A DIRECTION

The Purpose of This Volume

As suggested in the Introduction, the purpose of this volume is to
offer an answer to this question: What do Christian theology and
ethics have to offer public life in our globalizing epoch — an era in
which the public spheres of life are much expanded and highly differentiated? To pose this question, of course, is to raise the issue of
the relationship of theology to the development of large scale social
systems, an issue that few try to address and many find odd. Yet, I
believe, this is one of the most important and most neglected issues
of our times. I will not only argue that Christian theology has much
to offer, I will propose that certain normative themes in it do directly
pertain to the most important social ethical issue of our times — the
creation of an ethos, a moral infrastructure for a worldwide civil
society that could lead to a highly diverse, cosmopolitan civilization — if the formation of that infrastructure is guided by a viable
worldview. If that is to happen, it must both be rooted in a valid
theological stance and it must be able to engage the empirical conditions it proposes to address. This is so not only because we must
ever respond to new, sometimes threatening, developments that put
our views of our faith and morals in doubt, nor only because some
developments manifest phenomenon against which we must render
prophetic judgement, although both of these are surely true. It is
true also because certain influences from the classic Christian traditions of theology and ethics are at least partly responsible for the
patterns and deeper dynamics that are driving globalization. To ignore these influences will mean that we cannot understand what
is going on in these patterns and dynamics, recognize their inner

moral and spiritual content, act to enhance what is right, good and fitting or to constrain what is wrong, evil or unfitting in its effects.

Many of the dynamics and structures that are manifest in globalization appear to many to be nonreligious and quite amoral — conditions of economic life, for instance, that are ordinarily not seen as having a spiritual base or ethical significance. Yet, as already suggested in the Introduction, many of the developments that shape globalization are culturally approved technology — e.g., info-engineering, bio-engineering, geo-engineering and socio-engineering (management) — that are laden with religiously shaped ethical convictions and assumptions, and the economic developments that many call globalization are based in substantial measure precisely on them. The capacity to participate creatively in these dynamics and the ordered spheres of life that give them structure are inhibited, distorted or ignored if these convictions or assumptions are not recognized as part of the fabric of a social ethos and critically assessed by the people. Yet these dynamics and structures are not confined to a single society. They reach over the barriers between peoples, nations and political economies in ways that have been advanced by the orthodox, catholic, ecumenical and evangelical impulses of Christian thought and life in the past. They are now having delayed and often indirect but potent effects.

Many of the difficulties that people have with the idea of globalization are due to the failures of contemporary theologians and ethicists (including pastors, priests, and professors of religion) to recognize and take responsibility for the historical impact of Christianity on the various powers and spheres of society that have generated it and that sustain and renew it. Other difficulties come from the correlative failures of social scientists, historians, and economists to acknowledge that much of what they study in this area is rooted in, shaped by or legitimated by principles and purposes central to Christian thought. Some social scientists and critics are oblivious to these factors, and reject the very idea that religion could be an important factor in social history, because it is not important in their lives or disciplines, and they cannot imagine how deeply it influences others or the presupposition of the historic disciplines and society as a whole, even if they acknowledge how it is influenced by other factors. But it is an intellectual fault of major proportions. In fact, religious motivations and convictions, and the realities to which they point, have had, still have, will have and should have profound effects on how societies, cultures and civilizational possibilities work in the age of globalization.[1] While the resurgence of (especially conservative) forms of religion has perplexed, even frightened, those who thought that the religious phase of human history was past, and many view religion as the by-product of psychological needs or social forces, best kept out of public discourse, no one has succeeded in keeping it in the past, in the private emotions, in class or ethnic confines or out of the public squares.

A more perilous mistake with regard to globalization is when religious leaders take such nonreligious, anti-theological and or amoral social theories about globalization as definitive, and then use their theology as a club to render their moral judgements against it for being so. They act as if the views they have blindly adopted actually grasp the realities of social history, and as if theologically based ethical pronouncements or actions could make any difference now if their analysis of the structure has no place for religion as a causative factor when there is no presumption or argumentation that such convictions have done so in the past.[2]

Although theologians and pastors often appeal to their hearers to relate their faith to their daily lives, they frequently do so in a way that suggests that they must judge and overcome the cultural patterns and social dynamics of life — without accounting for the fact that they have been shaped by hundreds of years of religious influence interacting with material needs, wants and interests or that some of this shaping is right and good. In no few theological circles today, there is a high contempt for modern culture and western society, as if its main contours bore no trace of authentic moral or spiritual conditioning over the centuries. Others seek

---

1. But see Peter L. Berger, ed., *The Desecularization of the World* (Grand Rapids: Eerdmans, 1999) and David Martin, *On Secularization: Towards a Revised General Theory* (Burlington, VT: Ashgate, 2005) for recent overviews of the debates.

2. This is the peril of Rebecca Todd Peters' simplified overview of current perspectives on globalization as they are widely viewed in liberal Protestant circles: *In Search of the Good Life: The Ethics of Globalization* (New York: Continuum, 2004). Holding that globalization is essentially economic, she treats neoliberal, developmental, earthist (ecological), and postcolonial perspectives, claiming that the first two are doomed to failure and the last two can be strengthened to reprogram globalization by grass-roots, faith-based community organizing activism for a new democratic socialism. This view offers a faulty analysis of the past, a thin vision of the present and a futile view of the future.

a pure faith untouched by the tendencies of modernity. In consequence, practitioners in the many complex spheres of social life, and who try to attend to the messages of these religious leaders, are seldom reminded that the meaning which they find in their work, their culture, their society and political order is loaded with the incarnate residues of moral and spiritual values derived from historic theological influences. In the long run, they can only make sense of what they do, or reform it, if those values, principles and purposes were identified, critically evaluated, and utilized in fresh ways to address the new contexts of life that they have helped generate. If that does not happen, people will increasingly find themselves trapped in habits of thought and activity that they cannot understand, worshiping in a faith community disengaged from the common life and thus living with an alienation from the world their faith helped shape while grasping only fragmented bits of the meanings on which it rests. They will remain in a state of not knowing whence their scattered preferences and practices derive or not recognizing that the moral and spiritual powers embedded in them are dormant realities full of promise. With no consciousness of the deeper rootage and potential flowering of these religious meanings, the various spheres of life in which people dwell can be captured by morally and spiritually corrupting ideologies that flatten life's potential meanings and make ethical principles and purposes incoherent.

This fault is partly due to the fact that much of theology focuses on the internal life and thought of religious institutions. This is not entirely wrong; indeed it is indispensable in measured proportion. As the great theologian, who was also the prime minister of Holland, Abraham Kuyper, argued a century ago: each sphere of life has its own sovereign integrity and must wrestle with its own "principium" — the central dynamic and patterned purpose by which it is normatively governed.[3] Thus, lawyers must focus on the internal content and logic of law as they apply it to particular cases, doctors must focus on the medical diagnosis and practice of medicine with regard to particular patients with particular maladies, and airline pilots must attend to the mechanics of flight and the distinctive weather conditions on each flight. So also the church needs specialists who seek to understand the content and logic of particular

---

3. See, especially, his *Principles of Sacred Theology* (Grand Rapids: Eerdmans, 1954).

doctrines and constellations of faith held by specific set of believers. But all these spheres of life stand under a Sovereignty that is greater than their own integrity, and makes it possible for each to interact cooperatively with other spheres. Still, there is a threat: the focus of each can become so exclusive that it denies or filters out attention to the embedded normative dimensions those fields or to the relationships that the specific sphere has to other spheres. After all, the reason for the existence of lawyers and the law has to do with the attempt to grasp and enact justice and to prevent or resolve the inevitable conflicts in areas of social interaction other than the law itself. The reason for the existence of doctors and medicine has to do with the discernment and actualization of wholesome living while facing the reality of inevitable suffering and death, much of it caused by working conditions or communicable diseases as well as of hereditary flaws and aging. The basic existence of these fields has a deeper base and a broader, deeper context of meaning than any particular area can represent. So clergy and theology must be concerned with the beliefs and values, principles, purposes and practices that form the church and the believers as they seek to be faithful participants in the community of faith and in the common life that now is global in reach. They do so on the basis of warranted claims about the sovereign God, and the only God worth worshiping cares about many things besides the already pious at prayer under the steeple.[4]

Some traditions seem to address public issues in a way that is not distinctly helpful. Often the appeals to relate faith to the common life focus on specific issues — characteristically today, poverty and wealth on the left and sexuality and abortion on the right, with each using what they call theology as a megaphone to shout at the government to regulate them. This does not only reinforce a statist view of public life, but also overestimates what political means can do to shape personal decisions about economic and sexual life. Although there are notable exceptions, few seem to address the structured fabric of those institutions where people live — corporations and families for example. Yet these institutions have built into them convictions, principles and purposes that sustain an ethos. Often, they are what bear the meanings that enable or inhibit people's

---

4. See the chapters by John Witte Jr., on law, and Allen Verhey on medicine in vol. 2 of the *God and Globalization* series, Introduction, note 2.

ability to develop their potential, find a purpose in life or become responsible agents of the repeated reformations necessary to sustain meaningful identity and a viable social life in a globalizing era. That ethos, and the characteristic institutions of civil society which embody it, is a primary formative influence on both personality and politics. Yet, the members of the complex institutions of contemporary life live as if the realities they face and the work they do in these contexts must exclude any overt reference to theological and ethical considerations. That separation alienates theology from life, impoverishes faith and deprives the institutions of the common life of both a full measure of meaning and an articulate morality. The results are preaching, teaching and ritual with little grasp of their implicit moral, social or political amplitude, and a host of practices, policies, institutions and society with an incoherent spiritual core, understood by specialized sciences that pay little attention to the normative basis of truth or justice or healing or faith on which they depend.

In contrast, the claims of this volume will be that Christian theology and a social ethic based in it can, indeed must, learn from the various social and historical sciences and from the practitioners in their various spheres of society, and that efforts to think theologically or to make moral judgments without reference to these turn out to be gnostic esoterica or spiritual froth. The reverse is also true: the various social sciences can, indeed must, learn from the theological and ethical sciences, and efforts to interpret history or society without reference to them turn out to be or incoherent or flat. The two need each other, and if the connection is broken the results falsify the depth and width of both personal and social life.

What We Have Done: A Brief Review[5]

In the previous three volumes of this set, a remarkable team of scholars has charted other ways of understanding and addressing our situation. They have drawn on theology as well as other fields of scholarly research to identify the scope of globalization as a world phenomenon, to interpret the social history from which it derives,

---

5. Those who have read the first three volumes may wish to proceed to the next section. What follows here is a brief summary of the conceptual framework, stated more fully in the "General Introduction" to the series in vol. 1, here modified by the contributions of the essays written on specific areas for the subsequent volumes.

and to suggest ethical themes to guide life and thought in it. Their essays are organized into the three volumes according to a basic view of "the powers" which drive the formation of civilizations; each "power" is organized by institutional clusters sharing primary norms and common ends, which we call "spheres." Each sphere has a distinct role in today's social and historical life and functions more or less in accord with its own pattern of "best practices"; yet each interacts with every other sphere to form a society guided by a central faith-based worldview and an implicit ethos. These are shaping and being shaped by the dynamics and structures of globalization.[6]

The first set of dynamic powers, with corresponding spheres of institutionalized patterns of life to nurture, express, and constrain them, are present in every society and are called the "principalities." A second set is those which, having evoked new kinds of institutional spheres, become dominant only in modernizing or modernized complex societies, and are treated as the "authorities." And a third set, the "dominions," refers to the great religious "metaphysical-moral visions" or "worldviews" that provide frames of reference for whole societies and organize the relationship between the powers and spheres of the first two sets in distinctive ways.[7] In each of the spheres of life our authors have identified religious and ethical influences at work in the dynamics and structures of globalization and have treated them in theological terms.

The basic social entities are, of course, socially embedded persons who live and move and have their being in the midst of clusters of

---

6. The concept of "spheres" is drawn from Abraham Kuyper, *Lectures on Calvinism* (Grand Rapids: Eerdmans, 1931) as mentioned in volume 1, and as also used by Karl Barth, *Church Dogmatics*, III/iv. The term, as well as "the departments of life," was used by Ernst Troeltsch, *The Social Teaching of the Christian Churches*, trans. O. Wyon (New York: HarperCollins, 1932). These concepts refine the medieval theological notions of the "estates" and the Reformation's "orders of creation," the number and structure of which was thought to be fixed. Some Marxist theorists use the geometric term "sectors of society," but the focus on occupational groupings (also present in traditional Asian hierarchical theories) or on class analysis is much too narrow to grasp the global dynamics. All, however, intend to identify the key social matrices that allow human life to flourish and constrain tendencies to chaos or exploitation.

7. As indicated in earlier volumes, these terms are drawn from Paul's use of the terms "powers," "principalities," "authorities," "thrones" (see previous chapter), and "dominions." I use them because they suggestively link psycho-spiritual dynamics with social ethical patterns of life that have positive or negative commanding significance. The use is intended to reinforce the claim that theological insights are critical to the analysis of the global patterns of life.

institutions that make it possible to survive and flourish in distinct environments. Persons may decide to exit one or several of the institutions into which they were born, but they almost always form new relationships or associations to live out their lives, modifying their cluster of institutions. Although all "spheres of society" stand under certain universal ethical principles, each also has its distinctive functions and is constructed to host and guide the "powers" that energize human life, so that they may actualize their potentiality and purpose. Thus, in every society familial institutions are formed to nourish, guide and constrain the impulses of human sexuality that are both necessary for the propagation and nurture of the next generation and for fostering experiences of self-transcending ecstasy and bonding affection. These impulses and their expression can also become destructive and idolatrous, by fostering the worship not only of body parts or functions, but also of genetic gene-pools by the making of genealogical heredity the center of a collective identity. This "principal" power is symbolized by the term "Eros."

Similarly, economic institutions are formed to meet basic human needs, to invite the creativity of human labor, and to fulfill the desire for an abundant life. But these can become idolatrous also, in, e.g., gluttony and greed or by thinking that possessions can be spiritually salvific, as conveyed by the term "Mammon." Political institutions are organized in order to insure order and law, to provide defense and to do for all what cannot be accomplished by people alone or by groups voluntarily — all of which requires the disciplined use of coercive means. This "principality" is symbolized by the term "Mars," which can also become idolatrously deified in statism, dictatorship or the kind of militarism that celebrates the nobility of violence. Further, cultural institutions are developed to facilitate communication and to express concerns in all the spheres already mentioned, and to articulate aesthetic sensibilities through disciplined forms of the arts. These are symbolized by "The Muses," and can become idolatrous also, when humans worship their own creativity and impose it on others as if no spiritual force outside the self could be the source of inspiration.

In each of these areas of human activity, the pertinent sets of practices and institutions form a "sphere" of life. These are ordered in their interaction by an operating patterns of values, principles, purposes, virtues and normative stories which together form an ethos. In other words, hovering over all these interlocked but distinct systems is a regulative set of beliefs and practices (which we call "Religion") that routinize the reigning metaphysical and moral vision of a social unit and relate it to profound sensibilities that a transcendent realm provides the precedents and expectations by which the whole is to be guided. When that transcendent sensibility, the ethos it shapes and its distinctive social architecture is disrupted — as in times of great social transition, such as is the present case with globalization — its "powers" are unbound, sometimes freed from conventional fetters that prevent their creative functioning, and sometimes becoming ends or idols in themselves. Persons suffer, essentially because institutions begin to fall apart and a community becomes unable to defend itself against stronger societies that are more cohesively organized. Tribes have been decimated by stronger cultures or become absorbed into kingdoms; kingdoms have fallen to empires or become a part of great civilizations. The dynasties of ancient China, India, Africa and Meso-America succumbed to modern colonialists. Ancient Rome fell and, recently, the Soviet Union collapsed, as did the apartheid regime in South Africa. They all tried to concentrate all functions of the spheres under one, unified sovereign concern — racial, economic class, political authority, cultural dominance or monolithic religion. Not only do such regimes not work practically, the "gods" — including the quasi-religious "secular" ideologies of nation, race or class that demand loyalty and a confession of faith — failed in sociotheological crises of confidence. Fewer and fewer believe in these systems any more, and they demonically seek to preserve themselves by wreaking havoc on their members and neighbors, until that system falls apart or is defeated by a spiritually, morally and socially superior civilization. Tragic examples in the West were the attempt to replicate a romanticized feudalism by establishing slavery in a land that had no peasants (until it was defeated in the American Civil War) and the attempt to create a racially pure "society" in central Europe (until Nazism was defeated in World War II). The zeal to conduct these wars was fueled by religious and ethical movements that attacked the evils at work in the ethos of societies based on false faiths.

These clusters of spiritually, morally, and socially ordered spheres exist because the "powers" that drive life are both necessary and subject to distortion. The basic powers — Eros, Mammon, Mars and the Muses — can induce quasi-religious feelings of transcendence, experiences that grip human souls and link persons to groups, which is why marriage and the ecstasy of intimacy, business and the joys of reward, governance and the blessings of victory and peace, and cultural institutions and the euphoria of artistry are celebrated by all the world's religions. They can also, arguably better, be understood as divine gifts that remind humans of what we already sense: we live under a normative transcendent reality that is more than any one of these alone or all of them together can construct or grasp. This sense was classically called a "prereligious" *sensus divinitatis* — but what is today more often called "spirituality." As already indicated in the Introduction, when it is organized into a "creed, cult, and code" and is incarnated into cultural and social forms, it is called "a Religion" and it begins to shape the culture and society in ways that mold them to its defining principles and purposes.

The capacity to develop an awareness of transcendence is thought to be an intrinsic part of human consciousness, unless people have that awareness damaged by misshapen or damaging religion itself, in which case various forms of anti-religious ideology become the substitute faith. Such dynamics are necessarily operative in every society. Moreover, if this "spirituality" is not attached to a religion that incarnates something real, true, just and merciful, it will drift with the winds or become attached to something unreal, false, fanatical, unjust and cruel. This is the fact that accounts for much critique of religion.

The basic definitions of what is real, true, reasonable, just and merciful are articulated in a variety of ways, of course, and each way guides the formation of traditions about what is the best way to order these powers. Indeed, the "powers" behind generative and bonded sexuality, cooperative and effective production of wealth, constitutional government with human rights and relative peace, and orchestrated beauty are not only based in our glands, our digestive tracts, our brawn or our brains, but are often seen as spiritually inspired and ethically formative. Still, these powers are subject, like persons, to deep and dangerous distortion if those who use these powers fail to see that they can be taken for granted and become idolatrous when our final trust is put in them. If the powers lose contact with their divine source and norm, or begin to control the other powers to enhance their own potency, they become pompous and destructive internally as well as to those other spheres around them.[8] The classic traditions speak of that as being "demonic." If one of the spheres fails to simultaneously facilitate and channel the power that drives it, or begins to cannibalize other powers, destroying their integrity, or if it cannot be reformed by both the functional pressures of the other spheres and the recovery or reconstruction of a valid spiritual vision with a viable ethic, the whole is likely to implode, and the people suffer greatly. A new and larger vision is needed to reconstruct a more comprehensive articulation of those decisive convictions that can give disciplined and reasonable licence to these powers. Many believe either that modern civilization is imploding sexually, economically, politically and culturally, due to globalization; others, including the authors of this series, see the prospect of a larger vision in it, one that could, under certain conditions, reconstruct the common life.

A Short Genealogy of Today's Globalization

Some societies and some of the spiritual, religious, and ethical visions that hold them together generate reconstructive transformation. That has happened in the West, and it may be useful to trace some of the key developments in Western history that brought us to today's globalization.[9] Of course, as I have already noted, many people see it only as the economic phenomenon of capitalist expansion, one that, they say, is bringing the destruction of cultures and a degradation of society and nature. In fact, as was repeatedly suggested in the first three volumes, and as we will attempt to show in this final volume again, many of the changes in regard to the extension of the influence of corporations, technology and markets, and the increasing disparities between the very rich and the very poor, are due to noneconomic factors that have shaped economic changes.

---

8. Early in the twentieth century, the great reformer-theologian, Walter Rauschenbusch, identified "powers" such as these as "super-personal forces of good and evil," "forces" potentially subject to conversion and reform. See his *A Theology for the Social Gospel* (New York: Macmillan, 1917). His efforts have been criticized much during that century; but as we face a new wave of social change, now on a global scale, a revival of interest can be found in C. H. Evans, *The Social Gospel Today* (Louisville: Westminster John Knox Press, 2001).

9. Here I expand on a theme mentioned in the Introduction — the theological, ethical and social developments that made today's globalization distinct from that of the Silk Road and that of the age of exploration and colonization.

It is not that economic interests and developments are not important; they are. There is no land in which the general population does not want things to get better economically, and by "better" they mean more jobs, more productivity, more money, more commodities in the market, more access to technical training, and more possibilities for good food, clean water, substantial housing, and opportunities for education, cultural expression, health care, and voice in determining their own future.

But only some kinds of changes that could bring these possibilities are viewed as socially, morally, and spiritually tolerable, and many are viewed as unacceptable. In most Socialist, Buddhist and Islamic regions, for example, there is a strong tendency toward the concentration of centralized national power in ways that inhibit participation in global development, although legally socialist India, officially Buddhist Thailand and mostly Muslim Malaysia, have begun to develop quite rapidly in recent decades, due to the adoption of deregulation, liberalization, and privatization. The reason for the concentration of power is quite different in each case, religiously and culturally, yet the pressures to reconcentrate it remain high. However, most of the modernizing changes that diversify the society have proven to be less degenerative of the society's religious core than predicted, but more reconstructive, although not without internal resistance.[10] Still, the majority of these changes have enhanced the prospects of a new societal vitality, reduced the likelihood of the powers becoming totally autonomous, created a wider interdependency between peoples and regions, and brought relief to much suffering.

Some religions, indeed, invite, even demand, constant reformation and not simply the preservation or restoration of past patterns of life, and they do this because they give the various powers a disciplined, but reasonable, freedom with a sense of a positively transforming destiny, expecting that, under certain conditions, the powers can help heal the disabilities, injustices and evils of historical life. They encourage the various spheres of society to develop a relative autonomy while demanding that each obey the first principles of right and wrong and to see that its own good is in relationship to ultimate ends beyond its own well-being. The problem, for some

---

10. On this point, I commend the careful treatment of the empirical evidence found in Robert E. Baldwin and L. Alan Winters, eds., *Challenges to Globalization: Analyzing the Economics* (Chicago: University of Chicago Press, 2004).

religions or faith-based societies, is that the first principles of right and wrong, as manifest in the principles of human rights, when introduced or adopted, disrupt long-term cultural practices (e.g., regarding the role of women or low-status groups). Further, an expanded vision of the common good can override class, tribal, caste, or national loyalties, fracturing a previous localistic sense of the solidarity of an "us." Other religions and societies — several branches of catholic and ecumenical Christianity and the cultures rooted in them, for instance — thus, not only developed an independent center of power by forming a socially active community of faith, they also develop systematic ways of linking the principles and purposes they cultivate to each of the basic spheres of life. Even more, they helped create new powers and spheres that become increasingly important in complex, more highly differentiated societies. As we have seen in volume 2 of this series, the development of certain theological orientations in the late Medieval and early Reformation periods has led to another species of the powers, beyond the primary "principalities," that have become the "modern authorities" as manifest in the "high professions."

In anticipation of what will be spelled out more fully later, we can say that "modernity" was born after a long gestation in the West out of the marriage of early Catholic Christianity and Greco-Roman culture, and was nurtured by the reform movements of the last Middle Ages and educated by the Reformation and its fraternal twin, the Renaissance. In the process Christian theology broke with the primal communitarianism of its Hebraic parent (and, in principle, with all fixed gene-pool identities), yet it claimed to be the true heir of its ethical and prophetic wisdom and its urban-centered visions of a messianic age yet to come. These it joined to the philosophies and political-legal systems of its context in an effort to establish in the midst of time a concrete social emblem of that Godly realm of truth, justice and beauty which transcends historical actualization. Challenged by the rapid expansion of Islamic civilization from the seventh century on and stimulated by both the civil initiatives of the free cities of Europe and the rise of Protestantism, new spheres of life were generated, such as international trading companies, banking firms, faculties of law, medicine and the "mechanical arts" (engineering and technology). These had all been nurtured inside the church for centuries, but they were transplanted into the public square, expanding it exponentially. Religious

and philosophical renewals expanded with the material transformations, selectively legitimating them and refining their forms, uses and
morals. Together, after a long courtship and a sometimes conflictual
marriage, they gave birth to the Enlightenment, which in some circles was anti-Roman Catholicism and dogmatic Protestantism. Still,
the Enlightenment was claimed a wondrous child of faith by liberal
Protestants and progressive Catholics, although Christian Fundamentalists and sectarian obscurantists repudiated this "bastard"
offspring.

These developments, however, generated new spheres of life
based on a kind of institution that was called the "voluntary association." People were not born into these, as they are into families,
tribes, ethnic groups, castes, classes, nations or cultural-linguistic
groups; instead these groups can constituted for a "rational" purpose. People who chose to join, or were elected into membership,
covenanted with the new group to abide by the rules and to dedicate
themselves to the more specialized purposes in society than those
found in the communitarian patterns of primal societies. As modern physics has not only discovered but created new "elements,"
so also modern societies have not only discovered latent potentialities that they nurtured into relatively autonomous "powers"
but have constructed new spheres of human associations to cope
with them, recognizing that these are constitutive of complex societies and decisive for the differentiated human personality structures
that they require. These new spheres, each with a distinct sense of
professional expertise, invite, among other things, a sense of the
individual — one able to engage in the voluntary construction of
one's own personhood by selecting a pattern of memberships and
forming new loyalties to professional or social groups.

Although the theological contributions to this genealogy will be
exhumed and examined in greater detail in later chapters, we must
indicate now that these new patterns of organization were not, to be
sure, brand new or spontaneous. They developed out of a specific
religious tradition, the Christian one, that is rooted in a theology
of grace, manifest in Creation (disrupted by the Fall); in Providence
(with its Law, Covenant and Vocation, often broken); and in the
promise of Salvation (accomplished, in principle, in Christ, but not
yet fulfilled). This grace was advanced and made incarnate in society most obviously in the formation of a new kind of institution, the

church. This new center of brotherhood and sisterhood is, in principle, distinct from the patriarchal family, from a feudal economy, from an imperial politics, from an ethnically defined culture and from every territorial religion. The church drew its models of organization from the Hebrew synagogue, the Greek *ecclesia* and Roman "mystery cults," although it modulated all of them. In contrast to all these traditional patterns, the church was to become an association of those seeking or committed to the gracious source of life and meaning, drawn from many backgrounds and roles in society. This association engaged in a theological and ethical reformation of all the traditional faiths it encountered. It reinterpreted previous pieties and began to reshape the understanding of the soul and the fabric of society because it claimed that it had ultimate evidence of an historical *novum*, the Christ event, that pointed to a new epoch in human history that in turn pointed toward the ultimate future, symbolized by "the New Jerusalem" and a new heaven and earth.

This new kind of historical institution in society, of which the church is the prototype, became complex itself, and it reached, in principle, across many boundaries. It generated a series of relatively autonomous distinct institutions that were accepted and legitimated in long and complicated struggles. As we shall mention in later chapters again, the faith-based university, led by credentialed "masters," gradually became the dominant center for education and research. Moreover, a system of codified, constitutional law based on biblical concepts of "divine law" joined to ideas of the *jus gentium* and *lex naturalis*, as interpreted by qualified lawyers and judges, became the distinct sphere of civil law, beyond scriptural command, tribal custom, imperial decree, or monastic rule. The church, the universities, and the law also formed the social space for scientific medicine and hospitals, rather than relying on traditional treatments at home by midwives, shamans or barbers. And architects, engineers, and inventors organized complex constructions beyond the home or the castle or the barn, bridge, mine or mill. Indeed, by the scientific development of agriculture, mining, and means of communication (from harness and contour plowing to metallurgy to bell towers), each was legitimated by Christian theories about the necessity of establishing human dominion over nature under God's watchful eye, and the need to use the "mechanical arts" to improve human well-being and to manage nature's condition. In short, education, law, medicine, technology, ecology, and the formation of distinct institutions that specialized in dealing with them, in many ways made it possible for people to, at least partially, extract themselves from the interlocked, primal "principalities" in which they had lived, and to form new spheres of life by "covenanting" under God, together, each with a special sense of "calling" with reconceptualized notions of "nature" and "virtue."[11] These "authorities" of modernity have established models now followed by hundreds of other "professionals" who have developed expertise in specialized areas — including, especially, management.[12]

As these new professionals became linked to economically rewarding endeavors, and to new spheres of practice and association, they enabled the expansion of European civilization and facilitated the spread of the faith by encouraging missionary activity, which we now treat as the age of exploration, the industrial era, and the colonial period — all preludes to contemporary globalization. These developments were, of course, deeply disturbing to the more traditional patterns of life where family, economic, political, cultural and religious life were intertwined in local cultures with distinctive sensibilities and practices. The results still disrupt life wherever modernization challenges tribal or feudal or nationalistic cultures. Yet, where this does not happen, indigenous peoples become more isolated, and fall further and further behind in terms of the wider social, economic, cultural and political markers of development. Only

---

11. In volume 2, I identified these "powers" as "authorities" of a distinct kind, for they are historically novel areas of moral concern and are theologically laden, in spite of the fact that in modernity most have attempted to declare their independence from religious matters, although they are more driven by theological assumptions than is often recognized. In addition to these "professional" spheres that deal with the "powers" of *ars et scientia* (Education), *lex et jus* (Law), *salus et morte* (Medicine), *techne et ingenie* (Engineering), two other "trans-religious" authorities have emerged in modern society, the concern with ecology and of cross-cultural virtues, as seen in "exemplary persons" (Mahatma Gandhi, Bishop Tutu, Martin Luther King Jr., the Dalai Llama, Mother Teresa, etc.). This signals a kind of ethical universalism focused on ideas of "nature" and of "virtue" that are not constants over time. See the essays in vol. 2 by Jürgen Moltmann and Peter Paris, particularly. Finally in this area, I mentioned the new trans-national regulatory institutions, exemplified by the World Bank, the IMF, the WTO, etc., which are called the "regencies," a translation of the New Testament term "thronos."

12. William F. May documents the expanding list of professional fields, and points out the power that they exercise in contemporary life. Yet he also notes that many feel powerless and seldom think of their work in terms of ethical principles or contributions to the common good, thus tending to think that they work and live in a moral vacuum. This is a prime consequence of the loss of a sense of vocation. See *Beleaguered Rulers* (Louisville: Westminster John Knox Press, 2001).

the radical traditionalists of such cultures, and the anthropological romanticists who hate modernity and want the world to be a living zoo of distinct cultures and peoples, seek to celebrate these possibilities as the youth from them go to the cities, as parents seek modern medicines for their children, and as aluminum or plastic utensils are adopted instead of clay pots and woven baskets.

This European expansion of the "authorities" not only generated new spheres of life and conceptions of nature and virtue that have disrupted the "principalities" at home and abroad, it facilitated the consciousness of personal autonomy and the relative independence of the various spheres of life from each other, and especially from any overarching religious set of convictions — each personal or social unit living according to its own preferences, abilities and ends. This is especially the case where many nation-states, including former colonies, had an officially established religion designed to serve as a societal glue in otherwise differentiating societies. But as the various spheres became more distinct, it became less and less obvious what need these spheres had of religion or for theology. Of course, traces of the religious roots remained in many of the rites of the authoritative institutions — the official holidays, the wearing of ceremonial clothing at special occasions, the rhetoric of duties and privileges, and the codes of professional conduct (although progressively denuded of any overt theological reference — which seemed to many increasingly quaint). Moreover, many persons felt a "calling" to work out their destiny in one or another of these areas of endeavor; they worked for, as well as in, an area of expertise or station in one of the spheres, often with great excellence and dedication. Still, the internal fabric of these authorities themselves become less consciously rooted in a theological vision, and more and more in what enhanced the interests and influence of those in the particular sphere. Such developments triggered the prolonged debate about modernization and its relationship to secularization. Modern societies and people no longer had need, it was thought, of religion; and theology was given over to the articulation of the creeds of various sects for a remnant of believers.

Simultaneously, the European expansion also brought a wider exposure to other world religions, societies, and cultures, relativizing the sense that any one religion had a clear and final grasp on the nature of the divine and that any society or culture was a unique manifestation of divine intent. Yet that same discovery brought fuller awareness of the fact that not only societies or cultures were influenced by religion, but that whole civilizations were. It became clear that the colonial administrator, the successful trader, the cultural anthropologist, as well as the judge, the doctor, the teacher, and engineer, and the missionary had to understand the broader traditions that shaped peoples in their own cultures. How could one understand the respect for authority in tribal life without noting the religious significance of the "spirits of the elders" or in the familial and imperial life of China without reference to Confucianism's "filial piety," the significance of caste hierarchy and ritual purity in India without Hinduism's view of *samsara*, the autocratic kingdoms and apathetic priesthoods of South-East Asia without knowledge of Buddhism, or the simultaneously legalistic and spiritually theocratic Mid-East without paying attention to Islam's *shariah*. It cannot be done. And the question was posed: can or should we attempt to understand the West, even in its apparently secular globalizing impulses, without reference to Christianity? Many tried; many failed.

As it spreads from Catholic- and Protestant-influenced lands, globalization is sometimes understood in political "imperial" or "neocolonial" terms only (especially in regard to European influences) or economic and technological terms only (especially in regard to Anglo-American influences). In the introductions and essays of the first two volumes of this series, as well as this one, we have explored such perspectives, and have repeatedly noted that they miss the religious factor. Volume 3, therefore, treats some of the key ways in which the great world religions have shaped great civilizations in the past — along with dominant conceptions of human nature, basic attitudes toward civil society and the various powers and spheres of life, a sense of the character of the bio-physical universe and of human virtue and, above all, an awareness of the strikingly different views of salvation and human destiny. That volume offered a series of scholarly glimpses of how they might shape a global civilization, and be reshaped by globalization should they become a dominant force in defining the future.

Religion in the World's Civilizations

It is quite clear that the ancient primal religions, plus Confucianism and Hinduism, had long proven that they can form enduring civilizations. This is so, although the primal societies not drawn into the

Han-Confucian patriarchal empire or into the Hindu caste system have tended, in the last several centuries, to adopt one or another of the converting religions, Buddhism, Islam, or Christianity — in each case bringing their traditional beliefs and practices with them, and creating new syntheses in the process. It is also the case that Confucianism and Hinduism, while undergoing efforts at renewal at the moment, have been deeply disrupted by modernization and by sustained challenges from the converting religions. The result is, of course, an enormous range of pieties and practices in each of these religions, especially at the interface with other traditions. Yet, each religion has its own more or less stable integrative norms of coherence that seldom are totally obscured. The full meaning of the integrative norms may be disputed or differently arranged by some within the system, but long term devotion to one or another of the great "dominions" — the "powers" of the world's faiths — symbolized by The Elders, Master Kung, Lord Krishna, The Buddha, The Prophet, or The Christ have, in all sorts of direct and indirect ways, influenced the great civilizations of the world. These "dominions" ("lordships") have shaped the basic understandings of what is proper in the professional spheres of complex societies, and how people ought to live their economic, familial, political, cultural lives.

As was spelled out in volume 3, the "religion" (actually, more of an ontocratic philosophical ethic and aesthetic) of Confucianism, for example, has been traditionally deeply intertwined with loyalty to an imperial central government and to its local replication in the clan-based family, and to the honoring of the educated elite as servants of the imperial unity and as moral exemplars for the people. That of Hinduism is tightly tied to a hierarchically organized system of extended families (castes and subcastes) and region (which includes ethnic and linguistic differences) which determine social and economic status. Islam, on the other hand, as a religion is almost indistinguishable from a legal, political and male-dominated network of tribal linkages, although its radical monotheism points in principle to an overarching universalism also. Buddhism has branches that resemble, in distinctive ways, each of the above, depending on the particular tradition, in part because it does not clearly have its own distinctive view of a normative social order (it is essentially royalistic in South East Asia, borrowing from the Hindu *Arthashastra* tradition, more hierocratic in the Tibetan tradition and supportive of the War Lord traditions, and sometimes of Imperial orders, in East Asia).

All of these dominions share certain characteristics, so that we can call them "religions," and we can see that they all favor certain first principles of ethics. They all know that everyone should honor that which is holy, and neither slander nor blaspheme it; and they believe that all should respect parents and elders and observe certain holidays. Moreover actions such as murder, rape, lying, stealing, etc., are believed to be against the moral law, and they also believe that one should be hospitable to strangers. Believers in all of these traditions gain comfort from prayer and meditation, and find solace in their distinctive pieties. They also have socially overlapping commonalities — all must deal with the "powers" of Eros, Mammon, Mars, and the Muses and they all form institutions in the various spheres of life to guide, sustain, and constrain these that can be recognized as comparable to what the other dominions have formed, even if they are shaped differently.

Yet each religion has a distinct sense of past, present, and future that reflects also differences from one another in doctrine, practice, and, most important for our project, in their attitude toward the way civilization is to be formed or reformed to approximate the vision of the ideal society. These differences fundamentally influence their adherents' attitudes toward what is acceptable in education, law, medical practice, technology, political leadership, ecology and definitions of virtue, even if they do not consider themselves to be deeply religious. Of course, these attitudes are also influenced by material interests and the pragmatic sense of what works to benefit the groups to which they are most loyal. They also influence their attitudes toward the modern authorities in general, with those who embrace them becoming less orthodox in a traditional sense, but often profoundly committed to the revitalization of the culture which older religious traditions sustained. Those who resist the modernizing changes, the Fundamentalists in all these groups, oppose them in principle — while, often, they adopt or adapt them functionally even if they cannot quite dedicate themselves to the values that the changes bring with them.[13]

---

13. I think that the evidence for these developments is dramatically present in Thomas L. Friedman's *The World Is Flat: A Brief History of the Twenty-First Century* (New York: Farrar, Straus & Giroux, 2005), with its special focus on India, China, the Islamic World and the United States. This is so even though he seldom mentions

As to the West, the modernizing movements that sought to have done with traditional Christianity issued, on the one hand, in the romanticized neopagan world of the Fascist Axis which attempted to subordinate Christianity to national racist policy, and, on the other hand, in the militantly secular ideology of the Soviet empire (which was exported to the Maoist regime in China, and to many radical movements around the world). These had to cultivate personality cults (from Hitler and Stalin to, e.g., Idi Amin and Che) and compulsory mass rituals to generate a consensus that allowed them to keep their fragile grip on power. Against these, other modernizing movements have formed modern Liberal ideologies that are not overtly anti-religious or anti-theological, but become so if Christian (or any other) theology or religious ethics claim access to basic and universal truths and to be able to comparatively evaluate different religious orientations or convictions or practices on these bases. Yet, as Rousseau already recognized, they discovered also that political and economic power needs to have a spiritual legitimacy which it cannot supply by itself; thus it will try to create an ersatz religion, calling it patriotism or freedom or fidelity to identity, to mask a lack of genuine religious authority and integrity. Thus, "civil religion" is formed.

In spite of several kinds of Enlightenment fundamentalism among the intellectual elite of Europe (and among the elites of the former colonies who studied in the West as well as in many parts of the American universities), the convictions of most of the people incarnate in most of the various spheres of life in the world of Western modernity remained basically Christian (or Judeo-Christian, for these two sister faiths have mutually influenced each other not only over the centuries, but dramatically since World War II). This is so even if many are forgetful or ignorant of its dominant religious vision embedded in the fabric of its civil society. They became secular, but they are secular in a Christian (or Judeo-Christian), not in a Confucian, Hindu, Buddhist or Islamic, way. It thus came as no small surprise to many philosophers and social scientists who predicted the secularization of the world on the basis of their own forsaking or denial of the Christian heritage that it, like the other

---

the primary cultural forces or religious traditions that predispose these societies to move in the directions he reports.

world religions, is now in various stages of resurgence under conditions of globalization, and the kind and quality of the recovery
and recasting of this religious vision is altering how the globalizing
forces are adopted or resisted.[14]

Not only in the West, but in most places around the world, globalization is being generated, received, or resisted according to the
nature and character of the region's normative "dominion" and according to the relative strength and independence (from the state) of
the "authorities." The exception to this generalization is that many
Christians who have accepted a Marxist or Liberationist analysis of
capitalism also resist globalization, as I discussed in the Introduction. In contrast to these leftist economistic views, it is useful to note
that only some religious "dominions" formed the "principalities"
and "authorities" in such a way as to condition its host society so
that it is inclined to support the powers that generated globalization
or now embrace it. These have selectively generated, adopted, inhibited, or rejected the dynamics of globalization, interpreting them
from their own spiritual and moral points of view, and thus the
distinctive patterns of its principalities and authorities. Most have
sought the material benefits of globalization, some while seeking to
hold onto values of their traditions that make it difficult. Others
have adopted the managerial and technological methods produced
in the West, while actively attacking the religious and cultural values, especially as advocated by secular materialistic views that claim
to have made them a part of the West. And, indeed, no few religiously or intellectually alienated people in the West adopt other
religions or join the protests against the West for reasons that have
to do with the rejection of the religious and moral convictions that
favor globalization.

This highly compressed genealogy of certain western trends toward globalization is a narrative overview of our first three volumes,
as I see the implications of the various contributions and discussions
by our authors. I suspect, of course, that not all the authors would
interpret the results of our dialogical process exactly in this way, and
I am certain that not all the authors have followed the scholarly debates about the nature of globalization in the same way. The main
reason for reviewing these contributions in this volume is to give a

---

14. See Peter L. Berger et al., *Many Globalizations: Cultural Diversity in the
Contemporary World* (New York: Oxford University Press, 2002). See also note 1
above.

clearer picture of where the discussions and the resources consulted have led us. The various spheres of civilization that have been designed to express, constrain, and channel the powers of life — the principalities, authorities, and dominions of the world — are presently in disarray and without a compelling religious vision to guide them. The traditional power that did guide them in previous great civilizations, the Christian religion, especially as critically shaped by theology, is doubted as a resource able to do so today by many who are among the world's best professional authorities, and many of its religious leaders. Yet, no treatment of a major social and historical phenomena, such as contemporary globalization, is complete without taking these factors into account, as has been already stated. The neglect of religion as an ordering, uniting and dividing factor in a number of influential interpretations of globalization is a major cause of misunderstanding and a studied blindness regarding what is going on in the world. This has direct implications for how we view the possible contributions of a Christian theology and ethics in relation to globalization.

Having reviewed what we have done in the first volumes, we find that we now extend our efforts to clarify the direction in which we found ourselves moving. In this way, we include certain aspects of intellectual and social history that contribute to the project. Thus, we shall have to treat some of those who have seen, and not ignored, the global role of religious ethics.

Representative Figures[15]

A number of contemporary scholars have clearly recognized the remarkable importance of religious influences in the economic, political, cultural, familial, and professional dynamics and structures of globalization. The deep continuity of religious belief among most populations of the earth persists, and skeptics are shocked by what appears to be a dramatic religious resurgence that falsifies the widespread assumptions that secularization is an inevitable part of modernization.[16] I will here comment on three of the well known

---

15. An earlier version of this section was delivered as a paper at the Festival of Theology and the Arts, celebrating the tenth anniversary of the Truth and Reconciliation Commission in South Africa, in March 2005, at the University of Pretoria. My thanks to Piet Meiring, organizer of the event.

16. One of the key pioneers of this recognition is Peter L. Berger. See notes 1 and 14 above. The recovery of the post-Marxist recognition of the importance of religion,

figures whose work is widely cited in the literature on globalization, each of whom represents a major contribution to one or another facet of the issues to be addressed in the remainder of this book. One who has recognized the new pluralism of religions, but sees the prospect of an ethical commonality among them is Hans Küng. The disputatious Catholic who has often argued that unless there can be peace between the world religions, there cannot be peace in the world, and whose understanding of Christianity is open to the recognition of ethical universals in all religions. Thus Küng has not only studied the world religions comparatively with specialists from other faiths,[17] but also has given himself to the work of the Parliament of World Religions and the UNESCO Commission on Global Ethics, and other groups seeking to find the common ethical grounds that, he holds, the great faiths share.[18] His numerous publications represent one of the most extensive efforts to identify the normative content of the world religions, and to urge the adoption of statements supporting those principles of justice, such as human rights, that can serve at least as aspirations for all the peoples of the world. In this, in my view, he has surpassed any of the known efforts to develop an ethic for the world on philosophical grounds. He has also drafted proposals about a "global ethic for global politics and economics,"[19] using principles that, largely, echo the Ten Commandments. Undoubtedly, Küng's work represents a creative, idealistic strand in globalization research: it clarifies the standards of right and certain measures of good to all and for all in ways that all, in principle, could subscribe, whatever other disagreements they have.

---

after the failure of the "New-Left" and most liberation movements can be found in his revisionist treatments of the legacy of Max Weber: *In Search of an East Asian Development Model* (New Brunswick, NJ: Transaction Press, 1988), and his *The Capitalist Revolution* (New York: Basic Books, 1988). See also the recent volume by Scott M. Thomas, *The Global Resurgence of Religion and the Transformation of International Relations* (New York: Palgrave Macmillan, 2005).

17. See, especially, Hans Küng et al., *Christianity and the World Religions: Paths to Dialogue* (New York: Doubleday, 1986); and *Christianity and Chinese Religions* (New York: Doubleday, 1989).

18. See the references to his contributions in the essay by Yersu Kim, in vol. 1 of this series; and in the essay by Diane Obenchain, in vol. 3.

19. See his *Global Responsibility* (London: Oxford University Press, 1991), *A Global Ethic: The Declaration of the Parliament of the World's Religions* (New York: Continuum, 1993), which he edited with Karl-Josef Kuschel, as well as his *A Global Ethic for Global Politics and Economics* (New York: Oxford University Press, 1998).

Further, Küng's work in these areas reflects, just below the surface, the great tradition of a God-given "natural law" by which human reason, bestowed and guided by grace, can recognize, articulate, choose as guides for action and approximate in life the fundamental moral laws that allow greater human flourishing, facilitate the establishment of greater degrees of justice and more nearly overcome the evils of human history. This allows people from divergent traditions to honor the righteousness and virtue to be found among those of another faith.

We should note, in this regard, that many Protestants who admire Küng's contributions and support his work, this author included, are doubtful about the adequacy of the concept of "natural law," because of a more profound sense of the reality of sin that taints the use of reason and distorts both the will and the passion for life. This fosters disorder in God's intended order in ways that prevent reason, will and passion from being used in the best ways. Further, some interpretations of natural law confuse the normative, moral meanings of the term with "laws of nature," rendering a much too strong physicalist interpretation of the natural world, as if it is what it should be. In either case, the use of the term says very little about the fact that "natural law" is God-given, leaving the impression that humans can, by their own abilities, without the further need of grace, revelation, forgiveness, justification or guidance, attain righteousness. But it is not obvious that humans can, only by the observation of the laws of nature, simply do what is right or be good. This kind of moral naturalism or deism is not valid theological.

Moreover, without the awareness of the fact that all persons are created in God's image, and are equally in need of God's continuing grace, most interpretations of natural law tend to relegate some people to inferior status, suggesting that there is a natural hierarchy of peoples. Küng is alert to this issue and recognizes that various forms of racism and sexism, and the caste system, are based in this view. Others use evolutionary theory to explain such matters, and conclude that some peoples are naturally less evolved or that the laws of competition mean that it is a world marked by no other moral logic than the "bloody law of tooth and claw" in which the strong defeat the weak. Richard Weikart has argued recently that Darwinism "smoothed the path" for Nazi ideology in regard to war and race. While the idea is denied by some respected evolutionary thinkers, the evidence seems quite compelling.[20]

It may be that we shall have to avoid interpretations of natural law that have such totalizing effects, but we surely cannot go without any basis for a humanity-wide ethics, which is what Küng is after. It may be wise to speak of a *justitia originalis*, as did some of the church fathers and, more recently, Reinhold Niebuhr, in the Neo-Orthodox tradition, or of "general revelation," as did several Reformers, or of a "common grace," as did Abraham Kuyper in the neo-Calvinist tradition. In these expressions, the necessity of a reference to God becomes clear, although, like some "natural law theory" intends, it becomes possible on this basis for humans to recognize the dignity of every human, including those of other faiths, cultures, genders, ethnicities and social ranks. It is this that allows the contemporary scholar Michael Perry to write simply that "certain things ought not to be done to any human being and certain other things ought to be done for every human being."[21] The work of Küng seems to me to have demonstrated what those who drafted the UN Declaration of Human Rights also discovered: it is difficult but possible to come to some agreement about the first principles of right and wrong, even if there is disagreement as to what best accounts for that possibility.[22] These laws were not only paradigmatically delivered by God to a specific people, as the Jews and Muslims hold, but were, in some sense, "written on the hearts of all persons," as Isaiah thought possible and Paul thought actual. They are, by reason and revelation and functional necessity knowable by all.

---

20. R. Weikart, *From Darwin to Hitler: Evolutionary Ethics, Eugenics and Racism in Germany* (New York: Palgrave Macmillan, 2005).

21. M. J. Perry, *The Idea of Human Rights* (New York: Oxford University Press, 1998), 5.

22. In his new book, however, John S. Nurser documents, on the basis of previously unexamined archival resources, the role that Christian theologians played, largely behind the scenes, in drafting the UN Declaration. See his *For All Peoples and All Nations: The Ecumenical Church and Human Rights* (Washington: Georgetown University Press, 2005). It supplements and expands Mary Ann Glendon's treatment of the role of the Roosevelt and of several outstanding Catholic philosophical theologians: *A World Made New: Eleanor Roosevelt and the Universal Declaration of Human Rights* (New York: Random House, 2001). These careful historical works demonstrate, I think, that Arthur Dyck's argument that theology is not necessary to the development or ratification of human rights because people of many faiths have endorsed it looks quite superficial. See his *Rethinking Rights and Responsibilities*, rev. ed.(Washington, DC: Georgetown University Press, 2005).

Küng's representative engagement in these issues reflects the fact that humanity is, in some sense, "hard wired" by the way we are created to live under a moral law that we did not make up. Even if we have a difficult time coming to agreement about the details of what that law entails in every case, or how it came into being, we can reasonably debate these matters and recognize that they are of ultimate importance. This pointing toward a universal moral law with a divine source that we almost know and to which we can appeal when all earthly appeals are exhausted is an indispensable factor in forming human character and civil society. On this basis human beings seek to establish just laws that govern the insider and outsider, the high and the low and call us to confess if wrongs are done, reconcile with enemies and revise unjust laws.

Many who may hold to such a view of universal moral truths, however, may also point to another set of factors that also shapes our human moral prospects. In this regard, Samuel P. Huntington has offered a widely discussed book that not only seemed to many to have provided a prescient account of why 9/11 happened, but also offered an influential corrective to many of the interpretations of our global situation with which our previous three volumes also argued.[23] I turn to Huntington's work because it confirms one of the major arguments of this series of volumes: religion is an unavoidable factor in understanding how social history works; it shapes cultures that form civilizations, and it sometimes induces conflict. While we can identify certain religiously based normative commonalities, other religiously based factors incline civilizations to clash in certain ways. At the same time, as we shall see, Huntington does not seem to understand other points that these volumes have stressed — theology can and does critically interpret and reconstruct religions and offer an ethic to redirect the dynamics of how human history works. At least some motifs in Christian theology can provide the moral and spiritual architecture for a society where the violence of the clash is potentially reduced.[24]

---

23. Samuel P. Huntington, *The Clash of Civilizations and the Remaking of World Order* (New York: Simon and Schuster, 1996).

24. It is quite possible that other theologies can do so as well. See the remarkable little book by Jonathan Sacks, Chief Rabbi of Great Britain, *The Dignity of Difference: How to Avoid the Clash of Civilizations* (London: Continuum, 2002).

Must Religions also Clash?

Religion not only offers us high ethical ideals, some of which overlap quite strikingly, it also brings clash and conflict in real social history, and the issue of how history works is a key question for any interpretation of globalization. Affirming such pathos, Huntington cites his work as an aspiration "to present a framework, a paradigm, for viewing global politics that will be meaningful to scholars and useful to policy makers."[25] Unlike Huntington, this project on "God and Globalization" is less centered on politics and international relationships, insofar as these terms depend on an understanding that politics has to do with the accumulation of power to establish a governing institution that comprehends all other institutions internal to a society in a given territory and controls international relations through its diplomatic and strategic policies. Instead, this project is more focused on how people in all spheres of life can understand the dynamics of globalization and seek to guide the various institutions of civil society that influence the accumulation of political power. Nevertheless, one can see in this volume and in other closely related writings of Huntington a quest for a basic model of how things work in human history. It involves the cultivation of a "mental map" that offers a suggestive way of interpreting the masses of data that investigations into globalization produce. He writes:

> World views and causal theories are indispensable guides to international politics, ... Simplified paradigms or maps are indispensable for human thought and action.... [If] we deny the need for such guides ..., we delude ourselves. For in the back of our minds are hidden assumptions, biases and prejudices that determine how we perceive reality, what facts we look at, and how we judge their importance and merits.[26]

He is surely correct in this. And, as Küng can best be understood to stand critically within the great tradition of Catholic "natural law" traditions, Huntington stands critically within, and in some sense surpasses, a more recent scholarly tradition with a notable pedigrees and many advocates. This is not because most people are aware of how and when these worldviews were generated — they

---

25. Huntington, *The Clash of Civilizations and the Remaking of the World Order*, 13.
26. Ibid., 30.

are generally not — but because they have become conventional frameworks for interpreting history. Indeed, specialists doubt details of his analysis in regard to this or that region of the world or with this or that historic development. He may well need some correction of that sort, but our interest is in the basic presuppositions behind his interpretations.

Huntington is clearly aware that he is working in a tradition of macroscopic views and may suffer the fate of other efforts to draw large and comprehensive mental maps. Huntington does not deal with G. W. F. Hegel, who offered an early and influential philosophical logic that could explain much of "universal consciousness" — the famous "dialectic" by which Hegel interpreted "world historical developments" — although he remained a rather decided Prussian nationalist.[27] But Huntington does refer to Henry Buckle,[28] whose fame in the 1850s is now largely forgotten. He is nevertheless notable as one of the first thinkers to try to develop a comprehensive theory of the pending global, historic transformations to a world system beyond national and international ones. Influenced by Comte's scientist view of progress, as well as certain themes from Adam Smith, Buckle set forth an account of the material interests, rationally guided, that he thought would bring a world civilization. He provided a macro-vision of what was going on, and what people ought to do about it. The Victorian world of colonial expansion was hungry for such a vision and it devoured his view. Theology at the time was not providing a larger vision able to guide expansive societies, although it had taken the "world missions" movement seriously. For Buckle, the scientifically and materially advanced nations would inevitably conquer weaker ones, then spread their rational approaches to life with them, to the benefit of all. The competition this entailed was the natural logic of history, a view that anticipated and influenced both Darwin in the realm of natural science, and Engels in the realm of social theory, and, through the latter, Marx, who welded this view to his inversion of Hegel.[29] Such views drew the mental maps by which

---

27. Especially his *Philosophy of Right* (Germ., 1821; Eng. trans. T. M. Knox: New York: Clarendon Press, 1952).

28. See, especially, his *The History of Civilization in England*, 2 vols. (London, 1857, 1861).

29. A contemporary postmodern attempt to rescue this view can be found in Michael Hardt and Antonio Negri, *Empire* (Cambridge, MA: Harvard University Press, 2000), as discussed in the Introduction.

many then, and many still, read the world. What does the logic of history require of us, according to Buckle? Expand, by science, education, technique and military action, as required, for material and rational prowess are the harbinger of a new world, displacing obsolete, irrational traditions.

But rationalist materialism driving a modernizing, nationalist expansion did not convince all then or now, as the collapse of Marxism-Leninism seems to confirm, but as Darwinian-based "rational choice" capitalists have yet to learn. Others also sought to interpret the massive changes on the horizon of modern world history. Drawing on the romantic view that each "people" has a distinctive, collective "soul," as already suggested by Rousseau and Herder, but expanding their ethnic focus to a Eurocentric view more generally, Oswald Spengler developed another widely influential view, one that anticipated current accents on "multi-culturalism" by vocal opponents of "materialistic, rationalistic and individualistic western cultural imperialism," as the litany of critique has it. Spengler presumes the social and spiritual sovereignty of each nation.[30] Each "people" expresses its own genius in a characteristic religion and generates its own ethical norms, just as they do the various forms of art and architecture. In this "cultural anthropological" view, each group thus has its own way of ordering the internal relationship of its parts, and each had to be understood entirely in terms of its own genius and morphology. "The West," Spengler argued, expanding the concept of "a people," is in decline for it was losing its own inner genius and being swept into a universalistic, materialistic and rationalistic, indeed a soulless uniformity, with no basis in the hearts of the people or their traditions. He resists precisely the dynamic of the sort Buckle described. Thus, what all are to do is to reassert our own distinctive spiritual collective character.

Certainly, this view can go sour, as it did in the political theology of Carl Schmitt, court theologian to Hitler, who reasserted the spiritual-ethnic definition of "a people," and argued that each people must have its own "political theology" and must decide which other peoples are friends and which are foes, making peace

---

30. *Decline of the West*, 2 v., Ger. 1918, 1923; translated by C. F. Atkinson (London: Allen & Unwin, 1932).

with friends and war on any foe that threatens the sovereignty, gene-pool identity, and spiritual genius of a people. Whether using such view to defend cultural pluralism, as have a number of anthropologists over the last century, or to adopt a policy of "us" versus "them," as have the Fascist movements of recent times, world history is defined by a cultural anarchy of variety and particularity. Each opposes the "soulless sameness" that universalizing modernity imposes on the world — by opposite strategies.[31]

Another great exemplar of determinative general philosophies of history is found in Arnold Toynbee's twelve volume series, *A Study of History*.[32] But rather than concentrate on the logic of material development or on the "genius" of "peoples" and their monadic cultures, Toynbee writes of "civilizations" — great complexes of relative integration, such as the Greco-Roman world, or those of China or India. Each of these may have within it a number of states, societies or prominent cultural forms, each with subcultures and ethnic groups, yet they form an "organic" unit that, over time like a great sequoia rises, flourishes, shades out much below it and then — as usually happens — begins to lose its vigor. Toynbee further notes that some great civilizations form the "shade" for centuries, sheltering many subcultures, and others die early. The latter do not develop a refined complexity, endure long enough, generate the confident courage to influence others or to get others to adapt to the core values which the civilization seeks to advance. The message: gird up your loins for the challenge of civilizational formation, seek extended survival, and be aware that others may try to displace you.

What these interpretations of globalization's "great transition" into a new world order share is that they basically ignore religion as a causative factor in shaping civil societies, states, cultures, and

---

31. In a volume dedicated to Edward Said, author of the widely regarded *Orientalism* (New York: Vintage, 1979), Fredric Jameson and Masao Miyoshi extend aspects of this argument in *The Cultures of Globalization* (Durham, NC: Duke University Press, 1998). The argument is made also by many theological-Liberationist theorists in their critique of Francis Fukuyama's thesis about "the end of history," by which, Huntington rightly argues, he means the end of the era of Marxist class conflict and, for that matter, of the historical dialectic. See Richard H. Roberts, *Religion, Theology and the Human Sciences* (Cambridge: Oxford University Press, 2002). The footnotes to these volumes indicate scholarly and populist alienation from a Western master-narrative (identified with the homogenizing evils of capitalism), and a marked affirmation of multiculturalism.

32. (Oxford: Oxford University Press, 1934–61).

civilizations, although several others acknowledge religion as an expression of social and cultural developments. However, Huntington does not. Rather, in a certain way, he attempted to integrate these several perspectives, to use their main insights, and to reorganize them by including the factor that they tend to ignore. He has put on the table of discussion the idea that contemporary world history is largely to be defined by the growing self-consciousness of large civilizational units, beyond peoples, societies, states, or cultures, that now supply the primary organizing principles of social life. More strikingly, Huntington argues that religion is the decisive factor in forming the deep contours of civilizations and their guiding cultural loyalties and patterns. Of course, he knows that the various institutions of the common life — such as families, universities, corporations, ethnic communities, and of course states — will continue to be agents in social history, but they will always be shaped by the ways in which their religion and ethics influence their material interests over the long haul. In arguing these points, he further argues what none of the previous alternatives affirm, that we cannot understand how history works if we do not recognize the inevitable power of religious worldviews and of the ethics based on them. These are the spectacles through which people read life and they provide normative visions of the right and the good by which people preconsciously make judgments and define their aspirations. These decide how people interpret life, change or intentions.

Huntington argues, with repeated reference to Max Weber and his disciples, and to the views of Christopher Dawson, one of his mentors, that the common life and the world situation cannot be understood if attention is not given to the social functions and effects of religious ideas and values as they are incarnated in the dominant culture of large civilizations. At stake, in every instance, is the question of how history works and how religious ideas influence the mind maps by which we interpret the events of the day. In a speech that Huntington gave to the Ethics and Public Policy Center about his work and its reception, he speaks of the end of secular ideology as the dominant force in politics. Today, politics is and must be religious. He said:

> During the twentieth century, a secular century, Lenin, Attaturk, Nehru, Ben Gurion, and the Shah (for instance) all defined the identity of their countries in the secular century's

terms. That has changed, the Shah is gone, the Soviet Union is gone, and in its place is a Russia that in public statements iden- tifies itself... explicitly with Russian Orthodoxy. In Turkey, India, and Israel,... political movements are challenging the secular definition of identity. Politicians (everywhere)... have found that religion either is crucial to maintaining... legiti- macy... or must be suppressed because it presents a challenge to... legitimacy.[33]

After all, peoples, economies, societies, states, cultures and civi- lizations tend to be much the same in the sense that we can study them comparatively, see how they similarly adapt to similar mate- rial conditions, and know that we are comparing like with like; but they develop differently because they are bent in different directions by the ways in which distinctive religions, each with its own differ- entiating features, influence culture. One of the tasks of the policy maker (like the theological ethicist!), thus, is to clarify how regu- lating convictions have become wedded to and normative for the organization of economic, sexual, political, cultural, and especially civilizational life, and then figure out which courses of action best fit the basic, religio-cultural values and are both practicable and just.

When Huntington's most famous volume is read in connection with other writings of his, especially two volumes which he has co- edited since *The Clash of Civilizations*, various dimensions of this argument are illuminated. One volume is edited with Lawrence C. Harrison, the noted economist who spent years working in Latin America on development projects and became convinced that eco- nomic change cannot take place without a previous religio-cultural and ethical change. The title is *Culture Matters: How Values Shape Human Progress*;[34] and the other, already mentioned (note 14 above), is edited with Peter L. Berger, called *Many Globalizations: Cultural Diversity in the Contemporary World*. In the first it is ar- gued that religious values are the most important, regulative factors in economic development, although most liberal and radical econo- mists remain skeptical and cannot imagine that this is so. In the second, they argue that globalization, while clearly a universalizing reality in which the rationalization of the economy is taking place,

33. "Religion, Culture and International Conflict After September 11," *Center Conversations* 14 (June 2002): 1.
34. New York: Basic Books, 2000.

is not homogenizing the world, but is taking quite different forms in each distinct civilization, primarily because of the ways in which the dominant religious and cultural values receive or resist or selectively adopt or adapt these rationalizing forces. It is such themes as these that give his constructive position a distinctive shape, for each religiously based civilization is treated by him as a kind of massive system of incarnated convictional complexity, which comprehends several societies that have organized patterns of familial, economic, political and cultural fabrics. Each civilization, like giant geologic tectonic plates, has emerged into prominence out of a long history in ways that displace, incorporate or subordinate interpretations that focus on material forces or state policies and local subcultural habits and traditions. Yet, a kind of anarchy reigns between these plates, creating massive fault lines in the world scene that are likely to clash into one another.

When this book came out, it was subjected to critique by many social theorists. Many thought they had disposed of the volume and its hypotheses, for most, not unlike the noted British scholar of globalization, David Held, suggested that religion was and is a mostly benign by-product of psychological and cultural forces that takes different shapes under changing material and political conditions.[35] While some endorsed Huntington's correlative argument that these tectonic plates have internal fault lines based on religiously shaped subcultural groupings, which could or should be overcome by attending to nonreligious economic and political interests, more doubted that the religious effect on cultures generated external fault lines that would inevitably clash. Huntington in fact, argues both points and believes, quite pessimistically although he would say realistically, that these tend to cause volcanic eruptions of violence and earthquakes of social destruction, "fault-line wars." Of particular focus is the inevitable clash of Islamic and Western traditions. He says we must meet this challenge and contain that threat.

What has he done? Huntington has assembled an enormous amount of data about the various areas of the world which specialists predictably say are more complex than he allows. Those arguments will continue. But if one sees the basic mental map that

---

35. See my critique of this view, as argued in Held et al., *Global Transformations: Politics, Economics, and Culture* (Stanford: Stanford University Press, 1999), in vol. 3 of the *God and Globalization* series, Introduction.

Huntington has constructed, it is possible to compare him to his key predecessors, whose heirs and disciples show up in footnote after footnote. Like Toynbee, Huntington has a civilizational focus; but unlike him, civilizations are not organically conceived. They do not rise and fall by natural forces like living sequoia. Civilizations are products of religious and cultural formation, and they demand relative political and material integration under those values or they fail. Like Spengler, he holds that cultures are each quite sovereign and that cultures are spiritually guided; but unlike Spengler, culture is not the expression of ethnic or national genius — it derives from historic transcendental convictions that shape the values of the dominant culture and thus also ethnic or national identity and political and economic forms of life that increase or decrease social power. In addition, like Buckle, he expects that some material and rational forces will come to dominate a civilization, although not by material and rational means alone. Darwinian and Marxist forces may be at work in human history, but it is the spiritual and moral cultural factors that often decide the outcome of clashes. They determine the sense of collective identity that steels the will to engage in struggle — not, incidentally, because everyone is conscious of religious influences in their lives, they are not; but because certain religious assumptions have become so routinized into the ethos that they become second nature, the moral soul of the civilization. That constitutes the core of the social fabric in which people live, and they tend to interpret their familial, cultural, political, economic and professional interests in such terms — sometimes, of course, as false ideologies, sometimes as rationalized interests, but most profoundly as faith convictions.

But Huntington's mental map may have faults of its own. He does not seem to imagine any real possibility of a critical analysis, comparative evaluation or transformation of these determining religious convictions, doctrines and practices. Religions and religiously shaped cultural values seem to be pre-given and fixed and not something subject to development, criticism or reform, although they form the dynamic moral and spiritual inner architecture of economies, societies, cultures, and civilizations that do change. His work has these faults for two reasons. He does not seem to recognize any basic human or religious commonality that makes it possible for dialogue, exchange or discovery of mutual interests and values between religions, such as those first principles recognized by

Hans Küng. Religions, their ethics and the cultures they form are seen as discrete, fixed units that appear to be unable to change or grow, although the study of religion and theology shows that cross-religious borrowing and cross-cultural adoption is frequent and the development of doctrine as faiths spread into new cultures is unending in every tradition. This fault seems to me to be clearest in a more recent study, a book on contemporary challenges to American national identity.[36]

Another limitation is that Huntington does not expresses any interest in theology as a discipline that can critically compare and evaluate ethical constellations of principles and purposes or religio-cultural clusters of conviction. Thus, only conflict seems to take place at the religio-cultural-civilizational fault lines. Further, he does not point to any criteria by which one could decide whether the religions he says are so important in forming civilizations share any criteria of truth or justice by which one could discern whether or not some of the conflicts are worth fighting for and others are not. I think it is evident that, in fact, most religions do share a number of common criteria of considerable significance, as Küng has argued, and can agree that some conflicts are not worth fighting for, even if many custodians of religious ethics have been delinquent in tracing these out. Nor does he consider the possibility that one religious discovery or revelation can unveil what is pertinent to all peoples in all religions, cultures and civilizations, and that this can be peacefully debated over time between religions. Yet, many who have been involved in cross-cultural experiences and dialogues know that it takes place all the time, even if many remain satisfied with their Spengler-like dogmatic sectarianism. Of course, there are differences between the great traditions that are not likely immediately to find consensus, but theological visions think in long-term perspectives. In short, the analysis of this book and its attendant writings suggests that certain kinds of theology must take on the task again of mental map-making as well as an interpretation of history.

---

36. See his recent *Who Are We?: The Challenges to America's National Identity* (New York: Simon & Schuster, 2004) in which he argues that America is built on Anglo-Protestant values now having a resurgence in Evangelicalism and under threat from the tendencies to celebrate "multiculturalism" in America — especially at the hands of Hispanic (Catholic) traditions — although his entire volume endorses multiculturalism in the world.

Huntington is important because he redefines the size of our context, the parameters of our social vision. His view is broader than most political, social scientific and religious views. The "new world order" that concerns him is not only based on material interests, political power, cultural genius, and the tendency of civilizations to rise and eventually fall, although he knows these play a role. He knows that religion must also be considered as an independent variable. Still, he tends, at the decisive point of studying religion, to have, functionally, a "flat heaven" view. He does not imagine, at least he nowhere suggests, anything like the height or depth of vision of an Augustine, Thomas, Luther, Calvin, or Edwards, or for that matter of a Dante or a Milton — let alone that of a Buddha, a Śankara or al-Sháfi'í; but if civilizations are formed out of such visions, and if they last longer, reach wider, touch deeper, and influence all within them more than we are often aware of, they cannot be freeze-dried as not subject to change. Many of the present debates about the role of religion in politics are a thin, confused manifestation of great struggles about this fact, seldom illuminated by the theologians and ethicists of our day, and obscured by Huntington when he appeals, without criticism, to the "identity politics" expressed in some Anglo-American chauvinism. I agree with some of the key values he identifies (essentially Protestant-forged and influenced by "common sense realism"): respect for individual dignity, constitutionally ordered democratic polity, a regulated but generally open economy and efforts to provide equal opportunity in education, employment, etc. He is, I think, more right than wrong on these matters, both as to their historical roots and their continuing significance; but he offers no fundamental basis for holding these convictions other than the fact that they are ours. That will not do in a global context that is populated by more than American Christians and Jews.

In short, he does not seem to know how to work with the kinds of metaphysical-moral visions that are incarnated in these patterns of life except to note that they were generated and sustained in a culture of which he is a part. He sees no religiously based universal definitions of a master narrative or shared justice, and if we do not develop superior vision to his for our world he may be tragically right about the inevitable clash of his culture with all others.

A Third Option

The third major figure I want to treat is that feisty Anglican Arch-
bishop Desmond Tutu of South Africa. This is a figure who has
endorsed Hans Küng's proposals for a global ethic and who has
lived through one of the deepest clashes of civilizations since World
War II and the Cold War — the kind of clash within a nation
state that also is a clash of civilizational models and ethnic identity. Yet Tutu's dominant contribution has not been the clarification
of ethical principles, nor the realistic assessment of how cultures
and civilizations work; it has been a vision of the future. He represents the kind of vision found also in Pope John Paul II and Martin
Luther King Jr. He represents, further, many of the socially engaged
clergy and activist laity around the world. He knows we must recognize the terrors of the past and the tragedies of the present and
probably future, but that these are not finally definitive for our
world, and that we need not be trapped in them. He argues that
through confession, repentance and forgiveness peoples can find
the prospect of hope and reconciliation that can have an effect
in our times, even if the ultimate reconciliation with God, begun
in Christ, is an eschatological vision yet to be manifest, and then
only as given by God.[37] In this, Tutu is not led either by a quest
to articulate first principles, although he believes in them, nor by
a quest for a tough-minded assessment of sociopolitical reality, although he knows that we shall all have to form a polity able to
contain conflict in human affairs until the Kingdom comes. It is
that vision that a godly kingdom will come, one that anticipates
the possibility of a new reconciled human existence that commends
him in this trio. His is a spiritual vision echoing John's revelation,
formed by inspired gifts, poetic imagination, artistic creativity and
both prophetic courage and priestly care.

We cannot avoid recognizing the facts that all profound religious
orientations wrestle with the attempt to articulate the first principles
of right and wrong, and can, in part, be assessed accordingly as
they embrace efforts to establish human rights for all. Moreover,
a profound analysis of human societies, cultures, and civilizations
will reveal that religion is an inevitable factor at the core of these,
and that it shapes, in particular ways according to the kind and

---

37. See his *No Future Without Forgiveness* (New York: Image Books, 2000); and
God Has a Dream: A Vision of Hope for our Time (New York: Doubleday, 2004).

character of the religion, both the identity of the civilization and the ways in which it will deal with the likely clash of it with other civilizations based on other premises. But neither the philosophical-theological ethical task alone, even worked out in intensive dialogue with those from many world religions, nor the social scientific and politically realistic recognition of the role of religion alone, given its tendency to generate civilizations inclined to clash, nor these together, fully open the door to hope. On this point one must turn to those dynamics of faith that include but also transcend even the best ideals of theological ethics, and of tough-minded social analysis and prudent political planning. Tutu is a living icon of human hope.

I would suggest that these persons represent in their work highly visible examples of the three most important modes of thought that need to be brought together in our approaches to the global future; they reflect some of the basic tasks of theological ethics.[38] We may not approve of everything these figures have done or said; but we need an idealism that can clarify principles; we need a realism that is able to form, reform, and defend the values that allow open, complex societies to function; and we need a vision with a process that ever pulls us toward a new future. Each of these figures offers a significant element of what surely will be needed if we are to avoid the perils of the globalizing forces that now characterize today's new social developments.

In the case of Bishop Tutu, he helped engender the Truth and Reconciliation Commission that began to heal the wounds of South African society after the horrors of Apartheid came to an end. It is a model that has also been tried in some dozen other conflicts. As an activist-pastor, he has caught and conveyed, time and again, the Christian vision of an eschatological possibility, a glimmer of a redeemed future where, in a new heaven and on a new earth, there appears an image of a new heavenly city, a city set on a hill, whose builder and maker is God, that may be approximated on earth by a process of truthful confession and reconciling forgiveness. This vision may be overtly Christian, yet it recognizes the dignity of other faith commitments, and invites all who will to join in the procession toward a healing civilization. It differs from the vision of the future

---

38. See the subsection "The Tasks of Theological Ethics" in the General Introduction to this series, vol. 1. That formal argument is taken up again in the Introduction to vol. 3, with specifications of how and why the world religions agree in part, have overlapping concerns in part and fundamentally disagree especially on eschatology.

of other religions, to be sure, yet it appears to have had a dramatic effect on the South African transformations that are still unfolding. And here is the genius of it: its poetic, imaginative, inspired qualities ever play a role in dynamic social change, also in globalization

On these kinds of points, one can pray about it and be motivated by it, but one cannot argue for it in the same ways that one can about the first principles of justice or about formation and defense of religiously based values that must get woven into the social institutions of the common life. No, a vision of the ultimate end of life and history in one sense remains a vision, the data that would confirm or deny its truth is not fully available in history. But when this vision is vivid, the substance of the good it portrays loops in on the present from the future and prevents mere moral idealism or mere tough-minded realism. It changes our orientation and thus our actions in the present and invites us to become agents in service of the vision. It inclines us to help construct the conditions and shape the possibilities of a different sort of future.

Awareness of such factors as hope and promise that point toward a vision of the ultimate reconciliation of life and history with all that is holy beyond time is a matter that Mark Heim has taken up precisely in regard to the new global awareness of religious pluralism.[39] The world's faiths may be able to discover a common awareness of the first principles of right, and each of the enduring world religions has had its core values become incarnate in a culture and in the institutions in the common life, generating variably ordered, but analogous civilizational patterns that can be comparatively studied, even if they clash. A Christian or a Buddhist can recognize the integrity of a Muslim or a Confucian family, even if they disapprove of purdah for women in the one or all the duties of filial piety in the other, for example. But in this area of a vision of the ultimate end of things, matters differ. And the essential reason why they differ, why they read and apply the same first principles of ethics differently, and why they shape the institutions of civilization differently is that they have different assessments of why it is that life in this world is so problematic, why it is fraught with so much difficulty and distress, conflict and anxiety, disease and death. They differ, in short, in their view of what we need to be saved from and what

---

39. S. Mark Heim, *Salvations: Truth and Difference in Religion* (Maryknoll, NY: Orbis Books, 1995). This book is also treated in the Introduction to vol. 3.

we can be saved for. Thus, the religions differently explain why it is that humans are inclined to do wrong, and they differ in how they order and weight the various spheres of life that we all need for life to flourish.

Let me extrapolate his argument this way: if the underlying difficulty of our existence is that we break community with our ancestral ways and its natural harmony, and thus lose our collective identity, we must recover and reenter into the primal spirituality of our forebears and their relationship to nature. If the fundamental problem of the human condition is that we are too much attached to others, things, the world, or even to our selves, another religion, Buddhism, for example, can offer a way of becoming detached and finding the bliss of "no-thing-ness." If the basic issue is that we do not obey the laws given by God that set us aside as a people, and follow instead the laws of the world, Orthodox Judaism or communal sectarianism may well offer a holy pattern of life that allow us to approximate the fulfillment of those laws. And these views differ from a desire for the ultimate end of *Moksha* (release from the cycle of rebirth by the reintegration of the personal soul with the divine Oversoul) as taught in dominant schools of Hindu thought, or the hope for a place in Paradise as Mohammed was inspired to announce in the Islamic view. Indeed, it would seem that even religiously sanitized ways of pointing to some ultimate hope, expectation, or belief in an ultimate destiny — the happiness in contemplation of Aristotle, the perpetual peace of Kant, the perfect classless society of Marx, or the cultivated virtue of a comprehending, harmonious (if patriarchal) Empire of the Confucian — are quasi-religious visions. The Christian vision of the Kingdom of God, may have a place for these other possibilities; but its central feature is that the Reign of God is working within and among us by the power of the Holy Spirit and has its culminating destiny in the reconciliation of peoples and God in "the New Jerusalem." This is based in the conviction that humans are alienated from God, each other, and the divine intent in creation, and that God is providentially bringing about a reconciliation that we cannot accomplish on our own. What is the fundamental problem with humanity and what has, does, can, or could overcome it? This question can only be answered by hope, which is the substance of faith, and is made manifest in the love of God and the neighbor, the mark of which is a just, open and pluralistic civilization.

In facing the issue of globalization, anticipated in our ethnically, religiously and culturally plural societies, we cannot shortcut dealing with the diversity of eschatological visions that seek to portray the ultimate normative destiny of humanity and the cosmos. But we also are disinclined to forfeit the vision of the future as a divinely given complex civilization to which all the people may bring their gifts. Yet, we have not made an argument for that. The more profound, the more difficult issue is to define which kind of religion, or what sort of metaphysical-moral vision, could and should shape the emerging global civilization that is on the horizon. This is a question that demands a public theological response, one able to address the context we face.

In the following chapter, I will define what I mean by a public theology by tracing its roots, its allies and its opponents. That will prepare the way for chapters in which I shall flesh out its content, in chapters respectively having to do with "Creation and Nature," "Providence and History," "Redemption and Promise," and "Development and New Jerusalem." The idea of a "public theology" using such biblically based themes, I will argue, is critical in the face of those changes that allow and even promote globalization, including the economic aspects of it that preoccupy so many. The question is whether it can accurately assess the religious and ethical aspects of the new developments in ways that are able to endorse and defend its dynamics where that is warranted and to help reform or redirect its trajectory where it is not.

– *Chapter 2* –

THE APPROACH

"PUBLIC THEOLOGY"

What Does Public Theology Do?

"Public theology," I believe, is the most important theological development today in terms of its potential capacity to address the issues posed by globalization.[1] Many fascinating gains have been made in the studies of the biblical scriptures and traditions, using historical and critical tools of analysis, and attention to non-Christian traditions is well underway. Most of these, however, understand religious texts and practices in terms of their local *sitz-im-leben*, that is, in terms of their particular contexts of origin or use. Such studies feed the efforts to develop a public theology insofar as they reveal a capacity of the critical thinker to transcend his or her time, space, tradition and conception of the holy or divine. A grasp of previous or alternative contexts is publicly accessible, indicating that trans-contextual understanding is possible.

Today globalization demands the recognition of a wider public, one that comprehends and relativizes all the particular contexts in which we live. A new kind of particular context-transcendence is required. Thus, a number of scholars around the world are attempting to develop a public theology, for it has become a serious question whether a society or civilization can be sustained on the basis of either a purely local and particular faith, or a purely secular basis that claims to transcend all religion and theology.[2] In fact, the moral

---

1. I should make clear at the outset of this chapter that the approach to public theology used in this volume is not necessarily shared by the other contributors to the first three volumes, even though the essays they wrote are organized by what I take to be a public theological conceptual framework, as reviewed in the last chapter.

2. In May of 2007, an assembly of leaders from twenty-five centers for the study of public theology around the world met and formed "The Global Network for

fiber seems to go out of a society or a civilization if it is not sustained by a compelling vision of transcendence to continually fund its spiritual capital. People's material interests and felt needs are, of course, always present, and many decisions are deeply influenced by them; but people also want their interests and felt needs to be guided and fulfilled in ways that are ultimately valid and thus in accord with the principles of justice and a more ultimate purpose.

A public theology, it will be argued, differs from those forms of fideism that assert purportedly universal and absolute beliefs on the basis of a presumed infallibility of one or another tradition's scripture, or on the basis of any materialist fundamentalism or humanistic metaphysic that denies the possibility that transcendence could or should be that resource in life or thought. All of these have gained influence in recent centuries, although it is difficult to understand how an intense conviction could form or guide a society or civilization without having a argument as to why it should be believed, or how a scientist view can be honestly held without acknowledging that we live in the world where meaning, truth, justice and beauty transcend what can be accounted for by material cause or common consensus. Over time, these simply hold no promise for grasping or guiding the dynamics and structures of globalization.

While the term "public theology" was first developed in America, it is rooted in the classic, western Christian tradition and its themes and directions seem to have resonance for many beyond the West. Indeed, non-Western perceptions of it and contributions to it may help western advocates of it refine its form or extend its content by responding to the globalizing "powers" — the principalities, authorities, and dominions — and the various spheres of life discussed in the previous volumes and chapters, as the non-Western forms of these appear in other contexts. Indeed, as we shall argue, certain themes in Christian thought may well be universal in their content and ethical significance — although it is clearly the case that other themes in this tradition can only be seen as accidental or occasional. The emergence of a potentially global civil society that relativizes every local context reinforces the need to quest for the more universal themes. It is likely, thus, that certain insights that derive from outside the Christian tradition, themes from, say,

---

Public Theology" under the leadership of Will Storrar of the Center of Theological Inquiry, Princeton. The new *International Journal of Public Theology* was also launched, edited by Sebastian Kim.

philosophy, science, other world religions or the cultural accomplishments of non-Christian peoples may aid us in identifying or refining the decisive, universal themes in Christian thought, and in proposing transcultural motifs that can and should be acknowledged and adopted by Christians as a part of their public theology. Clearly, if there is one thing that globalization has already shown, it is that trans-national, cross-cultural, multi-ethnic, poly-linguistic and inter-religious encounters of many kinds can and do take place, and that many make sense and have some kind of fundamentally shared basis. Awareness of these is what is constituting a new public beyond the local contextualism of many current analyses, in spite of the fragmentation that many celebrate in postmodern thought. This forces the hand of theology to clarify what, if anything, it has to offer this more comprehending situation.

It is with these concerns in mind that I state the purpose of this chapter: it is to clarify the term "public theology" as it has been and is being developed, and to identify certain key sociotheological motifs that may well transcend the U.S. context in ways that invite others to join the discussion, to revise its myopias, and to test whether they actually have wider resonance and pertinence. Indeed, research centers and projects focused on this topic have appeared in Germany, Scotland, South Africa, Australia, Korea, Hong Kong, and Beijing as well as in America.[3]

---

3. Besides those resources referred to in the footnotes that follow, the following serves as a representative list of substantive books published in this area: Victor Anderson, *Pragmatic Theology: Negotiating the Intersections of an American Philosophy of Religion and Public Theology* (Albany: State University of New York Press, 1998); John Atherton, *Public Theology for Changing Times* (London: SPCK, 2000); John Bolt, *A Free Church, A Holy Nation: Abraham Kuyper's American Public Theology* (Grand Rapids: Eerdmans, 2001); Don Browning, and Francis Schüssler Fiorenza, eds., *Habermas, Modernity, and Public Theology* (New York: Crossroad, 1992); Linell Cady, *Religion, Theology, and America Public Life* (Albany: SUNY Press, 1993); Jose Casanova, *Public Religions in the Modern World* (Chicago: University of Chicago Press, 1994); David Fergusson, *Community, Liberalism, and Christian Ethics* (Cambridge: Cambridge University Press, 1998); Duncan Forrester, *Christian Justice and Public Policy*, Cambridge Studies in Ideology and Religion 10 (Cambridge: Cambridge University Press, 1997); Michael Himes and Kenneth R. Himes, *Fullness of Faith: The Public Significance of Theology* (New York: Paulist Press, 1993); Robin W. Lovin, *Christian Faith and Public Choices: The Social Ethics of Barth, Brunner, and Bonhoeffer* (Philadelphia: Fortress Press, 1984); Robert McElroy, *The Search for an American Public Theology: The Contribution of John Courtney Murray* (New York: Paulist Press, 1989); Jürgen Moltmann, *God for a Secular Society: The Public Relevance of Theology* (Minneapolis: Fortress, 1999); Robert Simons, *Competing Gospels: Public Theology and Economic Theory*

To argue that theology can make a difference in globalization, of course, presumes that ideas and symbols and worldviews of a religious sort can and do make a long-term and decisive difference in social history, and that theology and theological ethics are key disciplines in the critical examination, refinement, and guidance of religious conviction and social-ethical orientations. I have elsewhere argued, in some detail, that theological and theological ethical principles are like cybernetic dynamics: relatively low-energy systems, such as symbolic formulations, that can guide high-energy systems over time if they are connected to the spheres of life that constitute a society or a civilization and functionally help the various spheres to function well. They usually work indirectly through, e.g., the cultural, educational, and jurisprudential systems and penetrate other spheres of life — politics, business, technology, for examples — of a civilization and often quite directly through the convictions of the people who organize and manage the institutions in these spheres.[4] They also work through the religious opinions of the wider population, but these usually set the preconditions for the reception and diffusion of theological and ethical influences. It may be, as social theorist Francis Fukuyama once told a gathering of students while discussing his book on "Trust,"[5] that genetics plus economic and power interests may drive the society some 40, or 70, or 90 percent of the time (nobody knows the exact percentage), but what is more interesting is the remaining percentage. That involves the imagination, cultural concerns, values, and commitments of people as these relate to the fabric of the common ethos in which they operate. These shape the kinds of interests that are acceptable and they legitimate certain kinds of power, and indeed, what kinds of partners in marriage people choose, and thus the future of the gene

(Alexandria, NSW, Australia: E. J. Dwyer, 1995); and Max L. Stackhouse, *Public Theology and Political Economy* (Grand Rapids: Eerdmans, 1984).

4. I have tried to deal with some of these issues in previous works that, like this one, take up the often neglected issue of Christian Theology and Ethics as they relate to and can give guidance to large-scale social systems. See my *Ethics of Necropolis: On the Military-Industrial Complex* (Boston: Beacon Press, 1971); *Ethics and the Urban Ethos* (Boston: Beacon Press, 1976); *Creeds, Society and Human Rights: A Study in Three Societies* (Grand Rapids: Eerdmans, 1984); and *On Moral Business: Classical and Contemporary Resources for Ethics and Economic Life*, ed. with Dennis McCann, Shirley Roels et al. (Grand Rapids: Eerdmans, 1994), all efforts that I think lead to this one, although there are perspectives and judgments revised here due to the larger context.

5. *Trust: The Social Virtues and the Creation of Prosperity* (New York: The Free Press, 1996).

pool. In short, economic and power interests and material patterns of causation are shaped by religious influences over time. People consciously or preconsciously fuse their "spiritual interests" with their "cultural interests" and their "material interests" in ways that confirm or challenge, stretch or reform an ethos.

Theology, as I am using the term here, is the discipline that seeks to determine what, if anything, in these "spiritual interests," particularly as advanced by one or another religion or religious leader, is valid. It investigates the degree to which any of these spiritual interests accord with what we can know of what is divine, holy, or "absolute," while theological ethics seeks to discern what is right and good in these spiritual interests especially as they get woven into the ethos of the various spheres of life and for an enduring relationship to the actual fabric and possible prospects not only for personal virtue and piety, as important as they are, but also for social justice, the flourishing of the common life, and the quality of ends implied by the resulting directions of public trends.

Public Theology and Modern Philosophy: An Impasse?

In a globalizing era, when a new and wider public is being created than most of the world previously imagined possible (and which some of the world vigorously resists), new patterns of personal commitment may have to be criticized or nurtured and some possibilities in society may have to be opposed or assisted in order to find a more universal, genuinely ecumenical and authentically catholic way of speaking theologically and ethically about the increasingly common life. That is so for at least two reasons. One is that the Enlightenment project attempted to speak in universal terms on the basis of reason alone; this has proven to be significant but fragile.

The Enlightenment project is rooted in great measure in the traditions of late medieval and Reformation thought, which were decidedly shaped by the recovery of classical humanist materials in the Renaissance as well as by the traditions of earlier Christian theology.[6] It also, however, sought to overthrow those forms

---

6. See, for example, Joshua Mitchell, *Not by Reason Alone* (Chicago: University of Chicago Press, 1996). Also, see the exemplary efforts to comprehend globalization with no reference to the theological roots of their own thought in "The Challenges of Globalization: Rethinking Nature, Culture and Freedom" in *The American Journal*

of confessional dogmatics imposed on the citizenry by nationally established churches that inhibited the advance of human rights, science, democracy, and economic development. The contributions that the Enlightenment made were often scientific or philosophical restatements of certain implications of the basic assumptions of previous theology. They wanted to engage the sciences, other religious traditions, the pluralistic professional worlds of a postfeudal laity and the growing proto-democratic sensibilities of the population more directly than in most preceding eras.

To be sure, all these aspects of thought and social development had been present in key strands of theology for centuries, as we will see in the next several chapters, but they were often submerged by imposed confessional dogmas. In overthrowing the state-imposed theological dogmas, the Enlightenment philosophers often, unnecessarily, also threw out those strands of theology that enhanced the prospects of thought and social development; but they did not overthrow the idea that a doctrine should be state imposed. However, it was no longer a religious doctrine that the Enlightenment imposed — or rather, it was no longer a theologically rooted doctrine. As a result, the attempts to develop a polity, an ethic, a society and thus a civilization on a basis of reason alone turned out to render a statist nationalism freighted with interests, passions and presumptions that are less universal, reasonable or self-critical than theology necessarily is. This is so, because the latter sees itself accountable not only to reason, but also to humanity and history and, beyond these, finally to the God who is greater than what any rational argument, collection of humans or period of time can represent. In fact the reliance on reason alone has sometimes been destructive of the wider ranges of human understanding that claims of "rationality" obscured. In many instances the bright lights of the Enlightenment and their disciples, through their impact on culture, law and education, justified a colonial imperialism by the European states in the "North" and the "West" over the "East" and the "South" in ways that later invited a "hyper-modern" revolutionism in all the world. If people would not abandon their other (traditional or religious) ways of thinking, the state would force them to become "rational."

---

of Economics and Sociology 66, no. 1 (January 2007), ed. by Steven V. Hicks and Daniel E. Shannon.

In reaction to these developments, we have seen a second set of challenges. On the one hand we have seen the dramatic return to premodernist and postmodernist celebrations of tribal, ethnic, or national identities, often backed by neofundamentalist, sometimes violent, interpretations of religion. The examples of the Sudan and of the Balkans, of Northern Ireland and of the Mid-East, of Sri Lanka and of Afghanistan come to mind. So also, in the West and more specifically in regard to theology, we have the neosectarian re-assertions of particularist communal convictions, some of which claim to represent a "radical orthodoxy" that seeks to delegiti-mate modern culture, philosophy and social theory.[7] It is alleged by these perspectives that the capacity to speak in universalist terms is impossible, as the failure of the Enlightenment's "liberalism" demonstrates. Thus, it is said, if we are not to return to an imposed secularist dogma — at the hands of a rationalist "liberalism" — we must try both to overcome "critical thinking" and to reclaim "our tradition" as a faith community or "our identity" as a people. Such appeals to heritage or peoplehood not only risk a romantic idolatry of antiquity or ethnicity, they tempt us to the perils of a new anti-liberal creedalism, as one can see, for example, in Wahabi Islam, Indian Hindutva, Myanmar Buddhism and American "Christian nationalism."

However, no one ever "returns" to a tradition just as it was, just as no one can leave a rooted tradition entirely behind. The past is ever recovered selectively, and selective accents demand critical decisions in the present as to what is to be left as part of memory only and what is to be remembered as a resource for renewal and thereby gets lifted into a new prominence. These decisions demand an argument as to why we should make them. Besides, the call for a return leaves aside the possibility of the incorporation of new perspectives or the prospect of a new creative synthesis of faith and reason, will and loyalty, persons and identities. In sum, the current widespread reactions to the fact that the Enlightenment had limits are, at the very least, overstated, and if they are radically pursued will lead to a Nietzschean dead end. They make religion a private concern of a certain group's irrational passion, with theology

---

7. See, for example, John Milbank's notorious *Theology and Social Theory* (Oxford: Blackwell, 1990). Milbank is not alone. See the substantive critique of other exemplary figures in Roger Gustavsson, "Hauerwas, *With the Grain of the Universe,* and the Barthian Outlook," *Journal of Religious Ethics* 35, no. 1 (2007): 25–86.

nothing more than its mouthpiece, and not a matter of the critical evaluation of the religious convictions and actual choices of the people to see what in these might indicate something of God's truth, justice, and mercy in the midst of an emerging global civil society.[8]

The reactions against the Enlightenment do, however, signal another key task of theology and of theological ethics: these fields are not only interpretive of what is going on in regard to religious thought and life, nor are they only analytic about the relative moral adequacy of various religious and social developments; they are also proposals as to what ought to go on. That is, they recognize that every theology is a proposal about how to read the socioreligious environment, and about what should be believed and lived out according to the highest, widest, deepest and most comprehending reality we humans can conceive. Every theology, as proposal, has to meet the test of public reception — according to what manifests the truth, justice, and mercy of God and what the public can internalize from it and weave into the fabric of the common life to enhance their moral, spiritual and material existence. In this sense, public theology is quite practical.

At this point, one of the presuppositions that makes public theology attractive is revealed. This is the conviction that it is the duty of theology to provide a reasonable proposal with regard to the moral and spiritual architecture and the inner guidance system of civilizations. I believe that this is an urgent matter, for all the world seems to be plunging toward global interactions that are perilous and potentially destructive yet simultaneously inviting and transformative, and many of the deepest presuppositions driving this trend are rooted in that combination of Christian theology, Enlightenment thought, and material interests which is in part a confirmation of Christian theology and in part a protest against its own foibles.

Public theology seeks to explore whether there is a way through these impasses. It seeks to identify those genuinely universalistic dimensions of divine reality and of human existence that are indispensable aspects of theology and that are, often just below the

---

8. I should point out that I am using "religion" and "theology" less in the senses made influential in the past century by the genius of Karl Barth, and more in the senses implied by those streams of scholars who struggled with the problem of modernity that stretches from Schleiermacher through Kuyper, Troeltsch, Tillich, the Niebuhrs, Moltmann, and several of the Catholic Social Encyclicals and their interpreters, plus several post-Marxist social theorists from Weber to Parsons, Berger and Robertson (see chapter 1 of vol. 1 of the *God and Globalization* series).

surface of the present, shaping global developments. Moreover, public theology will seek to ethically guide, repair, or resist those developments that have proven to be deceptive, unjust or misdirected. It does not make an idol of modernity or pretend to be prophetically against it while benefiting from it. Instead, public theology intends to selectively put modernizing developments on a more secure basis by exposing, and where appropriate correcting, the submerged theological assumptions that are internal to them and sustaining of them. Such an intent entails the belief that theology as a critical and constructive discipline is, properly, a mode of public discourse that both interprets the key areas of the common life in ways indispensable to the historical and social sciences, by pointing out the religious and ethical presuppositions that are operating in a given ethos, and simultaneously offers normative ethical guidance for the reformation and sustenance of a viable civil society, the basis of a civilization.[9] It further assumes that for all we can learn from modern philosophy and science, theology can, in principle, contribute a deeper perspective on the nature, character and power of those factors that have shaped and inevitably will shape the common life, and its often-obscured moral content, than any interpretation that neglects theology. It can and does also address the more universalistic ethical issues as to what humanity ought to embrace and what to resist, what to keep and what to reconstruct in these areas. Further, in contrast to those who put religion in the category of irrational modes of thought, theology can clarify by the use of symbolic discourse what is at stake in these features of the common life that involve trans-rational resolve and relationship in a reasonable fashion. It can do these because it knows that we must take into account what others ignore or deny: that what is truly divine is the only truly universal reality, that theology can, in some serious measure, provide a more adequate basis of cross-cultural understanding, and thus that it can, in principle, point toward what is necessary for all in ethics, law, and society in a global era.

I shall try to compare and contrast sets of meanings that I think the term entails in regard to closely related ideas, especially where

9. The various "tasks" of public theology as it bears on the common ethical life are outlined in the "General Introduction" to the series in vol. 1, pp. 9–18. The interpretive-diagnostic, the critical-evaluative, and the prescriptive-practical action dimensions are stressed.

there seems to be disagreement about its meaning and usage.[10] Further, I shall suggest clarifications of some areas of its usage that have puzzled recent critics. In my view, the term is important in part because of competing understandings of the term "public," which is almost as controversial as the term "theology," as will become clear when we relate these more definitional matters to specific continuing debates over what they may imply as we look at particular issues today.

A Brief History of the Idea

The term first appeared in an analysis of the contributions of theological ethicist Reinhold H. Niebuhr by Martin Marty, the noted American church historian who was particularly interested in studying what it was that distinguished faith and church in America from that of Europe, from which America has drawn so much.[11] At the same time, he tried to sort out the several conflicting views about the role of religion in American public life, sometimes using terms already in currency such as "public religion" or "the religion of the republic." These matters were rather intensely debated after World War II. Western Europe (with its traditional established churches) was relatively weakened (and in some cases discredited for complicity) and the Soviet Union was extending its militantly secular influence on every continent. While, in one sense, America had emerged as a world power after the Spanish-American War of the 1890's, an event that reinforced its Protestant sensibilities, it had to face the fact that it had become a world leader in World War II and the last half of the twentieth century. This highly pluralistic nation,

---

10. Harold Breitenberg Jr. has documented the variety of uses of the term in his extremely useful essay, "To Tell the Truth: Will the Real Public Theology Please Stand Up?" *The Annual of the Society of Christian Ethics* (2003), from which I have drawn many insights with the permission of the author. See also his Ph.D. thesis, "A Comprehensive Public Theology . . . ," (Richmond, VA: Union Theological Seminary, 2004); Vincent Bacote, *The Spirit in Public Theology* (Grand Rapids: Baker, 2004); and my "Civil Religion, Political Theology, and Public Theology: What's the Difference?" *Journal of Political Theology* (July 2004): 275–93, of which this chapter is an expanded revision.

11. See "Reinhold H. Niebuhr: Public Theology and the American Experience," *Journal of Religion* 54, no. 4 (October 1974): 332–59 (of which Marty was the editor and David Tracy was the assistant editor); and "Two kinds of Civil Religion," *American Civil Religion,* ed. R. E. Richey and D. G. Jones (New York: Harper & Row, 1974), 139–57.

long ago founded on the basis of theological orientations that supported religious freedom, constitutional democracy, human rights and open economic opportunity, had to clarify its core values again.

In this context, the great Jewish sociologist Will Herberg published a widely discussed essay that spoke of the shared values held by believers in the United States. He wrote of the ways in which Protestantism, Catholicism and Judaism were more and more seen as sister denominations, branches of a single family that sometime met (and quarreled or celebrated together) on public occasions.[12] Herberg used the term "civic religion" to describe what they shared as the religious aspect of "Americanism," although he was also clear that each "root" of this shared canopy of conviction retained its own distinctive faith and practice.

Soon thereafter, another sociologist, Robert Bellah, published his famous essays on "civil religion."[13] He drew not only from Alexis de Tocqueville, but also from Emil Durkheim's adoption of the term which can be traced through Rousseau's *Contrât social* to Cicero's *De Legibus,* where he treats what cults should be permitted and which forbidden by law, so that loyalty to Rome's deities and civil order should not be undercut. Rousseau, of course, had adopted this idea of civil religion shortly before the French Revolution, and spoke of the necessity of each nation cultivating its own values and symbols to express the primal freedom of its people, and of its potential to cultivate a "general will" able both to overcome the influence of church religion and its dogmas and to solidify the collective consciousness of the nation. The displacement of the established Catholic Church by the French Revolution made Christian conviction a private matter. But, in its place, some kind of national system of moral values — a "civil religion" — had to be constructed. The idea that people should not only be able to chose their own religion, but that a people could and should invent their own caused the Christians, already incensed by the notorious removal of the Blessed Virgin from Notre Dame Cathedral and the installing of a statue to Reason, to oppose the idea of radical democratic reforms in church and society for some time.

In contrast to such a common denominator, invented cult, Marty used the term "public theology" to speak of those who drew on

12. W. Herberg, *Protestant, Catholic, Jew* (New York: Doubleday, 1955, rev. ed. 1960).

13. R. N. Bellah, "Civil Religion in America," *Dædalus* 96, no. 1 (1967).

overtly biblical and doctrinal sources to speak to public issues, pre-
suming that at least some of the terms used in these sources were
both publicly accessible whether one was a believer or not and indispensable to the shaping of the common life. While he focused on
Reinhold Niebuhr, who referred to a "Christian Realism" to identify Augustinian understandings of human nature and sociopolitical
developments in history, Marty also identified Puritan theologian
Jonathan Edwards, Christian educator Horace Bushnell, and Social
Gospel leader Walter Rauschenbusch among the theologians from
earlier periods who had influenced the American public and used
theological language to interpret and guide the basic ordering of the
common life. Moreover, Marty noted that Benjamin Franklin, Abraham Lincoln and Woodrow Wilson were key political figures who
drew on scriptural and doctrinal sources to guide the moral duties of
the nation. The contributions of all these figures differed from "civic
religion" and "civil religion" not only because they thought that certain biblical resources more accurately identified the root conditions
of human existence than did any theory derived from humanly constructed symbolic narratives for national identity, but because they
sought to identify the basic aspects of the human condition as it
stood under God and thus could see dynamics and structures that
were more universal than any earth bound speculation or national
heritage could render. Others issued critiques of "civic religion"
and "civil religion," saying that it merely made a religion out of the
American experience. Some suggested, more sharply, that it was a
new U.S. form of *Kulturprotestantismus,* populist self-worship, or
"American *Shinto.*"[14]

We may recall that many Roman Catholics were doubtful about
this for other reasons. Pope Leo XIII had condemned "Americanism" in his pastoral letter *Testem Benevolentiae.* He had as his target
the proto-democratic "trusteeism" by which the laity was taking the
leadership of the churches into its own hands and embracing democracy in both church and society — as in fact many Protestants
advocated on theological grounds. The American Catholic clergy

---

14. This particular critique came to my attention from the noted sociologist of
religion, my colleague Richard Fenn. He also pointed out that Bellah has, in fact,
drawn back from the use of the term civil religion in the face of such criticisms, and
while he did not cease being a sociologist, he turned to a more normative religio-
ethical language, as can be seen in his, et al., *Habits of the Heart* (Berkeley: University
of California Press, 1985).

also seemed to be eager to make the faith relevant to the democratic society in which they lived. They not only stressed the active life rather than the life of contemplation but adopted "modernist" views of philosophy and science rather than only holding to magisterial teachings. Moreover, many Catholics were beginning to develop an attitude of tolerance to the variety of creeds that most Protestants had already adopted, as was to become later manifest in the Federal and still later, National and World Councils of Churches. American Catholicism began to look less Roman and more like an elder cousin at the family reunion of Mainline (Protestant) Christianity, in spite of the extensive system of Catholic schools founded to prevent accommodation to a culture formed by Protestant biases.

The sociological recognition of an Americanist tendency to celebrate and inculturate Protestantism is an accurate perception of much of the national consciousness, one which has been subject to much criticism also by some Protestants. There is, for instance, a long tradition of "American exceptionalism," the notion that the United States is destined to become the New Israel, the model "city on the hill" referred to by Matthew. And it is so that America has offered, sometimes in imposing ways, some social, political, cultural, and economic patterns of its life to parts of the global future. More than one hundred "newer nations," for example have modeled their constitutions in part or in whole on the Constitution of the United States. Less nobly, many forms of popular music have been imitated around the globe. Yet, Americans know that every tradition, including our own, surely has to be critically examined to see what it can contribute that is of continuing value and what is dangerous morally and spiritually. Everyone remembers that Nazi Germany, the Communist Soviet Union, and *apartheid* South Africa had also developed national cults that can only be understood as resurgent pagan "civic religions" or artificially constructed "civil religions," and that the rest of the world had to oppose these.

At the same time, it could be said that the United States, as a land of immigrants and thus historically multi-ethnic and multi-cultural, anticipated other developments that we increasingly find around the world — peoples of many religious and racial backgrounds being able to find ways to live together, seldom without tensions, within the same civil society because the fabric of this society was woven out of a theology that shaped public life that basically legitimated such diversity.[15] This must be said with caution and contrition by any American, for this nation's toleration of slavery and our history with Native Americans is obviously subject to sharp critique. Still today, the basic motif of civil religion as it points to a patriotic self-celebration is a present temptation. It receded during the war in Vietnam, found a resurgence after the Fall of the Berlin Wall, was reenforced in the reaction to the attack on the Twin Towers and the Pentagon on 9/11, and declined again in the debates over U.S. policy toward Iraq — even if new debates persist about whether a society marked by religious freedom, democracy, human rights and economic well-being can be formed there or preserved at home as the U.S. struggles with national security.

Still, it is true that public theology as it has developed takes quite seriously the ways in which religion operates in a culture, in contrast to some dogmatic traditions that focus more exclusively on faith and revelation in ways that treat all religion(s) as an idolatrous social or cultural invention — rightly opposing what Rousseau has advocated. But from the standpoint of at least some forms of public theology, religion as it is believed and practiced in an ethos has to be examined to see whether it is the relative incarnation over time of authentic faith and valid ethical principles and purposes. It is the comparative and critical assessment of religion and its consequences that needs theological and ethical attention. I shall identify some of the key standards for making these judgments in subsequent chapters. But it is clear even now that we cannot affirm them as true or just simply because they are ours.

Perhaps it is ever the case that peoples develop a loyalty to, a pride in, and a kind of religious appreciation of their ethnic, national or cultural identity. And it is doubtless true that a certain appreciation of the genealogical pools and social institutions that brought each of us into existence is justifiable. Who does not honor certain kinds of limited patriotism, and the joyful savoring of distinctive cultural styles, idioms and achievements? People of many traditions might even pray in thanksgiving for them and pray divine protection of them. To interpret how such loyalties and practices develop and function, it is necessary to use public theology to identify

---

15. See the new studies of this question, from many perspectives, in Eddy A. J. G. Van der Borght et al., *Faith and Ethnicity*, Studies in Reformed Theology 4 (Zoetermeer, the Netherlands: Uitgeverij Meinema, 2003). My views are in "Religion and Ethnicity: A Public Theological Overview in a Global Era," 179–97.

the root convictions that have become routinized into those tissues of ordinary religious belief and practice that form a living ethos. Doubtless, it is also the case that none of these is beyond judgment, or the need of reconstructive guidance. And, for that task also, an ethically focused public theology is a stronger resource than a civic or a civil religion in itself, precisely because theology in this sense is less dependent on experience in one context on one hand and less dependent on a single confessional tradition on the other. In principle, it casts a critical eye on the religious self-celebration by any particularist group and seeks to cultivate a capacity to address the common life in terms that common discourse can grasp. In brief, it is not another name for a civil religion, but it acknowledges the power of religious dynamics in social life, and it seeks to identify the criteria for evaluating which dimensions of these are valid.

After all, the term "public theology" as used to characterize the contributions of Edwards, Rauschenbusch, Niebuhr, etc., is intentionally not centered on national identity, even if these leaders did intend to shape the common life and to aid religious believers and public institutions to form the habits, convictions and social ethic of the general population in ways that had implications for political policy. But at base, their conception of what they were about and the sources from which they drew had a more transcendental grounding and a more universal definition of what is public than any national set of values or civil religion, no matter how piously held, could be. That is also one of the reasons why the quest for a public philosophy does not fully suffice either.[16] The idea of "public theology" constantly swims against the stream of philosophers who argue that philosophy is the more universal human mode of public discourse, and that religion and theology are always particular, privileged, and closed to outsiders. But it may be the other way around: some kinds of discourse about God may disclose a *logos* of *theos* that comprehends the *sophia* of philosophy and gives a clearer object to its *philia,* and that simultaneously connects that *philia* and *sophia* to a framework that involves justice and mercy. Theology, of course, demands the idea of a divine reality that is

16. See, for example, Walter Lippmann, *The Public Philosophy* (Boston: Little, Brown, 1955). The list of efforts at nontheological public philosophy is long, and often focus on the attempt to define the "common good" without reference to anything overtly religious or theological. However, some Catholic and Reformed, religiously framed "worldview" philosophies that attend to social and political arguments approximate a public theology, as we will shortly see.

more comprehending than any deified values that a political order can construct, or any human love of wisdom can assure, although either may point toward it. One of the most important contributions of Reinhold Niebuhr was precisely on this point. He argued in his masterwork, *The Nature and Destiny of Man,* that philosophers do often identify issues and demand arguments to which theology must attend; but they also ignore the dependence of most philosophy on faith-based presuppositions that are less than universal in assumption and implication than the more universal insights on which theology depends. Thus, they miss the depths of human nature with its *justitia originalis,* sense of sin and need for grace, and thus too often propose schemes based on faulty perceptions of what is truly human, thereby endangering life and meaning.[17]

The term "public theology," rooted in such discussions and debates, was new; but it gained currency rather quickly, not because of its novelty or because the theological concerns to which it pointed were fresh, but because it seemed to capture wider and deeper strands of the classical Christian theological heritage, strands that are rooted in the interaction of biblical insight, philosophical speculation, historical discernment, personal awareness and social formation as these were dynamically and repeatedly resynthesized over time in new contexts. These strands were able to offer criticism of religion when it was tempted to idolatry or cultural chauvinism, and it could judge dogmatically stated doctrines that did not offer convincing reasons as to why we should believe the dogmas or offer just and merciful guidance to souls or societies. Indeed, a modest explosion of books on the topic has been documented.[18] Further, for the American scene, and for many in other lands, the model of Martin Luther King Jr. became a worldwide symbol of public theology in its activist mode, reinvigorating a tradition obscured temporarily by notions of the inevitable secularization that was to be brought by greater modernization, that theologians, clergy and committed laity may draw on theological resources as "public intellectuals" to

---

17. *The Nature and Destiny of Man,* 2 vols. (New York: Charles Scribner Sons, 1949–51). In vol. 1, Niebuhr deals with Darwin, Kant, Hegel, Marx, Freud, etc., and shows how each one has certain insights, and yet how each one misses some dimension of human nature that theology rightly identifies, and all should also take seriously.

18. See notes 3 and 8 above. More than a hundred articles have been published with "public theology" in the title. The number of related essays and volumes is enormous.

argue issues of justice in society. They saw themselves as deputies or agents of Christ, the prophet, priest and prince of peace who inaugurated the Kingdom of God. They were convinced that they must take responsibility for the spiritual and moral architecture of the common life as the Medieval Church had done with the collapse of the pagan Roman Empire, as the Reformers had done with the rise of early modern Europe, and as the Puritans and Pietists had done with regard to the advent of modern industrial society.[19]

More recently, indeed, a neo-Evangelical movement, which many call "the new religious right," to the chagrin of many "mainline" church leaders, has stimulated many active advocates on issues from abortion to welfare reform, marriage and divorce policies, gambling and the teaching of religion in schools, etc. They are quite visible on television, radio, and Internet media. They advocate the funding of faith-based organizations to engage in the building of housing for the homeless, job-training for minority and unemployed workers, rehabilitation and reentry programs for ex-prisoners and those with substance abuse problems, and the protection of freedom of religion at home and abroad. They do not claim that their theology is public, but they generate perspectives out of it that they seek to make powerful in society by political means and pressure.[20] This differs from what is happening in the southern hemisphere, where Pentecostal movements are changing society by the altering of social habits and institutions.[21] Neither the neo-Evangelicals nor the Pentecostals have a well developed public theology as of yet; but their leaders seem to see that social change is prior to political change, and some are in dialogue with both Catholic and Reformed theologians who have focused on such questions — as are some East Asian scholars who are raising these issues in cultures where Christianity is a small minority and they have little access to political influence.[22]

---

19. Three new works that address these matters in different but, I think, finally compatible ways are David Hollenbach, S.J., *The Global Face of Faith* (Washington, DC: Georgetown University Press, 2005); William Schweiker, *Theological Ethics and Global Dynamics* (London: Blackwell, 2005); William Storrar et al., *Public Theology for the 21st Century* (London: T & T Clark, 2004).

20. See Ronald J. Sider et al., *Toward an Evangelical Public Policy* (Grand Rapids: Baker Books, 2005). They do have issues that greatly concern them, and can often mobilize blocks of voters on these issues.

21. See, especially, the work of David Martin, *Tongues of Fire* (London: Blackwell, 1993); and *Pentecostalism* (London: Blackwell, 2001).

22. See, for example, Wijaya, Yahya, *Business, Family and Religion: Public Theology in the Context of the Chinese-Indonesian Business Community* (Bern: Peter

The deeper roots of such views and activities are found, of course, in those doctrines that, Christians claim, point to something genuinely universal — creation and sin, a providential set of gracious gifts that manifests a sustaining grace in the midst of tragedy and failure, and the promise of a meaningful and just ultimate future, which, Christians hold, is best found in Jesus Christ and is partly exemplified in Paul's encounters with other faiths in public spaces, such as the Acropolis, where he found it possible to engage the philosophies of the day. These roots were cultivated by some of the early saints of the faith, especially in Augustine's *City of God,* Thomas' writings on law and justice, the Reformers' teachings about the "orders of creation," "vocation" and "covenant" and the artful rendering of such themes by, e.g., Dante and Milton.[23] These efforts signal the continuity of today's developments of public theology with the classical theological heritage as it has now become partially incarnate in, passed through, and been refined by modernity.

The formative figures and authorities of public theology do not agree on a number of important doctrinal and ethical issues, but all presume that theology, while always related to personal faith, and partly derivative of particular historical communities, is at its most profound levels neither an individual piety nor a church theology that speaks only to gathered believers. Rather, it offers to all humanity a comprehensive way of interpreting and guiding the common life. Furthermore it does not draw from sources available only to a select or privileged group of the already persuaded. Rather it is engaged with the same questions that vex social analysts — family therapists, sociologists, economists, political philosophers, legal theorists, public health officials, anthropologists, cultural critics and journalists — as they try to discern what is going on in the world, whether things are as they ought to be and what, if they are not, can be changed.

Lang, 2003); and Zhibin Xie, of the Chinese Academy of Social Science, *Religious Liberty, Religious Diversity, and Religion in Politics: In Search of an Appropriate Role of Religion in Public Political Culture for a Democratic China* (Forthcoming).

23. Less remote shaping influences can be found in Ernst Troeltsch's survey of Christian "social teachings," Paul Tillich's "Theology of Culture," Dietrich Bonhoeffer's "ethics for a world come of age," Karl Barth's views on "church community and civil community," Emil Brunner's charter for the reconstruction of Europe after World War II in his much too neglected "Christianity and Civilization," and in Pope John Paul II's *Centesimus Annus* and *Veritatis Splendor.*

Public theologians generally have a high regard for the technical data gathered and analyzed by these fields, but they ordinarily do not think that the descriptive realities and especially the normative ones can be discovered by contextual social data alone. Rather, they hold that at the roots of social life are those powers, principalities and dominions, discussed in the previous volumes and summarized in the previous chapter, that are best grasped and evaluated in theological and ethical terms, and that point to what underlies the actual social conditions and to what stands over them in ways that allow us to evaluate and transform them as necessary, as well as debate about such matters with those not part of the faith.

Why a "Public" Theology?

There are two main reasons for the adjective "public." One is very simple: it is a modest protest against influential, and often allied, fields of political philosophy and political theology. One tends to make religion private, the other to make it a matter of state policy with the implied view that the government is and must be the only comprehending reality. Historically, however, philosophical discourse about the *polis* included discussion about all spheres of the common life. In Book II of *The Republic*, for example, Plato begins to open up the question of the nature of the *polis* by discussing matters of economics, sexuality, and morality (in the parable of the ring), and proceeds to discuss the different classes in society and the proper role of education, its arts and sciences, in shaping their character. However, there is a "statist" dimension to the argument insofar as all of these spheres of life are to be regulated by the central political order. Something similar can be said of Aristotle in the relationship of his *Ethics* to his *Politics*. Christian thinkers learned much from them, but they also challenged them and developed a theologically formed conception of the nature and character of the social order.[24]

Largely in continuity with the previous theological tradition, some arguments made by certain contemporary Jewish and Christian philosophers, such as Michael Sandel, Nicholas Wolterstorff,

---

24. See Oliver O'Donovan and Joan Lockwood O'Donovan, eds., *From Irenaeus to Grotius: A Sourcebook in Christian Political Thought* (Grand Rapids: Eerdmans, 1999), a masterful collection of major texts with discerning commentary.

and Michael Perry, have engaged the question of whether "religious" appeals can and should be allowed in public political discourse, in a context after the Enlightenment when many doubted that it should be allowed. They are in dialogue and debate with noted political philosophers, such as John Rawls, Kent Greenawalt, and Robert Audi who have, in slightly different ways, argued that religious believers must park their religious modes of discourse outside the public square, or at least restate them in theologically "neutral" language, for in that forum only "rational" and "empirical" arguments can be allowed.[25]

Several issues are in the background of this discussion. First of all, the dialogue and debate is framed in terms of "the public," which is seen as political, and "the private," which is seen as "personal." A church or a temple, a mosque, a TV ministry, is not seen as an arena of genuinely public discourse where people pray and preach in language anyone can learn, and engage issues fateful for the well-being of believers and nonbelievers and for the common good. Also, neglected are all those religiously generated organizations from colleges and universities to reading groups and hospitals, elder-care facilities and therapeutic groups for substance abusers, not to mention youth groups, prison ministries, singing societies, soup kitchens, disaster relief, etc., etc. These are seldom recognized as addressing "public" affairs. Often they are seen as incidental voluntary groupings where people evidence by ritual, preaching or teaching some otherworldly matters that are irrelevant to public matters, or demanding obedience to some allegedly comprehensive doctrine that is incompatible with both public reason and any other religious or moral views.[26] But such groups and institutions are, in

---

25. See, especially, John Rawls, *Political Liberalism,* paperback edition with a new Introduction (New York: Columbia University Press, 1996); and his "The Idea of Public Reason Revisited," *University of Chicago Law Review* 61 (Summer 1997): 765–807; Kent Greenawalt, *Private Consciences and Public Reasons* (New York: Oxford University Press, 1995); and Robert Audi, *Religion in the Public Square: The Place of Religious Convictions in Political Debate* (Lanham, MD: Rowan & Littlefield, 1997), with Nicholas Wolterstorff, of whom more later.

26. In previous volumes of the *God and Globalization* series, however, we have seen that all the world religions have some areas that involve commonality with each other (such as a leadership of trained personnel, and an endorsement of nearly identical deontological first principles), some areas where there are overlapping but not identical motifs (shared aspects of ethology), and only a few where there is a fundamental difference (especially eschatology). We shall return to these themes later in this volume in greater detail (see vol. 3, Introduction).

the view of public theology, the generators and bearers of the basic public social infrastructure that forms the ethos in which a political life takes place. The worldviews and the lessons learned, habits cultivated and social capital gained in these activities influence political outcomes more than is recognized.

It does seem, to some theologians as well as some philosophers, that religious faith is based on personal experience, private commitment or individual decision, and not much given to public or political discussion and deliberation, and it is true that if no individuals believed in a religion, it would be of psychopathological or archeological interest only. And it is so that much of religious language is metaphorical, symbolic, mythic and poetic in ways that are not always understood immediately on first hearing. But there is a logic to these modes of discourse, and such religious language is carried and utilized by a community of faith, often written in publicly accessible books and formed into distinctive practices and in publicly accessible institutions. It is not immediately clear that these are therefore nonrational, nondebatable or not proper to public discourse, and thus should not be allowed. To deny these features of public life — both ideational-symbolic and social-institutional — is simply to project an ideological definition of religion on a screen that does not fit most religion. No wonder religion seems so incomprehensible to some: their projection system generically distorts what it claims to portray.

Moreover, the claim that public reason is incompatible with comprehensive moral or religious doctrines is surely wrong. It may be incompatible with some parts of some religions, just as it is with some philosophies, but not with others, and probably not with key parts of all. Of course, Kent Greenawalt allows that legislators, for example, may be affected by religious convictions, but they should avoid reference to them in legislative discussion. In addition, John Rawls agrees that there is no necessary war between religion and democracy, for religion "may endorse a constitutional democratic society and recognize its public reason."[27] But this argument entirely ignores the direct theological influences on the historical development of the constitutional democratic republic and what actually

---

27. Rawls, "The Idea of Public Reason Revisited," 803. This argument implies, however, that the standards are entirely to be set by this form of public reason and religious language can only be admitted when it coincides with what is already established on nonreligious grounds.

has been, can be and is now allowed as reasonable in political systems that have one. Of course, some religions embrace constitutional democratic republicanism — they are its source and norm.[28] Once it is developed, others, religious or secular, have recognized its wisdom. The question is whether it can survive and flourish and constantly be reformed as needed if its root foundations are ignored.

A more complex argument is offered by Robert Audi. Audi begins with the "separation of church and state," and identifies three issues embodied in that constitutional principle. First, the state must allow the free practice of religion, within reasonable moral limits. Second, the state must not give preference to any one religion over any others. Finally, the state must not give a positive benefit or a negative liability to a religion, religious group or person, as compared to a nonreligious orientation, group or person.[29] Thus, people may (as they do) bring religion into any public debate. However, when making a policy for a whole society, only "secular rational" arguments can count. There must, in other words, he argues, be a point at which an "institutional principle of neutrality" must take over, although there may be areas of overlap. One can ask, however, whether Freudian or Jungian theories about human nature, or Darwinian or Marxist ideas about social life would count as "secular rational" arguments when it comes, say, to welfare or abortion or economic trade policies. Is it not so that these complex theories, each with an implicit metaphysical-moral vision, which some people hold with great religious conviction and zeal, would be privileged over any Catholic or Protestant, Jewish or Hindu perspectives on public matters if he allows them? Would that not give preference to one set of comprehensive doctrines, those without a reference to God, over those with such a key reference point?

It is surely true that the separation of church and state as an institutional concept rightly sees that no single church body should control the government, that one's religious membership should have no bearing on one's rights as citizen positively or negative, and it may imply that no citizenship should be determinative for

---

28. See, e.g., David Holmes, *The Faiths of the Founding Fathers* (New York: Oxford University Press, 2006); and Jonathan Hill, *What Has Christianity Ever Done for Us?* (Downers Grove, IL: InterVarsity Press, 2005).

29. In Audi, *Religion in the Public Square*, 4–8.

one's religious membership; but that separation actually leaves the door wide open for public, interfaith theological debate about the basic moral and spiritual fabric of the common life, especially in its prepolitical dimensions! And that will deeply shape politics.

The scholars who are in critical dialogue with these figures, however, usually offer other arguments than what I have thus far suggested. Michael Sandel holds that concepts of justice and of rights, as considered by both philosophy and politics, cannot be separated from the vision, usually religiously borne and refined by centuries of debate among religious scholars, of the ultimate ends of life. There is no compelling reason, Sandel argues, why these cannot be debated as reasonably as issues of liberal justice.[30] In another way, Michael Perry also argues for the inclusion of religious discourse in public debates, arguing that the full recognition of the dignity of each human and of a deep sense of the duty to care for the neighbor can only be secured by religious argument, and that an "ecumenical political dialogue" can allow divergent religious (and other comprehensive ethical views that function in people's lives as religious) traditions to find as much agreement on basic public issues as can purely philosophical discussion of political justice.[31]

Such arguments are vigorously supported by Nicholas Wolterstorff in his dialogue with Audi, and he adds the argument that the political form of liberal democracy may give space to debates about justice, but it does not resolve any of the contested questions under debate. He also points out that the position taken by those who want to force others to park religious and theological matters outside the gates of political life, or seriously constrain its potential role in public debate and policy making, are fundamentally discriminatory. They deny integrity to any religious conviction that teaches that persons should, on the grounds of their convictions, "strive for wholeness, integrity, integration, in their lives, that they ought to allow the Word of God, the teachings of the Torah, the commands and example of Jesus, or whatever, to shape their existence as a whole, including their social and political existence. Their religion is

---

30. Michael J. Sandel, *Liberalism and the Limits of Justice,* 2nd ed. (New York: Cambridge University Press, 1998).

31. Michael Perry, *Love and Power: The Role of Religion and Morality in American Politics* (New York: Oxford University Press, 1991).

not, for them, about *something other* than their social and political existence.... "[32] To exclude such views gives priority to those who are driven by ideology and claim neutrality, but are prejudicial.

The proposals that follow in this volume about a public theology are properly indebted to these Jewish, Christian and religiously tolerant "liberal" philosophers. They help clear the space for a public theology in those academic and political spheres which have narrow views of what religion and theology are all about. And yet, there are differences. The division between public and private, when public means "political" and "political" means governmental policy, is simply not adequate to sorting the fundamental issues. There are, as noted, aspects of religion that are fundamentally personal. But there are decisive dimensions of public discourse that are public but pre-political, to which political parties and governments must respect and protect, and these are nearly always religious in character, and the debates in this area are usually theological or ethical or both. It is these that shape personal beliefs and the predispose political orders to this or that particular polity. It is not, in this view, the responsibility of the church, the university, the media, the corporation, etc., which may be guided by this or that comprehensive view that is prior to their views of the nature and character of government, to actually make political policy; but if government makes policy that violates their sense of what is true, right, good and merciful, they may use their social influence as citizens to argue for its reformation — even for a regime change.

Why Not a "Political" Theology?

If there is a tendency in the debates over political philosophy to relegate religion and theology to the private realm, the tendency in political theology is to wed politics and theology too directly to the policies of government. In certain streams of Christian history and even in the development of doctrine in Europe, from Constantine to the Christian Socialists of the twentieth century, with parallels in the history of the religions of China and India — the emperor or war lord, the maharaja or the prince — the Caesars of the world dominated the entire society and determined its religious orientation,

---

32. Audi and Wolterstorff, *Religion in the Public Square*, 105.

functionally raising the political regime above the transcendent domain to which religions appeal. It was not only in the West that it was said: *cuius regio, eius religio* (whoever rules, his religion).

Thus, while the use of the term "public" is used in contrast to the idea that religion is and must remain private, it is against many widespread understandings of "political" theology.[33] However, public theology is not an anti-political view. No society can long survive without a viable political order; hell breaks out on earth without law and order. Indeed, Christian theology teaches that believers should be subject to those political authorities that foster good and are a terror to evil, for all such rulers are instituted by God. This means that no political authority is God or can be treated as holy, divine, heavenly or sacred, or worthy of ultimate respect; but that each must stand *under* the just laws of the ultimate transcendent authority who stands over every state, and who has appointed to every just state a functional role in fostering the protection and cultivation of human well-being in life and salvation beyond it.

This protest, thus, is based in the conviction that the public is prior to the republic, that the moral and spiritual fabric of civil society is and should be more determinative of politics than politics is for society and religion. The principles and purposes of the realm

---

33. "Public theology" has also appeared in German theology, especially as cultivated recently by a number of younger scholars whose work has been brought out in a series of volumes by Wolfgang Huber and an international team of editors. See W. Huber, *Kirche und Öffentlichkeit* (Stuttgart: Kaiser, 1973); and the series edited by him, *Öffentliche Theologie*, 12 vols. (Gütersloh: Chr. Kaiser, 1991–2001). My thanks to Dr. Prof. Heinrich Bedford-Strohm, a major contributor to this series, for drawing them to my attention. These volumes reflect the fact, as I see them from afar, that the older patterns of specific religions being established by the state have broken down, but a new relationship is under development. The question of the relationship of church preaching to public discourse was debated in the European context during the last half century under the powerful influence of Karl Barth's church- and dogma-centered theology and a number of ongoing discussions of the Barmen Declaration, one of the best-known anti-Fascist Christian statements. Yet, deeper in the social history are the lingering influences of the more radical political theologies of, for example, Carl Schmitt on the right and Ernst Bloch on the left, and the more reformist political theologies of Catholic Johannes Metz and Protestant Jürgen Moltmann in the middle. Public theology in these traditions seems often to be more "political theology," with much focus on giving direction to governmental policy. See Scott Paeth, "From the Church to the World: Public Theology and Civil Society in Dialogue with the Theology of Jürgen Moltmann" (Ph.D. Dissertation, Princeton Theological Seminary, 2004). There is significant evidence that some leading European scholars are modulating their views due to the influences from non-European developments. See Christine Lienemann-Perrin et al., *Kirche und Öffentlichkeit in Transformations-gesellschaften* (Stuttgart: Verlag Kohlhammer, 2007).

of God can be woven into the fabric of the common life, a process that can only take place when the people believe in them and seek to order their social habits and human relationships according to them. Christians, of course, believe that in Jesus Christ the realm of God entered into the midst of human life. However indispensable a government is and however much we should obey it, it is subordinate to what is more ultimate. Every world religion knows something of the meaning of the commandment, "Thou shalt have no other God before me." The only theologically valid government is thus a secular, limited one, for it is *under* what is truly divine — that is, under an authority and dominion where moral and spiritual principles and purposes govern what is woven into the fabric of the common life.

There were counter-movements to the tendency to have politics rule religion: when the church claimed a sphere of authority that could not be dominated by the political one, when religious assumptions shaped constitutional laws (historically rooted in the development of canon law) that constrained rulers, when electors or councils deposed emperors and believed that they had a right under God to do so, when universities fought for independence from both church and state control, etc. These were all classical examples of "public" life that recognized limits to governmental power, and established zones of social interaction that were able to shape the common life from the center out, and not simply from the political top down — or, for that matter, from a revolutionary movement of the bottom up (which usually only establishes a new top-down rule).

Public theology, thus, differs from political theology precisely in this: public theology tends to adopt a social theory of politics, and political theology inclines to a political view of society. The latter view is most common and tends to see the government as the comprehending institution of society. Politics, in this view, is dedicated to the accumulation, organization and exercise of coercive power for the sake of the enforcement of the edicts of a ruling party. That party may govern in a benevolent, authoritarian, tyrannical, or totalitarian way; but it is always deeply concerned with the power to guide, limit or command every subject or citizen and every other institution in a geographical territory. The threat of the use of force stands behind its actions. When it does not rule by naked force, it seeks legitimacy, that is, a recognition that its possession and

use of its power is spiritually, morally, or at least legally, autho-
rized — historically by heredity or acclimation, today by consent of
the governed.

A social theory of politics sees every political party and every government as subject to the more primary powers in society — those
spheres of life that exist prior to the formation of political orders.
And these spheres are guided first of all by the moral and spiritual
values that operate in and among the people as they develop the
fabric of their lives. In this view, political orders, regimes, polities
and policies come and go; they are always necessary, but they are
also a derivative artifact of those religious, cultural, familial, economic and intellectual traditions that are prior to government, and
every government is, sooner or later, accountable to them, and it is
where these are weak that the great Leviathans rise from the deep.
Where these are strong, a government that unduly attempts to control these sectors of social life will foment resistance, revolution and
attempts to transform the ruling parties or the form of government
altogether.

Public theology is at its strongest when it is, as already suggested,
based in the warranted conviction that the public is prior to the
republic, that the fabric of civil society, of which religious faith and
faith-based ethics and organizations are a decisive component, is
more determinative of and normatively more important for politics
than politics is for society and religion. Benevolent governments can
foment civil society institutions for some time, but the latter have to
assume responsibility for their own governance and moral integrity
sooner or later, and when they do they begin to shape the public
in ways that are beyond the capacity of politics to fully control.
And this public is found in public worship, public opinion, public
media, publicly held corporations, publicly accessible hospitals and
legal services, the public impact of independent professionals, and,
more and more, the Internet. Politics is only one area of public life,
and while it is perfectly proper for it to regulate limited aspects of
all the other spheres of life, it ought not dominate them, and it both
is and must be, over time, guided and regulated by them.

This is a critical point. Politics can and should have a comprehensive view of society and establish law and order in ways that serve
the spheres of life, so they can flourish without threats from internal or external violence. But, at the same time, the university can
critically examine all areas of social life and seek to tell the truth

by publishing studies about each of these areas, how they work and how well they work, and, with other educational institutions, supply each sphere of life with people trained to be experts in the various functions that must be performed to have them. Simultaneously, the economic sector must function in such a way that it can provide financial resources for the various spheres of life and generate enough wealth that society's members are not forced to be preoccupied with survival, and this must be done in a way that also supplies a sense of meaning in the work. If it does not do so, alternative economic efforts will be made, from black market criminality to revolutionary attempts to redistribute the fruits of production at the end of a bayonet, or the system will be declared to be morally bankrupt and an attempt will be made to reconstruct economics on some entirely transcendental basis — history has seen more efforts to build utopian communities than it cares to remember.

In a similar manner, the medical institutions of society must heal the sick, mend broken bodies, save people from disease and help people face the inevitable reality of death without needless suffering. If they do not or cannot, or do so only at exploitative costs, or do so only for those in positions of political power, other forms of medicine will be explored, based on other metaphysical assumptions and changing the fabric of society, or the pressure will mount in society to alter the political and legal arrangements. And so on one could go with the various spheres of life, each ethically constraining, guiding and utilizing the "principalities" and "authorities" in civil society for the common good, as argued in the last chapter. And, as we shall argue later in this volume, doing such things well is theological in the sense that it is a sacred duty especially of the professionals in these various spheres of life, and if the spheres are rightly organized and the professionals rightly motivated, they can be a means of grace and an opportunity for service to all in them. Moreover, if they do not function in these adaptive and meaning-filled ways, they will be experienced as empty of promise or even as demonic.

The debates that people have about these matters in their families, with their friends, with fellow workers, in their professional organizations, as they read the papers or watch the news, and especially in religious groups, involve struggles to discern what is fundamentally true, what is finally right, what is ultimately good and merciful in all these spheres. These debates, exchanges and arguments form the true public, and not merely private networks of interaction. It is one of the marks of tyranny that the political powers attempt to control these centers of ethos-formation, as we learned in previous centuries of imperial domination and in the last century in places where the Nazis or the Communists were in control. These debates bring people to common convictions about what to believe and what to distrust, what is worthy of loyalty and priority. These cumulatively, over time, bend politics in one direction or another; they grant or withdraw legitimacy to regimes. These networks of interaction should not be considered only private with public applying only to governmental policy making. Of course, political demagogues know that these things are both public and political, and they become masters at manipulating the symbols of trust, loyalty and priority for directly political gains; but a well-developed public will quickly discern the charade, and declare it illegitimate, no matter how much official political authority seeks to control the whole.

The Meanings of "Theology"

This leads us to what we mean by the word "theology" when it is coupled with this sense of "public." Some confusion exists on this matter for there are multiple kinds of theology. Perhaps the most familiar is "confessional theology." It is today often used to refer to intensely personal conviction, one given to us by nurture, tradition, socialization, or inspiration that we cannot fully grasp, and yet it grasps us in ways that we are in fact driven by it, approving the fact, even if we have not consciously made a decision for it. It also appears negatively when we hear something we cannot believe: "That's not my theology!" Another, more classical, level of confessional theology has to do with that which is formed by or for a specific community of believers — often, given the Constantinian tendency in religions around the world, at the behest of or under the supervision of government. Thus, each "congregation" or "denomination" has its treasury of doctrine that is manifest in its creeds, liturgies and hymns, and in its distinctive style of worship in a given territory. This is what is taught to the young citizen by catechism and practice, and is used to instruct converts. This theology articulates "what our community of faith holds as basic belief." In this area, there are notable differences between, e.g., Orthodox,

Catholic and Baptist theology, although they share much at other points with each other and with religious ethics generally.

Another understanding of theology, sometimes called "contextual," is based in the life experience of a particular subcommunity. It is an attempt to articulate the sociocultural sensibilities, including the memory of suffering and quest for hope that has been shaped by a distinctive collective history as interpreted in biblical terms. The last half century has seen a virtual explosion of Afro-American theology in the USA, Feminist and/or Womanist theology around the world, Dalit and Tribal theology in India, Minjung theology in Korea, Coconut theology in the Pacific Islands, etc. Indeed, contextual theology often views all theology as expressions of community experience, distinctively for an "us." It is in truth the "civil religion" of a particular class, caste, or cultural group, sometimes restated in biblical terms to challenge the ways creedal dogmas developed by someone else have been used to disrupt or dominate their society, or to demonstrate that a particular subculture has truths that ought also to be recognized as valid.

Still another kind of theology, with which contextual theologies are often in conflict, is dogmatics. It seeks to articulate the presuppositions and implications that are entailed in making coherent sense of the biblical revelation and/or of the classic creeds of the church based on it. Dogmatics thematizes what the faith, "rightly understood," has held or ought to hold. It seeks to clarify any apparent contradictions in the various formulations of the faith and to identify the orthodox understanding of sound teaching. It most often takes its departure from key elements of the narrative in the biblical record or in the development of doctrine in the history of the church, or some combination of the two. Of course, dogmatic theology is influenced by personal and communal confessional theology, and sometimes by the "expressive" motifs of contextual theology. But dogmatic theology seeks, at its best, to cast a wider and deeper net than any of these and to develop its contours in ways that bring the various confessions and expressions of faith into a coherent view of what the faith is fundamentally about, and thereby to shape or influence both personal confessions and various denominational and/or congregational understandings.

All of these are, of course, proposals to some smaller or larger group of the faithful and, as often as not, also get worked out in terms of practical theology, which is focused, as is widely acknowledged, on the development of theologically based practices of ministry in the church and for the people of the faith. It cultivates the arts of leadership, nurtures the kinds of spirituality, morality and habits of discipleship that evoke commitment, touches lives, builds personal character, forms the well-being of the faith community, engages in mission and both instructs the inquirer and sustains the believer by word and example, all within the traditions of accepted confessional, contextual, or dogmatic theology.

However much public theology may draw on these, and it inevitably does, its primary focus is on still another task of theology — apologetics. As I understand it, it combines aspects of the above and seeks to address specific contexts in ways that are faithful to the classical sources of faith and their ecumenical or catholic norms, and points toward the practical implications for life in society. It may differ in that it is willing to encounter secular, philosophical and non-Christian religious orientations to the world and to explain its claims in their language. It basically assumes what, for example, the translators of the Bible assume: the truths it contains can be stated in words and conceptual frameworks other than its own, although it also transforms the conceptual frameworks and the meanings of key terms by the translation process. And it is ethical in the sense that it takes them seriously as resources for discerning how it is that the truth, justice and mercy of the ultimate, formative and sustaining reality of the universe can be more fully recognized and actuated in the inevitably more inclusive and more variegated civil society. Thus it must show that it can form, inform, and sustain the moral and spiritual architecture of a civil society so that truth, justice and mercy are more nearly approximated in the souls of persons and in the institutions of the common life.

The idea that the faith should not only address believers at worship and not only in regard to their work in the world but also those not in the church and inform the shaping of the so-called "secular" spheres of civil society is often represented by certain themes in Catholic theology, both in its classical heritage that spoke of "natural law," and in its more recent development of the "social encyclical" tradition, when it addressed these not only to Catholics but to "all those of good will," as it gradually overcame much of its deep suspicion of democracy and human rights. The term "public theology" was little used, but the idea of a "Christian Social Philosophy," rooted in both faith and reason, was quite evident in such intellectual leaders as Jacques Maritain's work on human rights, John Courtney Murray's work on the compatibility of Catholicism and democracy, and John Ryan's work on economic issues. Such Catholic thinkers became spokesmen for the importance of theology's implications in public discourse. Murray, for example, quoted John of Salisbury when he asked "whether or not civilization, that is, civil order, civil unity, civil peace, is possible without what John calls in a beautiful phrase 'the sweet, fruitful marriage of Reason and the Word of God.'" [34]

This Catholic accent was cultivated further by a number of contemporary progressive Catholic thinkers such as theologian David Tracy, social ethicist Dennis McCann, and political philosopher Paul Sigmund, among others, each in different ways. They have drawn not only from the legacies of Maritain and Murray, but from a close encounter with Protestant theology and from the widening scope of Catholic social teachings from *Rerum Novarum* on labor by Pope Leo XIII, through *Quadragesimo Anno* on the ideas of subsidiarity and of solidarity by Pius XI, to *Pacem in Terris* by John XXIII, and perhaps most powerfully in the encyclicals of Pope John Paul II mentioned above. This tradition opened the door to major Vatican statements to the UN on racism, war, human rights, and pluralism, drawing ever from philosophical theology and shaping a message to wider civilizational issues. The contemporary theologian David Tracy (some of whose current views appear in the final chapter of volume 1 of this series) sought to find the basis of a truly catholic theology, and pointed out that although many today turn to experience to find a basis for common morality and meaning, experience turns out to be even more fragmented than doctrine, and provides no means to interpret itself. Yet we cannot lose the real sense of pluralism. Various modes of discourse are needed to discern its meanings. He identifies three: the church, the body politic and academia.[35]

---

34. Leon Hooper, *The Ethics of Discourse: The Social Ethics of John Courtney Murray* (Washington, DC: Georgetown University Press, 1986), 114.

35. D. Tracy, *Blessed Rage for Order* (New York: Crossroad, 1991) shows dependence on the work of the liberal Lutheran, Ernst Troeltsch, as well as on Catholic sources. His subsequent *Analogical Imagination: Christian Theology and the Culture of Pluralism* (New York: Crossroad, 1998) articulates these three "publics" that must be addressed by theology.

Not only Catholics, but a number of Protestants have followed this three-fold analysis and sought to extend this insight. Noting current global trends that in some senses supercede every national public, we have sought to redefine and identify a wider range of publics to which theology must speak. This wider range can be discovered, I think, by posing a series of questions. First, not only the church, but the "religious public," such as that of the Parliament of Religion, discussed in connection with the work of Hans Küng, as mentioned in the previous chapter, or as found in the encounter of faith with ideology,[36] can be identified by this question: What can and should be preached and taught among those who seek faithful living and thinking according to the most holy, and thus the most comprehensive, righteous and enduring reality to which humans can point? Obviously, no specific civil order is comprehensive; something more universalistic must be sought. Christians will, thus, want to speak of and argue for God as creator of all, as we will see in the next chapter. But these claims have to be tested now in new ranges of inter-religious encounters. We will have to be prepared, as Peter wrote long ago, "to give an account of the faith that is within us." (1 Pet. 3:15)

Second, also as Tracy already suggested, is the political public. The question here is: What is the best vision of freedom and order, and the most just organization of power, so that faith and thought, life and civil society can be protected from the forces of illegitimate violence from within and of disruption from without, in a multicultural world? Public theology, in other words, not only has to make sense in the faith community, it has to show that it can help shape viable institutions in all the spheres of complex global interaction, both those that are necessary to all societies, those that supercede national identities and political arrangements, and those that sustain the dignity and inner coherence of persons and the decisive networks of fellowship and exchange that connect them to others.

Third is the academic public, found by asking this question: What claims about truth can be called valid because they can best withstand critical analysis and offer convincing arguments or evidence for a normative reality that selectively supports what is valid in

---

36. See *A Dialogical Approach to the Value of Modernity*, where a collection of my essays on these topics, representing Western Christian views, is translated into Chinese and coordinated with essays by Bao Limin, general editor of the volume, representing Eastern and Maoist views (Shanghai, PRC: Scholars Press, 2000).

the present structure of life, as best we can discern, and points toward what can and should be altered in the face of informed critical
scrutiny? This implies that normative questions can be reasonably
discussed and judgments can be made with relative confidence.
Public theology in this regard is reluctant to draw upon those dogmatic claims that see no possibility of providing publicly defensible
warrants, and it is skeptical of those philosophical positions that
rule out discussion of theological questions before the conversation
starts. Thus, it finds philosophical theology and theistic philosophies
of religion to be allies, as is being attempted throughout the volume.

To these three publics we must add the economic public. This
area was historically presumed to be a matter of concern to the
household (or the extended family such as a clan, a tribe, or a
caste) in some ancient traditions, or of state control or of some
combination of the two when royalty protected the peasantry mili-
tarily and exploited them economically, or when rulers gave leading
families monopolies over this or that kind of trade in mercantilist
political economies, or when the state itself formed the factories
and ran the national industries in the days of socialist political
economies. But economic institutions and practices have, in substantial measure, begun to transcend the control of any familial or
royal household and of every nation state, and are now increasingly located in the modern corporation, which is the central locus
also of contemporary technological development. With the rise of
publicly held, high-tech, multi-national and trans-national corporations and of a largely corporate-regulated, global market system
of exchange, the economy has become an increasingly independent
public realm pulling millions into the middle classes, and leaving
some behind. Some scholars and no small percentages of public
opinion oppose this situation, speaking of the "economic colonial-
ization of the common lifeworld," and harboring deep suspicions
of corporations and markets, middle-class and bourgeois life-styles,
commodification and consumerism, profits and deregulation. Still,
the new public economy is sweeping the world.[37]

In regard to this area now, we must ask: What modes of production, finance, exchange and distribution, and what kind of an ethos,

---

37. See, for example, Hak Joon Lee's new study of the relation of Jürgen Habermas's social philosophy to Christian understandings of covenantal theory for a
public theology: *Covenant and Communication: A Christian Moral Conversation
with Jürgen Habermas* (Landham, MD: Scholars Press, 2005).

ordered by what theological, ethical, and legal principles, best engenders respect for human dignity, supports a variety of cultural life-styles, and allows humanity, worldwide, to participate in the creation of plenty without the destruction of the ecological order? The intense debates about the policies of the WTO, World Bank, and IMF are reflections of the fact that this issue is, as yet, unsettled. It is a matter that demands, I think, urgent theological and ethical attention, and there is evidence that these organizations are open to influence from Non-governmental Organizations (NGOs), including those based in theological ethics.[38]

Further, today, many issues of family life, technology, media, public health, and environmental issues are of great public concern, and many globalizing cultures and classical religious traditions are seeking guidelines for the new standards that must be developed.[39] But the standards advocated by some cultures and religions are in substantive conflict about how to morally and spiritually adapt to or reshape these developments. That is in part because the ways they are often advocated by the West and North, and received by the East and South, seem to be entirely mechanical and devoid of religious content and humanizing possibilities, although they are each substantially rooted in religious and doctrinal developments that drive them at a deep level. A public theological response could prove to be a substantive help in this new situation.

---

38. The World Bank Group, the IMF, and the World Council of Churches have been meeting to discuss how global poverty can be eradicated for some three years, according to the Ecumenical News Service. (April 2005). That signals a new prospect for the emerging trans-national civil society, centered in churches and advocacy groups working with new global regencies to form responsible patterns for development in a global civilization. It also challenges the church to develop a public theology focused on criteria of truth, justice, and mercy that can be understood in contemporary economic terms and functions in relation to corporations and international markets. The journal *Faith and International Affairs* raises a great number of the pertinent issues and may be more influential in the United States. It is usually written from a more Evangelical point of view.

39. Jonathan Chaplin, senior fellow at the Institute for Christian Studies, Toronto, in "On Globalization: An Exercise in Public Theology," *Comment* (Spring 2003), the best critical review of the first three volumes of this effort from a confessional point of view, called attention to Bob Goudzwaard's proposal concerning the normative "disclosure of society" as a criteria for understanding the adequacy of any serious perspective on the common life. (See his *Capitalism and Progress* [Grand Rapids: Baker Books, 2001]). This is very close to what public theology, as I understand it, intends as well, and that is why the continued accent on the spheres and the powers which they seek to order and transform is necessary.

However, there are objections to public theology in this mode. Some argue that theology has nothing essential to do with these several public spheres of life. They say that all theology is essentially based on a particular revealed source, and that the various scriptures do not address these issues, at least not in any clear fashion. Further, belief in these sources is entirely personal, not social, and thus it is a matter of individual expressions of faith, not of normative public argument as we have seen. Others say that it is, and should be, an articulation of a revelation given to special groups or of the faith of a particular believing community, especially the church, and that reliance on philosophy, historical developments, or social needs dilutes theology, or even displaces the norms of faith and revelation in favor of another set of worldly, artificially, and humanly constructed conventions. Furthermore, those in charge of public policy, not only in politics, but in the modern university, hospital, law court, corporation, labor union, etc., are simply not interested in these matters and don't see what they have to do with their areas of responsibility. In reply, advocates of public theology respond that while public theology does and must draw from such personal, confessional, dogmatic and practical emphases, theology in this mode has, above all, an apologetic emphasis. That is to say that if a theology is to be trusted to participate in public discourse it ought to be able to make a plausible case for what it advocates in terms that can be comprehended by those who are not believers. This case includes its ability to influence society in ways that generate greater inclusiveness, greater justice, and greater mercy. This is a test of its universality. It should be able to articulate its core convictions in comprehensible terms in many modes of discourse, explaining its symbolic and mythical terms, for instance, in ways that expose their multiple levels of meaning.

Moreover, advocates of public theology hold that not all claims about revelation and faith are of equal validity and can or should shape public discourse. It does not restrict this discourse by political means in the community of faith or in the society at large, but it engages patiently in extended (sometimes for life-times, even centuries) conversations and clarification of the promise or the perils of various comprehensive points of view. Public theologians hold that it is not only possible but necessary to assess them, according as to whether they accord with the most universalistic understandings of normative reality that we can find together, and whether they simultaneously give guidance to the formation of polities that are capable of including ongoing debate about the ultimate matters. In short, the doing of public theology involves engaging in discussing proposals that are debatable and subject to disconfirmation, not only to affirmation or denial, even if the debates go on for years.

Disagreement over this matter has, however, led to two wings of public theology. One is more deeply indebted to the fideist definitions of theology, and has allied itself to recent forms of postmodern thought, for both doubt that any universalistic arguments about such matters can be sustained, and it is deeply suspicious that others are advancing some artificial "spiritual Esperanto." This wing calls upon believers boldly to proclaim what can only be known through the eyes of a particular faith, for in public life everyone else is also presenting views that inevitably are also based on unverifiable and particularistic convictions. Believers in such theology thus can and must claim, and be granted, a place at the table of incommensurable discourses on the grounds of inevitable pluralism and the justice of fair access — although how one could defend "justice" and "fairness" for all at the table in this mode of argument is not clear, since these require the universalistic principles that fideist and postmodern arguments do not admit as possibilities.[40] Besides, if the discourses are incommensurable, why sit at the table?

A second wing argues that the purported break-up of meaning is overstated, and that the capacity of humans to learn each other's languages and to engage in meaningful debate about such matters as truth telling, honest argument, human rights, exemplary virtue, sound ecology, fair trade, good technology, quality medicine and just law suggests a deeper substratum of ethical commonality. In brief, this wing holds that theology is necessary in order to account for how and why humanity can debate such ultimate matters and give reasons as to why one account is more adequate than another, and how claims in this area need to be tested as to whether or not they offer an account equal to the alternative accounts of moral experience and normative assertions in part to test our own myopia and overcome our own parochialism. When these capabilities are exercised, we can properly say "Thank God!"

---

40. I understand this wing to be represented by Ronald Thiemann. See his *Constructing A Public Theology* (Philadelphia: Westminster, 1992). Cf., for another Lutheran view, Robert Benne, *The Paradoxical Vision: A Public Theology for the Twenty-First Century* (Minneapolis: Fortress, 1995).

Public theologians differ, thus, on questions of anthropology, epistemology and the relation of ontology to historicity. Thus, they also differ on the interpretation of "modernity." This Western development did not entirely deny that religion could be a powerful force in people's lives, but it doubted that theological matters could be reasonably defended and were necessary for civil society. Some saw the world religions and their elaborations into doctrines as the source of foolish conflict. They relegated both religion and theology to the private sphere of preferences, and denied them a public role, as we saw in recounting some of the contemporary debates about political philosophy. However, that is neither convincing as an argument nor confirmed by any demise of religion in social and political life.

Why a "Christian" Public Theology?

Implicit in the remarks about the various publics that are emerging and forming a global public is the prospect that a highly pluralistic global civil society could become the basis of a worldwide, complex civilization. The most notable fact about this development is that it is occurring without an integrated political order to guide it, although the United States seems to be operating as an unofficial hegemonic power, sometimes tempted to become imperialistic, to the great resentment of a number of other powers in the world, and the dismay of many Americans who do not want their nation to be imperialistic. If we are to avoid this danger to the United States and to the world, we need to see how it is that the various publics of an increasingly complex and worldwide civil society can be ordered into an inevitably pluralistic and dynamically, but viable, open and more just system than can any other system. Drawing upon certain basic biblical and theological themes, a public theology can provide the most adequate glimpse of that possibility.

We have already argued that one cannot understand the various cultures around the world without recognizing their religious worldviews as these are woven into their understanding of family membership, economic system, political order, and specialized roles of leadership. Our distinct question now is what Christians might have to offer to a world situation where a civil society is now being formed, without a clear political order, as I believe is the case. Does

Christianity have models of how to think about the ordering of complex civil societies that reach beyond any single nation state? I think
it does, and that it is implicit in two basic models (and weaker in
two others). One is the "hierarchical-subsidiary" model, developed
in recent centuries by the Catholics out of their modulation of a long
hierarchical tradition and given fresh articulation in the modern social encyclicals. And the other is the "federal-covenantal" model,
developed by Jewish and modified by Reformed traditions that draw
not only on covenantal theory, but that have also embraced aspects
of the "federalist" traditions of "principled pluralism" that led in
a long set of struggles to modern constitutional democracy with
guaranteed freedom of religion, press, science, economy and political participation.[41] It is sometimes named "that order which is
called freedom," and is held by many to be a social order that is
as close to how God wants us to live together as we have yet discerned. These models often appeared first in ecclesiology, then in
civil society, and, through the indirect influence of these, in politics — wherever a vital civil society developed, essentially at the
hands of the church. Both models imply that all areas of life are
under God, and pose the question as to how we should seek to
order their relationships while giving them the social space to make
their contributions to human well-being, under God.

Later in this volume, we shall return to these basic models; but
only after we establish what is the most distinctive contribution of
Christian theology to public life. This is the concept of a gracious
God who created the world and made humanity in the very image
of the Creator, who providentially gave humanity the spiritual resources to form and sustain a viable civil society in history, and who
promised to save humanity from our betrayals of that image and
those resources by pointing to possibilities beyond creation and history that we cannot ourselves accomplish. In short, we shall look
at the ongoing themes of protology, providence, and eschatology as

---

41. One of the best treatments of these options is found in James Skillen and
R. M. McCarthy, eds., *Political Order and the Plural Structure of Society* (Atlanta:
Scholars Press, 1991). This contrast was also drawn by James Hastings Nichols, *De-
mocracy and the Churches* (Philadelphia: Westminster Press, 1951); F. W. Dillistone,
The Structure of the Divine Society (London: Lutterworth Press; and Philadelphia:
Westminster Press, 1951); William J. Everett, in his *God's Federal Republic* (New
York: Paulist Press, 1988); and, as we will see in chapter 4, the Jewish political
philosopher who has a high appreciation of the Reformed tradition, Daniel Elazar,
The Covenant Tradition in Politics, 4 vols. (Piscataway, NJ: Transaction Publishers,
1995–98).

necessary foundations for a Christian public theology, and compare and contrast them to the offerings of other religions in terms of possible implications for our likely future. The next several chapters, thus, will offer a proposal in regard to the key Christian theological doctrines and ethical principles and purposes that invite and allow us to form the content of a pertinent public theology for our global era.

– Chapter 3 –

THE FIRST GRACE

CREATION

Toward Biblical Doctrines

After introducing this volume and identifying some of the key ongoing debates about the nature and character of globalization, especially as it is related to issues of faith, I reviewed, in the first chapter, the purpose, organization and basic motifs of the first three volumes in this set, pointing to the necessity of cultivating the various institutions in the several spheres of life able to harness, guide and constrain the "powers" that drive contemporary globalization. Further, I stressed the influence of religion on these various spheres and the woeful neglect of that influence by many contemporary analysts of the structure and dynamics of globalization, as if religion had played no part in the formation of the kind of civil society that has generated globalizing trends in some cultures or limited the cultural preparedness for it in other societies.

In my summary, I also noted that a number of ecumenical religious leaders simply adopt these secular points of view in interpreting globalization, yet expect that they can introduce a religious ethic based on a contemporary interpretation of the Bible or some theological doctrine that, they say, should alter the course of globalization or provide an alternative to it.

This is troubling, for it is not clear why, if religion has made no substantive difference in the past or in producing what is at hand in the present, it can significantly transform the future or effectively challenge the present. If it did shape the dynamics and structures of the past and present, and if religion is invoked to critique, resist and redirect those trends, what normative insights are so novel or discontinuous with the past so as to make people think a fundamental transformation is desirable, necessary or possible? Why should those who discern grace in globalization listen to them? In that context, I offered an analysis of representative perspectives of intellectual and moral leaders who do take religion seriously and have made a notable, if finally incomplete, contribution that helps us clarify the directions in which we must move.

Many of the secular voices who support globalization in the economistic sense are likely to pay no attention. A good number of them have adopted a neoliberal point of view increasingly supported by Darwinist theories of "rational choice," now sometimes called "evolutionary psychology," and see this as a new "natural law" theory. And many of those who oppose globalization as an economic phenomenon have taken liberationist theories that are derivatives of Marxism as their neo-orthodox view. Neither the "rational choice" liberals, nor the "class analysis" liberationists, I suggested, has grasped the deeper dimensions of the global transformations at hand, although there is some evidence for each of these views at certain limited levels of human experience. Individuals do make cost-benefit calculations and divisions between the rich and the poor do foster group sentiments of solidarity, preference and resentment in many aspects of social life.

I am also well aware of the fact that each of the social sciences makes the methodological assumption that it should try to explain as much of reality as is possible, and thus is tempted, by overreaching, to a reductionist view. Such views, however, are only valid when they acknowledge the influence of other factors and seek to discern what particular contributions to the whole are made by the specific set of factors they study. Human life and social history have many shaping influences, especially in the highly complex societies that have generated global developments. One purpose of the argument in this set of volumes is to draw attention to one factor that is decisive and largely neglected by economistic or other social scientific reductive analyses: religion. We focus on this for we think that there is strong evidence that it normatively integrates and provides the first principles and ultimate vision of purpose in life that orders the moral and spiritual meanings of that which other fields of study can supply.

In chapter 2, therefore, I proposed that we must think about global developments by coming at them from an overtly theological direction — for it is theology and theological ethics that most rigorously take account of religions as formative forces in social history and that test the adequacy of the moral principles and purposes by which they can and should shape the direction and organization of historical trends. If we want to grasp and guide what is going on in our world, which are key tasks of every theological ethics, we shall have to take these realities as seriously as we do the drive for survival, the calculation of costs and benefits, the dialectics of history and the various disciplinary quests for valid interpretation of social life. However, since so many Western intellectuals, including some religious leaders, view religious and theological matters as entirely private and personal, and basically unrelated to the dynamics of public life, I proposed that we examine the public influences of religion and, where appropriate, propose to reform or revise them by appeal to an overtly public theology.

In the previous chapter, therefore, I laid out a sketch of the history, forms and functions of what is now called "public theology," an understanding of theology that is historically informed not only by the classical traditions of Orthodoxy, Catholicism and the Reformation, but also embodied in the Puritan, Social Gospel, Christian Realist and Human Rights movements among mainline Protestants, in the modern Roman Catholic tradition of the Social Encyclicals and by the newer Evangelical engagements now expanding to a wider ecumenical vision. I suggested that all these have an affinity with those socio-political theories that give rise to a democratic ethos of civil society, which it in fact fomented when it developed the church as an institution distinct from the family or tribe and independent of state or empire. They thus have a bias toward a social interpretation of politics (rather than a political interpretation of society) and made the government a servant of the people and society, not a lord over subjects — a bias that clarifies how it is that theology can constructively induce creative changes in society. Wherever the core values of society are shaped around such ultimate commitments as these entailed, and become embedded in modulated human interests and the powers and spheres of the common life, the prospects of an open civil society is at hand. None of the spheres of life are today controlled by any single factor; but all of them seek moral and spiritual legitimacy, which can only come from an effective excellence in creatively using the powers which they were designed to guide. And the capacity to do that comes from a believed and believable metaphysical-moral vision or worldview, inevitably held religiously, that says: "doing that well contributes to the flourishing of the people and to the glory of all that is holy."

In the Introduction to this volume as well as in the two previous chapters, I made reference to the inevitable encounter with the great world religions and worldviews, and the civilizations they have shaped, now engaged with each other by mutual recognition, by the discovery of some areas of commonality, and by conflict over differences. In that context, I identified the chief purpose of this volume: asking the question of what a distinctively Christian public theology and ethics that seeks to engage and address the emerging global public has to offer to this new, massive and unavoidably transformative phenomenon. I suggested that it is a great deal. First of all, because much of what we now know as globalization has been shaped by the way key basic doctrines, many first advanced as minority reports, have become incarnated in the dominant ethos of modernizing civilization, an ethos now spreading over the world and being reshaped by its selective inclusion into other cultures, societies and religions. I did not, however, identify the central doctrines that bear on this situation, or seek to spell out how and why they have been and continue to be so important in a globalizing world. That is the task of this chapter and of the next two. Christian biblical themes and doctrines that claim to be of universal significance may well have direct implications for an ethic pertinent to the historic formation of a civil society of global reach. The treatment of all of these themes and doctrines is rooted in the conviction that it is possible to know something reliable about the God who is, and has been, above all, gracious, and that this grace has made, can make and should make a difference to faith, ethics, and social life and thus, indirectly, to all the complex spheres of life that are generating globalization.

"In the Beginning..."

Few doctrines are so disputed in theological history as to their implications for ethics and society as the doctrines of Creation and of Salvation. That is because they are so important. They are worldview constituting and are simultaneously held with ferocious devotion. Accounts of the probable beginning and likely end of the biophysical, sociospiritual world in which human life appears and historical developments take place frame the meaning of existence and influence every value in every ethos. In certain respects they define the whence and whither of life. Visions of protology and eschatology, the theories of first and last things, offer a view of how reality most likely was if we attempt to imagine it in its most primal condition, an account of why it is not like that now and a vision of what the most promising possibilities of the ultimate future could be. Mythic treatments of the beginning and the end offer a kind of punctuated narrative to establish a limited ontology and an ethically laden worldview. Narratives speak of historic change in time as characters interact with each other and their environments; but these narrative myths are told as if they constitute the basic preconditions that both allow and limit the possibilities of an effective ethic for and an ultimate consummation of existence. Most creation myths do this for a specific people and for a specific part of the earth.[1] (We shall return to the significance of distinctly Christian views of eschatology in chapter 5.)

The nineteenth and twentieth centuries, which saw massive historical change, also produced the idea of "world history" and saw the rise of historical scholarship in regard to religious texts, beliefs and practices, and, of course, various creation myths. These they subjected to the study of the particular social histories of the peoples who held to such religion. Thus, the early texts of the Hebrew scriptures were treated as redacted myths from diverse sources according to the historical and social situation of a people at later times. However, seldom in all the various editings and translations which these texts underwent was an effort made to relocate these texts as constituting the framework which made the later historical developments possible. Yet, Genesis, chapters 1, 2, and 3, and the related legendary narratives that condition that protological vision, might well have a certain preconditioning priority for understanding the historical development of all biblically rooted religions.

This is the reason: prior to the history of any or all of the "people of God," prior to the disclosure or casuistic application of any divine laws, prior to the composed songs of worship, praise or thanksgiving, prior to the inspiration of prophets and the anointing

---

1. See especially Robin W. Lovin and Frank Reynolds, *Cosmogony and Ethical Order* (Chicago: Chicago University Press, 1985); Barbara Sproul, *Primal Myths: Creation Myths Around the World* (San Francisco: Harper, 1979); and David Adams Leeming et al., *A Dictionary of Creation Myths* (New York: Oxford University Press, 1996).

of priests and kings and prior to the ordered formation of wisdom by sages are the primal myths of creation that point toward the basis upon which all the other dimensions of sacred theology become possible. The particularities of religion, culture, society and history depend upon an ontological order of being and of existential preconditions. That is what the creation myths articulate. Our interest for the present, therefore, is with the biblical view of creation, in part because it is written to apply to the entire bio-physical order and to universal humanity, and in part because it can easily be read as a contribution to public theology that has had profound implications for developing ideas that have shaped and do shape still the dynamics of globalization. When the earth is conceived as part of a cosmic whole, a graciously given form and substance by a creative spiritual and ethical reality, the classic insight that essence is prior to existence is manifest in time.

We can begin to see that the key themes having to do with creation are not essentially about the century-long and peculiarly modern debates that presume an inevitable antipathy between science and theology, where one side accepts the implications of evolution for cosmology, biology, anthropology, and epistemology and the other denies it. That is a debate between biblicistic literalists and scientistic reductionists which often hides as much as it reveals as pious and secular fundamentalists shout at each other, one in the clouds, the other in a swamp. The debates, however, do reveal two key questions. One is this: is it so that all that exists is the result of causes and processes devoid of any moral and spiritual meaning, or is there some kind of moral and spiritual meaning in or behind existence? The other question is this: what are the ways of knowing about reality? The deeper themes, thus, have to do with serious debates about the relevance of theological perspectives which presume that there is a creator God and thus a governing moral law and purpose in life, and the relationship of that God to the character of the bio-physical world and the humans that inhabit it, and thus to the social and cultural history played out on this stage.

Clearly, one of the pretheological but traditional religious ways of thinking about Creation has to do with a period in calculable time when all that we call "nature" was brought into being by a Divine Will in a harmonious and completed garden of innocence. This view is deeply discredited by science and not warranted by a careful reading of the biblical text. It is obvious to many that Charles Darwin's work has become a symbol of the multiple challenges that have been put to that kind of "creationism." Any honest observer will today acknowledge that the emergence of the earth and of humanity as a species was a slow and often violent process of mutation, adaptation and competition for resources that was often disrupted and had many dead ends. But acceptance of these facts does not demand the denial of every idea of a creator God, of a moral law or of a purpose in or for human life. That denial oversteps the limits of what science can prove. That is the insight that motivates many advocates of "intelligent design," although this is not the place to discuss the merits or difficulties of their arguments.

Indeed, without entering these contentious lists here, one can say it is quite reasonable to suggest that the simplest way to think about these issues is to presume the compatibility of some views of science and some views of theology, and to suggest that evolution is how God brought human creatures capable of a consciousness of their Creator out of the elemental dusts of the earth into a developing world already populated by flora and fauna. This allowed the drama of history with its sociocultural developments to begin on a marvelous and dynamic stage to which history and its drama is related. This view presumes, because it is the most elegant theory, since it cannot be refuted and because it leaves open further discoveries in this area, that God is, and is responsible in a profound way for the existence and development of the cosmos, the earth and all the creatures — even if many are not conscious of a creator. Indeed this view heightens human attentiveness to the probability that life has moral and spiritual meanings and dimensions not invented by humans. These are what are pointed to by the inspired imaginations that composed mytho-poetic stories that invite us to think beyond the mechanisms and processes of accident, mutation, adaptation and the survival of the fittest. In fact, that is reportedly how most advocates of evolutionist reductionism actually live — often having a very thin account of why they do so.[2]

---

2. The technical arguments about such matters are complex, detailed, intense and beyond the scope of my argument.

I have been deeply informed on these matters by one colleague at the Center of Theological Inquiry, John Polkinghorne, author of *Belief in God in an Age of Science*, rev. ed. (New Haven: Yale University Press, 2003), and a colleague at Princeton Theological Seminary, Wentzel Van Huyssteen, author of *Alone in the World?: Human Uniqueness in Science and Theology* (Grand Rapids: Eerdmans, 2006). One deals

We shall return to questions of evolution later in another connection, but for now we must put these considerations to one side as we consider the fundamental practical and social ethical issues pertinent to globalization in the idea of creation. A wide range of theoretical issues are implied in the protological claim that "In the beginning, God created the heavens and the earth, and all that in them is." It is a stupendous claim, one largely shared by Jews, Muslims, some theistic Hindus and a number of Primal religions which have a high, creator God, although we must immediately note that each of these traditions understands the reasons for and the act of divine creation somewhat differently. It is a claim basically denied by the Confucian tradition although there are traces of the idea in some parts of the tradition. The claim is denied also by non-theistic ("rationalist") Hindus and most overtly by Buddhists as well as by scientistic reductionists. Moreover, in speaking of these traditions, we must recognize that there are multiple strands of thought and understanding in each of these traditions, so that none of the great religions is entirely consistent within itself or perfectly congruent with any other religion on the understanding of creation or cosmogony. Still, each of the great religions has a general, predominant or characteristic stance toward the realms of divine, human, and natural realities portrayed in their basic myths, and it is fair to speak of these typical perspectives, and to compare and contrast them with other typical views, recognizing the varieties within each fold.

In this regard, the idea of creation entails a widely shared claim about the material existence of the bio-physical universe, the variety of its elements, dynamics and forms of life, and the distinctive place humanity occupies in regard to them. It represents in one way or another a hypothetical recognition that there is a divine desire to extend some glimmer of the glory and the moral and spiritual capabilities of the Creator both into the time-space/material continuum in which life, and particularly humankind, can exist, and into the identity of the human creature. Although the various religions articulate this dynamic of creative order and purpose in divergent ways, all these traditions believe that creation bears the imprint of divinity or a holy dimension that must be regarded, and that humans are, in

---

with physics, cosmology and theology, the other with contemporary evolutionary science and theological anthropology.

one sense or another, made in the divine image. This is so, even if most of them also recognize that something somehow has become disordered, distorted and dislocated, so that the meaning, spiritual integrity and ethics which are real and present are also threatened by death, illusion, deception, suffering, injustice or lovelessness.

The key motif in the Christian account is that the most powerful truth of the universe is this: a personal spiritual reality with a moral character, whom we call God, was before the world was, and that this reality will be when all the created realities no longer exist. This is a temporal way of saying that a supra-natural, supra-material reality comprehends, brings into being and sustains the enormously complex bio-physical world in which we live. This account both introduces novelty into what was not before and allows the created complexity itself to generate new constellations of existing entities both large and small by the interaction, rearrangement and construction of new parts or wholes. Indeed, the very idea of creation signals the claim that the world is real, and not an illusion, although it has a dependent, noneternal status. It exists for spiritual and moral reasons, even if many of its dynamics and patterns do not appear to have a clear moral *telos,* yet at its deepest levels it works according to divinely ordained laws, as well as according to a multiplicity of adaptive patterns specific to each part of its existence. That is, not only are there very general laws such as physicists, cosmologists, biologists and theologians like to ponder, there are also specific sets of regularities that govern distinct areas: those that pertain to virus mutations are distinct from those governing the migration patterns of the gnu on the veldt as well as those governing the movement of the tectonic plates. Each of these, and thousands, probably millions, more of these dissimilar patterns, may be studied and interpreted separately, and they may, in the long run, influence one another in various degrees; but they can also be comprehended by general principles and purposes that no particular study can fully reveal. Thus, the interaction of multiple kinds of ordered existential realities renders a complexity that does not implode but that involves a degree of contingency that creates new possibilities that sometimes work. That which is created has a kind of derivative creative freedom.

In response to a set of perennial questions that have been asked in many cultures, this view can say "yes" to the question of whether there is any divine intent behind the being of the universe, and thus, in some sense, a moral and spiritual meaning pertinent to the fabric of existence, including the human consciousness of it. Those who believe that God created the world can say "yes" to the question of whether there is any stable pattern, form or right order of things that we can know and in terms of which human existence ought to be conformed even amidst the contingencies of change. Humans who read the world through the eyes of creation can say "yes" to the question of whether there is any creational evidence that points to a moral law. At the same time, on the matter of whether novelty can be introduced into the bio-physical realm, so that creation has a history and the possibility of development beyond the initial pattern, the answer is also "yes." Further, on the matter of whether there is a *"sensus divinitatis"* built into human consciousness, so that we can recognize in the way things are some hint of a moral and spiritual meaning in both stable patterns and dynamic novelties, those who grasp the idea of creation can say "yes" as well. In short, is there a basis for arguing that there is in every human the possibility of coming to a theological "yes" to questions of whether there is an onto-theo-logical kind of order in the universe? It is on these grounds that we can find a justifiable basis for conversion from a chaotic world of multiple, unpredictable spiritual forces, to which premodernity was disposed, to a world of new rational coherence. It is also the basis on which to overcome the tendency to treat every question with a method of doubt, to which modernity is disposed, and to instead embrace a method that is governed by an ultimate trust. And it is the ground on which the suspicion of anything showing signs of stability to which postmodernity is inclined can be modulated by a hermeneutic of gratitude, at the most universalistic level, that there can be dynamic patterns that invite innovation yet manifest reliable continuities and facilitate warrants for confidence.

Creation Is Not Nature

If this is so, then there is a plausible if not provable ground for believing in a Creator God, and a reason for not believing that creation is the same as nature. In this view, it is wrong to hold the view that nature is the ultimate point of reference when it comes to meaning and morality. In fact, the creational view flies in the face of those who argue that to speak of "nature" is to speak of how things "really" are and, indeed, of how things ought to be. If that were so, then nature ought not be disturbed or disrupted; rather, it ought to be honored as "holy" or irrevocable as many classical pagan philosophers of antiquity, many contemporary conservationists and preservationists, and many advocates of traditional societies and religions functionally argue.

The theological idea of creation, indeed, implies that a series of questions needs to be put to naturalistic, and to nontheological humanist, perspectives. Is it not an implication of naturalist and humanist views that civilization itself is a threatening horror, since every civilization is built on a complex series of interventions into the bio-physical world, plus another complex set of social institutions intentionally designed to shape human identity and morality? Both the interventions in the bio-physical universe and in the inclinations of human nature draw on trans-natural and trans-human reference points that seek to make what is into what ought to be. These are not borne out by merely mechanical or organic analyses of what is, but are derived from metaphysical-moral visions, religiously held, that legitimate interventions or constructions. Such interventions presume, in short, three possible centers of reference: a geo-centric one, an anthropo-centric one, and a theo-centric one, with a preference given to some kind of a nature-and-humanity transcending one — dare we say, the theo-centric one.

If the members of a religion, culture or society take nature as the normative point of reference, they have chosen a geo-centric or a cosmocentric perspective, and they tend to contrast that with the arrogance of anthropo-centric views, and certainly with theo-centric ones which, they say in one vocabulary or the other, tend to exploit or dominate "Mother Nature." Today, of course, in our globalizing world, contemporary human technology is changing the face of the earth, and doing so at an astounding rate. It is rearranging nature by building complex cities and seeking ways to manage the new massive metropolitan areas, and by causing and ironically seeking to reverse global warming by technological means, while generating more and more value-added commodities for people to own and enjoy. This prevents millions from sliding back into the poverty of their natural state, even if it tends to threaten the ecosphere and perhaps the genotype. From a consistent "geo-centric" position, all this is basically an evil threat. The moral is that it would be better to return to the simple, "natural" ways of life, whatever that is.

Such a view, however, poses issues, issues that make such a return highly unlikely and morally suspect. For one thing, we must ask what it would take to persuade people to return to the simple life, to abandon the modernizing, urbanizing and globalizing powers and stop forming or participating in the spheres of life that channel life in that direction. For those who do not want to return, or do resist efforts to dismantle modernity, what kinds of police power would be required to force them to do so? The most dramatic efforts of the last century to persuade a people to do that did not work and thus they had to use more and more coercive means, which led to forced abortion and sterilization in China and India, and, in its most radical form, to the killing fields of Cambodia. Other possibilities come to mind: the *kibbitzim* of early modern Israel, now mostly incorporated into commercial cooperatives; the communes of the 1960s and 1970s, now mostly abandoned; and sectarian or monastic groups and some tribes scattered around the world seek to establish homogenous communitarian models based on preurban, preindustrial modes of life and religiously communal senses of identity. These, however, often become curiosities, a kind of sociological zoo, for tourists or anthropologists or romantics on temporary retreat. They may play a role in the whole scheme of things, but they are unlikely to provide models for grasping or guiding global civil society, even if they support themselves by producing otherwise obsolete craft products or organic foods or herbal remedies for niche markets in cosmopolitan centers.

Still, such groups pose useful questions to our globalizing era: "Do we have to live as we do now? Were not previous times better?" But such questions invite counter-questions. When is the ideal time to which we should return so that we can freeze that stage of development? When was life truly "natural?" Was it in premodern, prefeudal, or preagricultural societies? In fact, those who have the benefits of modern societies seldom want to give up their clean water supplies, their medical care, their longer life span, their options for travel, education and communication; and most who do not have these are trying to find ways to get them, not avoid them. Usually, those who are living in primal societies often accommodate their social behavior to dominant cultures — that is, to successfully incarnated concepts of what is what more humanly adaptive, nature-transcending and nature-transforming practices. In short, every geo-centric view has to come to grips with the realities of the anthropo-centric and theo-centric views.

Even an anthropo-centric view is not sufficient. For if we claim that humans have rights to such things as clean water, medical care, education, multicultural exposure, etc., and if the most morally concerned people in the world are striving to see that all have access to them, since they do not at present, there must be an implicit appeal to a normative view that transcends the present state of existence, one that cannot be derived from the study of nature as it is, or from the study of human existence as it is. And that normative view is most securely derived, Christians and many others hold, from nowhere else than a theo-centric view!

At other levels too, the questions of what is "natural" and what is "human" are being sharply posed. Is it natural that some percentage of the population is disposed to find intimate loving relationships best in the context of same-sex partnerships, a pattern that ought not only be tolerated but honored as having co-equal standing with most who, naturally, are inclined to dual-sex partnerships? In these examples, of course, "natural" means normally statistically probable. If this definition is used, the permissive attitude of contemporary western societies can be seen as in accord with "natural law" and "common grace" and as a progressive breakthrough. But if this is so, why should other patterns not also be accepted, since many find it perfectly "natural" in the definition also to have many casual partners or to endorse polyandry or polygyny. Since at least some are "naturally" attracted to preadolescents, why should there be laws against "child marriage," which has been viewed as quite natural in many cultures? Those who oppose these patterns usually have, functionally, another sense of "nature" — one that suggests that people are created in a mold that implies adult, heterosexual relations as the ontological and ethical norm, even if there are existential and statistical deviations from this norm. More broadly, this question about family life poses the issue as to whether there is any kind of a normative order not only for marital institutions, but also for economic, political, legal, medical, educational and cultural spheres of life that allows variations within the normative boundaries according to the abilities and social conditions of the partners in these relationships.[3]

---

3. It can be argued, of course, that there is no "essentialist" definition of marriage, or of the economic, political, legal, etc., orders or spheres of life, and that they are all are basically shaped by the cultural context, as does Marvin M. Ellison in *Same-Sex Marriage, a Christian Ethical Analysis* (Cleveland: Pilgrim Press, 2004).

We are on the brink of questioning how human nature is constituted. Should we encourage the taking of evolution into our own hands — since that is what new techniques of genetic engineering are increasingly able to approximate? If Darwinian theory is correct that natural selection has shaped the whole biosphere and thus of human history, then why not anticipate the process, decide what we think is the most humane definition of "the human," and engineer the future of humanity? After all, it may well be possible to "cure" a number of naturally occurring "birth defects" and debilitating illnesses and even improve the gene pool. And, since natural selection depends on the interaction of adaptive mutations and environmental conditions, modern bio-genetic engineering can be coupled with geo-engineering, as in urban planning, and social engineering (as in institutional management and governmental policy) to establish a new balance in the world. This would, of course, make Darwinian theory obsolete. It would be no more than a commentary on how the biological world developed prior to the practice of courtship and elder-approved match-making enhanced the human tendency to intervene in breeding processes. This seems to have been the case especially since the development of a human consciousness of God, which legitimated the formation of families and limited the kinds of approved sexual relationships. This desire to plan for certain kinds of offspring has of course been fostered by the development of modern medicine with its studied interventions into life and death processes, and with genetic coding and artificial insemination the prospect of programed reproduction of "designer children."

Such questions are seldom asked in most discussions about today's globalization, but they are emblematic of the kinds of challenges to naturalism and humanism that a creational view poses. Such challenges demand a more adequate examination of protological assumptions than most now seem to have. Similar questions

---

But that begs the key ethical and theological questions: what does and what should shape the culture beside the felt drives, the economic interests, the desire for political power, the attempts to manipulate the law, the ideological reading of medical evidence, etc.? For alternative views see Don S. Browning, *Marriage and Modernization: How Globalization Threatens Marriage* (Grand Rapids: Eerdmans, 2003); John Witte Jr., *From Sacrament to Contract: Marriage, Religion and Law in the Western Tradition* (Louisville: Westminster Press, 1997); my *Covenant and Commitments: Faith, Family and Economic Life* (Louisville: Westminster Press, 1997); and Arlene A. Swidler, *Marriage Among the Religions of the World* (Lewiston, NY: Edwin Mellon Press, 1990).

have been posed over history by other issues. Darwin himself puzzled about the breeding of cattle and the domestication of dogs as human interventions into the natural processes, and many features of science and technology were inhibited by both those natural law theorists and theologians who did not make a clear distinction between God's creation and the nature of nature.[4]

In view of our question, i.e., What can the Christian creational theological heritage offer to the understanding of globalization?, we can suggest that humans are so created as to be able to know something about God and God's justice — that is, God's law, God's purpose, and God's mercy — and that we can and should use that knowledge in the building of a global civil society. If that is so, we shall recognize that it could entail the reorganization of much of what is natural. Here we face the issue of the extent to which we can or should seek to intervene in what appear to be "pre-given" patterns and dynamics of existence, and take responsibility for managing life by geo-engineering, bio-engineering, or social and cultural engineering, each with global consequences. Taking up such issues in the context of a theology that sees creation as the first gift of God to all creatures, we should note, focuses our attention less on how long it took to get from the first creative moment, now called the "Big Bang," to the rise of humanity in the long history of evolution, than on accounts of the fact that all that is — existence, humanity, and eventually the course of human history — is rooted in a divine intent and has thus a certain conferred order, with malleable dimensions, and thus with both open opportunities and purpose to them.

The "Cultural Mandate"

In the first three volumes of this set, as I have mentioned, we have been introduced to some of the complexities of these debates as

---

4. The views set forth here are not only influenced by the essays written by Ronald Cole-Turner and Jürgen Moltmann in vol. 2 of this series, which I commented on in that book's Introduction; but by the debates between Thomas Derr, James Nash and Richard John Neuhaus in *Environmental Ethics and Christian Humanism* (Nashville: Abingdon Press, 1996), for which I was the editor. A discerning converging argument, which begins in different presuppositions, is found in W. David Hall, "Does Creation Equal Nature? Confronting the Christian Confusion about Ecology and Cosmology," *Journal of the American Academy of Religion* 72, no. 3 (September 2005): 781–812, which involves a sustained critique of both creation science and ecotheology.

they appear when looking at the particular powers and spheres that are present in the common life everywhere (vol. 1), those that are authoritative in complex societies (vol. 2) and those that dominate enduring civilizational systems over long periods of time (vol. 3). Here we need to ask, as it were, the previous questions, those which overarch the particular treatments of aspects of civilized life as they shape and are shaped by a globalizing era. Thus, we inquire into what capacities or abilities humans must have if a comprehending civil society (or possibly a global civilization) is to develop, and if we are to address its problems in a compelling way. It is to answer such questions that we also turn to protology, in order to gain clarity with regard to what cannot be altered without destruction and what may be managed or reconstructed where it is malleable and advisable, even morally mandatory, to do so. This means, of course, taking a God's-eye view of our prospects and asking whether there is anything like a knowable social, spiritual and ethical "right" and "good" way of approaching the issues and whether, if there is, it is related to anything we can discern in creation and history. In consonance with the intentions of this volume, we shall have to ask these questions by attending to key protological concepts in specifically Christian theology.

Certain concepts, Christian theology tells us, offer a promising point of departure for our next steps. I refer, of course, to ideas of "common grace" (and its close cousins, "general revelation" and "God-given natural law"), and to such motifs as the "cultural mandate" to "til the earth and subdue it," to be "stewards of the earth," and to "have dominion." We know that mores change and that doctrine develops. Can Christians who speak much about justification and redemption in Jesus Christ, and are, in principle, given an ethic of love and sanctification, at the same time speak compellingly of generic human abilities that offer a coherent account of how Christian and non-Christian human beings could responsibly participate in the potentially emerging world civil society? After all, globalization point toward a world where the parts are bound together in a dense network of interdependence in which Christians and non-Christians have to be able to co-operate on many fronts. The question then becomes whether Christian theology has a view of the human condition that offers a compelling and sustainable perspective on this set of generic abilities.

I pose these issues because they are decisive for all societies today, not only because many signs and portents point to a common future, but because even now every society is increasingly multi-ethnic and multi-cultural and multi-religious and thus is forced by internal circumstances as well as external pressures (and perhaps by divine will) to try to honor these differences. Simultaneously, they affirm those basic principles and over-arching purposes that could allow us to live with lower levels of hate, mayhem, distrust and terrorism — even if some advocates of ethnic and cultural values do not fully approve of universalistic principles or purposes. Since globalization is forcing cultures, peoples and religions to encounter each other, and we have come to acknowledge this variety more fully in the last few generations, we now have to clarify what it is, if anything, that is divinely given that makes the sense of normative inclusiveness valid. Can we identify anything as constants in all for all, and what common ground with "others" can, and ought, to be actualized — and what ought to be resisted to prevent homogenization or the normless acceptance of all possibilities?

It is not at all odd to again raise the question of the relation of "creation" to "nature" in this regard, especially when dealing with Christian understandings. For we now generally recognize that the narrative myths of the biblical account are apologetic in the sense that they were intended not only to make a statement about what humanity has to deal with externally and internally, but to challenge those faiths of the ancient world that were merely naturalistic or humanistic. Many in and beyond ancient Israel worshiped the earth itself — the rivers or seas, the sun, moon or stars, the spirits of the plants and animals or the dynamics of fertility. All these are given a place of honor in many religious worldviews. However, a creational theology doubts that any of these are divine, eternal, immortal, or capable of rendering moral guidance. They may be good, but they are incomplete. They have to be tended, attended to or cultivated by humans, under God's watchful eye, to make a contribution to culture and society. Human agency to cultivate nature, to have dominion over all of these examples of it, is demanded.

Moreover, and more controversial to some parts of the anti-theological scientific mind, to cultivate nature's potentialities suggests both that a culture is necessary to complete nature and that nature is, at least in part, malleable to moral principles and purposes that cannot be inferred by the scientific observation or analysis of the world in itself. However, modern science is deeply interlocked with technology, revealing an insight that was recognized by the ancient sages who wrote and edited Genesis. This can be seen in the texts that point to a "cultural mandate" given to all humankind.[5] That is, one species of creatures is commanded to "have dominion," to name the flora and fauna, and to cultivate the earth. Humans are to manage, protect and make the raw potential of nature productive as soon as humanity comes to have obligations beyond instincts. It is implied that humans are at some point given a consciousness that allows them to understand ethical communication — a consciousness that grasps the power of the word as the gift of a reciprocal interaction and as the capacity to conceive of a normative command given and received. This implies the subjection of the bio-physical universe to social laws and purposes that are not built into the bio-physical universe itself, although the potentialities that allow it to be so subjected are present. Indeed, this technological intervention along with the command to propagate the human species and "fill the earth" makes humanity both a sovereign agent over the earth and a subordinate agent of God in regard to the ends to be fulfilled. The distinctive difference between divine and human agency is that God creates *ex nihilo,* while humanity's creativity is dependent on what is already given to humanity or what develops in humanity's cultural and social contingency. The decisive myths of protology imply that it is a duty of all people to see the act of creation as an outpouring of grace, a gift of being to existence itself and thus to humanity, accompanied by a commanding invitation to humans to become servants of the Creator's purposes in cultivating and, thus, altering the world as given.

I have elsewhere argued that one can see the implications of this in the differences between the purposes of science and technology. Every culture has an interpretation of how things are, a version of "science," and every culture has its own "techniques" for working with natural resources. Only some cultures invite science and technology to join and establish the institutional matrices to facilitate

---

5. The term is Abraham Kuyper's, the Reformed theologian who became Prime Minister of the Netherlands a century ago. Portions of this chapter were delivered as a lecture in 2004 at Stellenbosch University, South Africa, where his influence was great if distorted. See Mary Stewart van Leeuwen's essay in vol. 1, where the term also is introduced.

that.[6] The purpose of science is to understand things as they are, and technology is used by science to crack open hidden information as to how things are, although we now know that the use of technology alters that which is observed. The purpose of technology is to make things other than they are, to turn things as they are into things that are deemed by humans to be as they can and ought to be in order to better serve human wants and needs — that is, to subject things to moral purposes by altering structure or function and thereby adding value. Technology uses science to measure the gains or loses in this effort, even if not all the purposes are equally moral.[7] This distinction and the reciprocal relation between the two implies that some aspects of the created order are constant, governed by the laws that are everywhere and always operational; and some aspects are malleable, patterns that are subject to modification and (sometimes radical) rearrangement.[8] The bio-physical universe, as a gift of the Creator, seems to have two levels: the ontological level, the underlying and sustaining regularities that allow things to be at all, and that never change as long as things exist, and the phenomenal level that can be modulated by human effort — as we can see in agriculture, herding and cattle breeding, city construction and urban planning, and technological production and commercial distribution, as long histories reveal. The former implies a mandate to protect and things fall apart if we do not; the latter is a manifestation of what we can do with that part of nature that is malleable. It is this that we have a mandate to make more efficient, more supportive of human flourishing; and the ability to do these things is to be seen also as part of the first gift of grace.

The long debates as to whether Christianity is responsible, as Lynn White Jr. argued many years ago, for the disruption of the "natural" ecological order because of its understanding of the cultural mandate has, I think, been proven to be true by a host of

---

6. See, for example, Toby Huff, *The Rise of Early Modern Science: Islam, China and the West* (New York: Cambridge University Press, 1995); and Alan Wallace, ed., *Buddhism and Science Breaking New Ground* (New York: Columbia University Press, 2003).

7. See my earlier *Public Theology and Political Economy: Christian Stewardship in Modern Society* (Grand Rapids: Eerdmans, 1987).

8. These definitions are implied on almost every page of John M. Staudenmaier's *Technology's Storytellers: Reweaving the Human Fabric* (Cambridge, MA: MIT Press, 1985). It surveys and summarizes the key finding of the journal *Technology and Culture* over its first twenty-five years.

ecologically concerned theologians.[9] But many took White's argument precisely in the wrong direction. They allowed their views of creation to collapse in face of the criticism, and so turned to a functional naturalism that does not maintain the creational perspective. They argued that when the process of creation was completed, according to the scriptures, God declared it "good," then proceeded to claim that since creation is good, we can take our moral clues from that natural goodness. Thus, many offer a critique of technology as evidence of a human arrogance. Few have pointed out the great benefits that have come from technology and thus from the creational command to have dominion over the bio-physical world. Seldom is it argued that, in fact, humanity has rightly engaged in the technological transformation of the world, and that we must today take wider responsibility for managing the earth in a technologically activist way. The destruction of the environment comes not from a stewardly commitment to manage the earth for human well-being, but from human domination of nature that ignores the fact that humans are to take responsibility for the bio-physical world under God's law and for God's purposes.

Such a view has enormous implications for globalization, for it implies that humans, according to their created nature as distinctive creatures and agents of God, are commissioned by God to form cultures and societies, and for this purpose have a divinely given ability to develop and use technology to change the world. This view is clearly at odds with any ontocratic view, with the views that honor nature as the source and norm of all that is good and with those scientistic views of the "laws of nature" that can see no other authority or mandate beyond the way things work. This is a view that, if consistently followed, would make modern technology with its instrumental reasoning a demonic force, except in some restorationist uses — a counter-force to be used when some other "artificial" force has disrupted the pre-given "good" order of things as discovered by science. That is, technology could only be used to return nature to the primal harmony that it presumably had before it was disrupted by human intervention. But even then, it is not clear how or why it became disrupted if everything is proceeding

---

9. J. Lynn White, "The Historical Roots of Our Ecological Crisis," *Science* 155 (1967): 1203–7.

according to laws of nature and they are taken as normative guides to human behavior!

The Image and Human Capabilities

What enables humans to engage in this intentional and divinely sanctioned intervention in the way things are, while protecting the ontological order of existence? The most accurate understanding of the biblical texts and the majority theological perspective is that this particular creature has a conferred dignity not present in other creatures, although to the eyes of material, natural and even genetic analysis, the differences are few and negligible. The dignity is accounted for by the mytho-poetic notion that humans are made "in the image and likeness of God" — the *imago dei*. That is, each member of this species has a dignity that is more like the core of the divine than that of any other creature. In much of theological history, this *imago* has been identified with the idea of a "soul" or a "spirit" that makes humanity unique among the creatures, although some ideas of "soul" entail the belief that each human has an eternal "piece" of God in his or her physical body, one which returns to God or to heaven or to the realm of the departed elders, when it is separated from the body in death. Some, indeed, hold that it may be reincarnated in subsequent bodies — as many Hindus and Buddhists believe. These are not the Jewish, Christian or Islamic views, or an implication of the biblical protology. The "soul" is not a ghostly substance that can flit bodilessly from state of being to state of being. It is the core animating reality of a person that does not exist before or after life except as known, willed and cared for by God. The *imago* is not a bit of God. It is similar to and like God, and it makes a living relationship to God possible without a human pretense of being divine or being identified with some cosmic spirituality.

This "soul dignity" is thus not innate, but conferred. It is a distinct spiritual gift graciously given to each person. This is the basis on which the theological tradition developed the idea of universal human rights that apply to each individual, and of the equal spiritual importance of each human person under God. Such ideas did not originate in primal societies where only the members of one's tribe were considered true humans or part of the decisive community of identity, nor did it arise in philosophies or religions where all is seen in terms of graded strata of hierarchical beings, with only those at the higher levels being worthy of greater respect — although the Hindu *atman* has been interpreted in this direction after contact with Christian and Islamic views. It is, instead, seen as a gift of God to each member of one species of creatures for their particular role in creation. The soul allows human persons to be in a spiritually aware relation to God and an agent on earth of God.

Moreover, the "soul" has a certain functional content. It is by God's reason, will, and affection that humans are endowed with precisely this set of abilities that allow us to manifest this spiritual dignity and a moral equality. These manifestations appear not only in the fact that God seeks to communicate with every human, but also it equips all with the abilities to respond to that communicative relationship and to participate in the creation of associations, societies and cultures, in order to made decisions in accord with a shared vision of the common good, and to form affectional relationships — although different human beings are inclined to do these things in various ways and proportions. Humans can, in other words, not only think about the possibilities of a communicating ultimate reality, but can take into account the interests, the reactions, the concerns of others and the consequences of actions and attitudes on others. In short, they can transcend themselves, the most important manifestation of which is to worship God, to bless and offer thanks to the Creator — reasonably, voluntarily and affectionately. Humans thereby recognize that they/we did not arrive at their/our identity, or at an awareness of their/our existence and the responsibilities of existence in history, or at a mandate to create culture and society beyond that which is instinctive for survival, alone. They/we can ask: What on earth does it mean to have a source, an identity, an object of veneration and an awareness of gifted capacities that are other than the way the rest of the created world is? The posing of the question itself renders insight into the understanding of the human creature, and, indeed, into the nature of the Creator.

At various points in the history of the development of theology, the nature and character of these capacities have been heatedly debated. Certain capacities are attributed to God — some of which could logically only pertain to God — omnipotence, omniscience, immortality, etc., but others could in a limited sense pertain to humanity. There are at least three of these. First, the capacity to discover in dialogue with others the intelligible in all the realms of

creation and history, and thus to figure things out, more or less —
a capacity which we call "reason" (*intellectus*), usually associated
with the mind, the basis for giving an account of things. Second,
the capacity to choose and exercise resolve since there is a certain
nondeterminacy in creation. To say that there is an intelligibility in
the bio-physical universe which humans can grasp does not mean
that all is preprogrammed determinism.

At no particular point in history can or does anyone have a complete rational account of all factors that would compel a single
rational choice, even if some choices are arguably and thus, reasonably, better than others. That is because the created universe
is open and manifests contingency in the interplay of ordered and
rational events and because human reason is incomplete. It is reasonable therefore to say that some determinations have to be made
by the "will" (*voluntas*) in history, usually associated with intention or the spirit, and without this capacity there could be only a
reduced sense of accountability.

Finally, the capacity to feel affection beyond the commonality of
reasonable argument, choices, resolutions or intentions. Thus we
develop ties of attachment to others and to objects (our homelands,
certain music or particular foods, for example) — a capacity we call
"care" (*caritas*) and which we usually associate with the heart. Writ
large, this capacity allow us to become bonded to God, causes or
things that are not extensions of ourselves. The capacities for reasonable thinking, intentional decision, and affectional caring, as signaled
by theological insights, are accurate estimates of human realities and
indispensable for grasping or guiding the dynamics of globalization.

Such capabilities cannot be clearly inferred by a purely naturalist or purely humanist perspective, for some people are born with
defects that make one or another of these capacities obscure, and
some have their ability to exercise these capacities distorted by bitter experiences. Moreover, some cultures inculcate the importance
of one or two of these at the expense of the other possibilities,
and thus leave some capacities less developed. But the theological
idea of the gift of the image allows us to recognize the human dignity and the human rights of even the severely handicapped and to
seek the development of their capabilities so far as possible.[10] These

---

10. I do not rehearse here the arguments about human rights that I have tried to
make in other books and articles, but the implications for human rights and thus
for a universal moral law should be obvious. See the debates about these matters

theological affirmations do recognize that such qualities appear in historical spheres of life that are other than Christian for, Christians hold, the Creator has conferred with the "image of God" the capacities of *intellectus, voluntas,* and *caritas* to all the Creator's favored creatures, humanity. These are marks of a "common grace" that are given to all. These charismic dimensions of the concept of creation are obviously universalistic in their theocentric cause and in their anthropocentric effects. We all live under the same God with fellow humans on the same earth. But it is also universalistic in its essentialist anthropocentric focus: we are first of all, and equally, creatures of God, made in the image of God, with animating souls brimming with conferred capacities. That is what we are first of all, although we are, of course, secondarily, of a particular gender, genetic code, culture, status and class, with distinct histories, strengths and weaknesses, and some are Christian who offer the account to all.

It is with claims such as this in mind that we can ask as to whether, from a "creational" or "common grace" point of view, with its inevitable overtones of what many Reformation theologians called "general revelation" and what the classic Catholic tradition called the "God-given natural knowledge of the Creator and of natural law," there is not a basis for humanity to discover, together, something of the substance of justice through debate and discussion. Some things simply are reasonable and lawful, yet at least partially subject to voluntary and resolute choice and formative of caring bonds that allow the creation of social bonds and deep concerns. Such themes appear in rich and complex forms of thought in ancient traditions, East and West, in classic Orthodox, Catholic and Protestant theologies, and those socially and ecumenically engaged parts of the Evangelical traditions.[11] In each instance, it requires rational communication and mutual understanding, the exercise of persistent will, and the cultivation of bonds of affection that encompass differences.

I am well aware, as I discussed in the previous chapter, of the deep suspicion of "natural law," and of anything seeming to affirm

---

in Elizabeth Bucar and B. Barnett, eds., *Does Human Rights Need God?* (Grand Rapids: Eerdmans, 2005); and Carrie Gustafson and P. Juviler, eds., *Religion and Human Rights: Competing Claims* (Armonk, NY: M. E. Sharp, 1999).

11. See Michael Cromartie, ed., *A Preserving Grace: Protestants, Catholics and Natural Law* (Grand Rapids: Eerdmans, 1997).

"natural theology" among many contemporary Protestant thinkers, and the contextual reasons for that suspicion are also well known. In recent theological history, for example, Karl Barth's radically eschatological, Christocentric theology and liberation theology's activist social programmatics helped save the church from being swallowed into racist (in neopagan Europe), classist (in neofeudal and colonialized Latin America), and culturalist (in, e.g., tribalistic South Africa) exploitations enforced by governments which claimed to be legitimated by a presumed "natural order" of things — enforced by the raw exercise of power. However, neither of these two powerful twentieth century theological movements generated the social forces that overthrew the tyrannical regimes, or have yet proven themselves able to form dynamic communities able to reform a viable civil society, or to engender new economic and political systems once those exploitative regimes are removed. In fact, in those locales where Barth is the strongest, the churches are dying — or withdrawing into a new counter-cultural sectarianism; and in those lands where liberation theology is strongest, the societies are falling apart — or being revitalized from the inside out by charismatic, Pentecostal movements that are often contemptuous of liberation theology. Neither a radical theological accent on the freedom of God, such as we find in the dialectical dogmatics of Barth, nor a radical accent on increasing human freedom, as we find in various liberation movements, can bond diverse peoples into common efforts to form or reconstruct those institutions for the common life that approximate justice, righteousness, and holy living. The ideas of the freedom of God or of a radical freedom for humans under oppression do accent the importance of the will in divine and human life. But it needs a supplementing accent on rational argument as to what is basically right, and on an emotive passion for a bonding loyalty that surpasses mutual interests, the interests of the church or any ethnic or class solidarity. Moreover, only these together can provide the basis for revitalizing human relationships to God and the flourishing of human beings in a more and more comprehensive social history that arguably points toward a vision of meaning and purpose beyond time and space.

In contrast to these movements, it may be that in focusing on this first great manifestation of God's grace, Creation, especially in its relationship to its constituent elements of the "cultural mandate," the *imago dei* and the human capacities (and as we will shortly see "the Fall") that are shared by all humanity, some commonalities can be found by public theology in our increasingly pluralistic societies as they anticipate and are drawn into a new global civil society. For one thing, if this claim is valid, then everything that is, including each person, is simultaneously real, an actual unit of existence that must be taken seriously, and dependent, limited, undeveloped and flawed, needing others to be. None are eternal, and no creatures, including we ourselves, while having a conferred dignity that must be respected, are autonomous. Moreover, nothing stays the same except the Creator and the laws governing the being of a dynamic creation that are behind everything. Many things and many people have come and gone, and neither the world itself nor we will last forever. God created and sustains nature, but it is unstable and un-reliable on its own. While nothing is constant or eternal, each thing has enough coherent order in it to be studied in a nomothetic way by the use of the gift of reason; but it also has enough freedom to be unpredictable in detail. Science, thus, can discover the patterns that, theologians say, reflect the intelligibility of the Creator behind the being of all creatures, but only probability can be found. Indeed, the sciences themselves have to be understood in terms of the shifting paradigms by which science proposes to grasp patterns in a partially contingent order and the dynamic possibilities it makes possible.

Further, each part of creation, those now studied by a plethora of sciences, is a system that interacts with other systems in ways that reveal enough contingency that nature appears to be not only ordered, but dynamically adaptive in some respects; it has not only a deep pattern that rationality can uncover, but a kind of "natural freedom." Due to this indeterminacy, humans can exercise their will and do intentionally intervene in the operations of the bio-physical world to control, within limits, this contingent interaction. In this implication of creational theology as an aspect of public theology, it is not only science in the modern sense that is made possible; technology is a matter of greater importance in generating and sus-taining our globalizing world.[12] Indeed, if we take the "cultural mandate" seriously as a divine command, it is a theological duty to become as proficient as possible in technology in order to exercise

---

12. Thomas L. Friedman's brilliant new work on globalization, *The World Is Flat* (New York: Farrar, Straus & Giroux, 2005), recognizes that technology is central to globalization and to the equalization of opportunity around the world.

our dominion, not as domination, but as agents of God's stewardship and cultivation of the Lord's creation. The practical implication
of this belief is that theology can interact with those who do not believe in a creator God in discovering what we may call the "ontic
laws of nature," while providing a stronger justification for responsible stewardship in the technological mastery of nature than they
can provide.[13]

The claim that God, in creating humanity, made humanity in
God's own image reinforces the notion of malleability of nature,
for the natural study of humans as evolved animals reveals that we
are very little different from the higher primates. And yet, it is humans who build the universities, develop the sciences and construct
both the airplanes and data bases to aid in the study of the primates — a quantum leap compared to the way primates study the
humans when they show up in the jungles or over the other side of
fences in zoos. Humanity is differently capacitated than any of the
other creatures.[14] We can, in some modest measure, think in more
abstract ways than the other creatures, discovering the patterns of
nature and of morality. We can also exercise some degree of freedom and, contemplating options, choose among possibilities in the
ways we relate to our bio-physical environment, our own bodies,
and other people. All primates, according to popularly available reports, also show preferences; whether they manifest a freedom of
the will is unknown, perhaps unknowable. Even further, we can
find affinities and affectional passions that link us to beautiful or
attractive things in our environment and to the splendor of divine
realities, and seek to create beauty in concert halls or museums.

---

13. I am at this point deeply indebted to several scholars, two of whom have made
contributions to the discussions of these matters at an Abraham Kuyper Center Con-
sultation. See *The Princeton Seminary Bulletin* 24, no. 1 (2003). See also theologian
Thomas Derr, *Environmental Ethics and Christian Humanism*, Abingdon Series on
Christian Ethics and Economic Life, vol. 2 (Nashville: Abingdon Press, 1996); and
environmental engineer Brad Allenby, *Observations on the Philosophical Implications of Earth Systems Engineering and Management* (Bratten Institute: University
of Virginia, 2002). See also the Introduction and chapters 3–5 in vol. 2 of the *God
and Globalization* series.

14. This is one of the key disputes about the work of the Princeton philosopher,
Peter Singer. See his *Animal Liberation* (New York: Avon, 1991). However, he admits, at points, that humans have a consciousness about their sensate capacities to
suffer pain, and a rational will to change social conditions when pain is suffered,
and relational capacity for empathy for other humans and for other creatures, that
animals do not have at least to the same degree.

So far as can be discerned, this too is evidence that humans are differently capacitated and known to feel aesthetic emotions.

Of course, the Genesis account points out these matters by showing how these capacities can be and prototypically have been distorted; humans can abuse the gifts given in creation, can mis-use the capabilities given with the *imago dei*. They/we can violate the boundaries of divine and created order and pretend, at least, to become the lords of all and judges of all good and evil — only to discover how ignorant and unreasonable, willful and irresolute or hateful and alienated from others and passionately committed to the self's interests humans can become. And in the process they/we blame some exterior subtle demonic agent or our closest human companions for the wrongs. If others beguile us, they are wrong; if we succumb, they are not.

The First Grace Betrayed

Humanity does not live in, never historically did live in, and cannot return to the idyllic dream-world of Eden that God must have had in mind for creation and for the favored creatures. The departure from innocence is not a necessary part of the created conditions, but it was from the start probable and perhaps inevitable. A rather large school of Protestant theologians, now largely forgotten but whom we should remember with high regard, the "Federalists" of the seventeenth and eighteenth centuries, accented the non-necessity of the departure from innocence when they spoke about a "covenant of works" that was part of the original design of creation. Their insight was anticipated in the view of some late medieval Catholic theologians that natural and supernatural graces were both present from the beginning of creation, but they were wilfully betrayed. Both groups rightly saw that the fundamental structure of God's relationship to humanity and of humanity's relationships to each other was given from the beginning as a kind of ontological fabric of existence that had also a moral dimension — a *justitia originalis*. But they did not fully see that whoever is more like God than anything else in the world, but is not God, is inevitably soon to reason and care about things in ungodly ways, as well as choose what is wrong and evil.

The divinely intended gift of existence and human life, with be-stowed dignity and capabilities, is disrupted by false reasoning, as suggested poetically by the way the symbol of fallen creation, the snake, questions the limits imposed by God by suggesting that God is an authoritarian tyrant who offers only totalized commandments about the tree of life and the fruits of the knowledge of good and evil. The distortion is compounded by the human complicity in the willful exercise of freedom that accepts that distortion of the truth and by breaking bonds of affection intended between fellow humankind. In consequence, when people think that they must, and can, avoid encounter with God, they/we discover not only that they/we are nakedly defenseless against life forces around and within us that alienate us from ourselves, our fellow humans and finally from God, but also they/we fail to see the illogic involved, the beauty obscured, and wilfully comply. Humans everywhere try to hide such facts from themselves, each other and divine scrutiny, and humanity is thus constantly under the threat of meaninglessness because we cannot fully perceive the splendid order, responsible freedom, and bonding passions that stand behind the complexity of existence. Whether this is occasioned by pride, by sensuousness, by anxiety, or by the arrogance of power cannot be easily determined, for humans are enslaved by all sorts of distortions of their dignity and their capacities, and thus become subject to suffering, pain, and death from which they need relief. It is for this reason that humanity must have not only a theology of creation, but a theology of history that points toward an end that is different from both the beginning and from our present experience. The implication is not only that nature itself is not only incomplete, needing tending and cultivation, but is distorted and distorting, thus needing, where possible, both restoration and transformation.

At this point, things become quite interesting from the practical and ethical point of view for two reasons: One has to do with the question of how to deal with established points of view which do not accept this kind of account. In this connection, we need to recognize that most of the great world religions have a conception of creation, and that they seldom see nature as the ultimate point of reference. That is, indeed, a distinguishing mark of "religions." We can debate with the representatives of the world religions the exact nature of this transcendence over nature and the ways in which we best come to know this, and presume that our debates about these theological issues make sense. This is one of the primordial forms of public theology. Jews, Christians, Muslims, theistic Hindus, some Deists and a number of panentheist philosophers could, in principle, debate these issues quite openly, implying a common possession of a rational capacity, although the will to do so is weak and the alienating power of the passion to protect the tradition for which each has most affection is so strong that the social bonds that could facilitate such discussion are undeveloped. Still it goes on in fragmentary and episodic ways.

The second reason is more difficult in a global era. It is the fact that some people doubt that a divine intelligence, a free will, and a caring affection is really behind the existence of the world, even if they honor brain power, make choices repeatedly, and love those who love them.

Some people doubt because they have been damaged by bad religion and/or arrogant, stupid or blatantly immoral advocates of one or another faith. Others doubt because they are basically one dimensional — they do not see the ontological depths of nature or the spiritual heights of any divine reality. They presume that someone must have made it all up, since they can only see on a horizontal plane; they are dead to the inspired art of, say, Dante and Milton, let alone to the wisdom of the great scriptures of the world religions. This is not the place to engage in a full-fledged discussion about theistic and non- or anti-theistic or atheistic worldviews, but some parts of the scientific community and some who hold to non-Western world religions believe more in nature than in a creator God, and more in a closed than in an open universe.

Today, more, showing themselves to be very modern, see only a primal accident that made the earth, and a contingent event that made protein, plus natural selection that made the microbes, plants, animals, especially the higher primates, all evolved by mutation and adaptation until, eventually, humans with their industrial-sized brains appeared. Then, these brains invented God to explain things otherwise not understood. These people do not believe that God made nature and us, but that nature made us and we made our god or gods in, or out of, our own imagination.[15] If it is true, we can

15. If I understand his intent correctly, I think my colleague Wentzel Van Huyssteen has engaged these views in his recent Gifford Lectures in terms of current scientific hypotheses about the paleontological evidence regarding the development of the higher capacities, and thus the human inclination to seek articulation of the nature and character of the divine realities that stand behind experience. See his

at least say that it is both natural and unnatural to think about the universal and the divine.

Moreover, if all great worldview hypotheses involving an open universe, where a divine transcendence is a force, are a product of ignorant imaginations, it can surely be argued that those who hold this view have a more difficult time accounting for the moral and spiritual character of their own intelligible, voluntary, and affectionate interactions with each other and the bio-physical universe than what the theological traditions convey. And we can argue with equal plausibility that life can best be understood in terms of an open system, one where "spiritual realities" influence "natural" ones, and a morality can influence social and cultural existence. Such debates are not only a matter of being faithful to revealed truths that are held by such tradition; they are theological debates, based on religious insights, about how life, the world and the universe really is.

Certain non-Christian religious views also are non-theist, but superior to anti-religious views, even if they are not all equally adequate in the eyes of Christian theology. Buddhist metaphysics, for example, is in certain ways compatible with certain aspects of contemporary scientific views, as held by some Christians. The environmental scientist and philosopher, William Cronon, for instance, has challenged the idea that there is a nonhuman or nondivine nature that can be taken as a measure of the right order of things. After all, humans have intentionally intervened in all sorts of natural processes for as long as these particular bipeds have been on earth. But not only have humans reframed their surroundings by intervention in them, "nature" is an idea, and

> [I]deas of nature never exist outside a cultural context, and the meanings we assign to nature cannot help reflecting that context. The main reason this gets us into trouble is that [the view of] nature as essence, nature as naive reality, wants us to see nature as if it had no cultural context, as if it were everywhere and always the same...so the very word we use to label this phenomenon encourages us to ignore the context that defines it.[16]

Alone in the World?: Human Uniqueness in Science and Theology (Grand Rapids: Eerdmans, 2006).

16. William Cronon, ed., *Uncommon Ground* (New York: W. W. Norton, 1996), 35.

Like the Buddhist, Cronon sees the world of "nature" as an unsubstantial construct of human consciousness. But unlike the Buddhist, he does not want us to detach from the illusion, but to take responsibility for the shape of that contingent reality toward which our construct points us. Indeed, Cronon is closer to the Buddhist ethic for laymen who do not become monks and continue to live in this world, where responsible engagement in society and culture as well as with the bio-physical universe must continue, where warnings of many hellish punishments await those who neglect their duties to "nature," to society and to religion. After all, it is from them that the begging bowls of the monks are filled. In brief, the difference is between the Buddhist idea of salvation and the idea of living in this life — a distinction Christians can see in the tension of an ethic of acosmic asceticism and eschatology or of protology and providence.

Traditional Confucian teachings bear some similarity to this view as well. They do not speak of where or what the source and norm of all existence is, as if there were a Creator God. The stratified portrait of existence, with nature at the bottom, society in the middle, and heaven above is presumed to be a preexistent whole; it is a primal ontocratic order by which all can be integrated into a relative harmony. Of course, disorder erupts — in "nature," in society, or sometimes in heaven, and the primal order must be restored by right ritual or a "rectification of names." The devastation of floods, for example, must be repaired and the waters of the rivers returned to their proper channels and uses, fathers must be more fatherly and sons must exercise greater filial piety, and the emperor and his literati officers must rule justly, exemplify virtue, and perform the appropriate rites to reestablish the harmony between "nature," society, and heaven. The idea of transcendence over this ontic whole by a divine reality is a foreign and difficult concept even to articulate in that worldview, in spite of some classical texts that see a "Heavenly Mandate" as a kind of impersonal creative principle.

That worldview did not provide for a view comparable to that of the vision of Eden, as did, evidently, ancient Tao belief, but it recognized something of a natural moral, and spiritual harmonious order, and thought it could be enacted in history. It thus made one of the world's greatest historic civilizations, constantly renewed by repeatedly realigning the order of things by natural intelligence, a disciplined will, and properly channeled affections that prompted efforts to cultivate a virtuous self in a virtuous society. Yet, there were anomalies. Ancient technologies that built the massive irrigation system involved a fundamental intervention into the natural order, but it was justified by the desire to adapt society into its traditional ontocratic structures all the more completely. Whereas the Three Rivers Dam Project is justified by a more eschatological vision — the actualization of a dynamic, complex civilization and world power based on a version of Marxist utopian thought and no small dose of Chinese nationalism.

When this worldview encountered, first, the Western missionaries, then the colonialists, and then the Marxist revolutionaries, with views that transcended the idea of a pre-given whole, the society collapsed and became viciously divided from within. Here, as we see in several traditions, life cannot exist if it totally disrupts that which is bio-physically pre-given; but it also fails if it does not recognize that some parts of the "natural order of things" are distorted ("fallen") and need to be transformed by human action that is obedient to a center of meaning and morality that is other than that order. The fundamental values that are to govern our lives do not come from nature, they come from culture, and, at a considerably deeper level, the core of culture comes from the ultimate religious vision — or they are merely imperialistic impositions.[17] Currently, in China as earlier in Korea, both at the scholarly level, and massively at the popular level, people are turning to Christianity as providing a better account of how to order souls and society than Confucianism did when it tried to preserve an ontocracy, and than Marxism did, when it tried to change everything by revolutionary action.[18] Neither can hold together a view of constant pattern in life and historically dynamic change with a normative ethical order in a technologically dynamic society. They each know some things about how the world works and about morality, they have generated magnificent art and noble exemplars of virtue, but the ethos they generate is sufficiently

17. These comments on Buddhism and Confucianism are informed by the essays written on the responses of these traditions to, and possible contributions to, globalization — one by Kosuke Koyama and the other by Sze-Kar Wan, included in *Christ and the Dominions of Civilization*, vol. 3 of the *God and Globalization* series. — and by my own conversations with Buddhist, Confucian and Taoist scholars in a series of yearly conferences in China, mostly sponsored by the China Academic Consortium between 1997 and 2006, and in shorter visits to Korea and Taiwan. See also Stephen Little et al., *Taoism and the Arts of China* (Chicago: The Art Institute of Chicago, 2000).

18. See David Aikman, *Jesus in Beijing: How Christianity is Transforming China and Changing the Balance of Power in the World* (New York: Regnery Press, 2003).

flawed that it needs something more. Cultures based on either of these cannot stand unmodified when faced with a better view.

These excursions into modern scientific and classical religious orientations that challenge our theological perspectives actually reveal something that I believe a creational theology and ethics, especially as revived by Abraham Kuyper, allows us to see — something that some of his closest disciples did not recognize. As Clifford Anderson, curator of the Kuyper collection in the Princeton Seminary Library, has pointed out, Herman Dooyeweerd, the great successor to Kuyper, saw a fundamental tension in Kuyper's thought, particularly in his view of "common grace" or "general revelation" as these are seen as given in Creation (and, indeed, in Providence) in contrast to "particular grace" as present for us in Christ and Eschatology.[19] One side is identified as the "Calvinistic" line — the view that Christians and non-Christians have different understandings because Christians see the world from the standpoint of the particular grace of Christ's redemption, and the other is identified as the "scholastic" line — the view that Christians and non-Christians can do science and politics together because the world and the human capacities to understand it bear within them traces of the primal ordering "logic" by which God created the universe.[20] Anderson proposes a reading of Kuyper, drawing on several of Kuyper's own pronouncements, that overcomes the tension in the antithesis between Christians and non-Christians by pointing to the fact that both Common Grace and Particular Grace are rooted in Christ, and they will be, thus, eschatologically rejoined, providing a united "canopy of grace" under which the believer can learn from the scientist.

For the theologian speaking in and to the church, Anderson's solution is neat and surely correct; but if there is nothing that we humans can do about this ultimate destiny, and if we are freed from worrying about that by the doctrines of election and predestination, it does not solve the practical question. Thus, Anderson's

19. Dooyeweerd is not alone in this charge. C. van der Kooi not only raises similar questions in "A Theology of Culture: A Critical Appraisal of A. Kuyper's Doctrine of Common Grace," in *Kuyper Reconsidered* (Amsterdam: VU Uitgeverij, 1999), which he edited with J. de Bruin, 95–101; but he calls our attention in his footnotes to the extensive controversies over these issues in the Reformed traditions.

20. C. Anderson, "A Canopy of Grace: Common and Particular Grace in Abraham Kuyper's Theology of Science," *Princeton Seminary Bulletin* 24, no. 1 (2003): 123.

Barthian solution is unlikely to carry the day in the university and in sociopolitical analysis or debate where public discourse of a different kind is required. On that front, I think it is possible to see in Kuyper (and the wider Reformed tradition that he, in this matter, best represents) another approach in regard to the nature of things in the world and history, and in the human capacity to understand them. It is this: at one very deep level the world has an ontological and ethical order that scientists, logos theorists, natural law advocates, cosmos-philosophy-oriented Hindus, Confucians, and Christians who see the importance of "common grace" can in part discern. They can do this because the human capacity for reason, guided by the will and passion to exercise it in the service of all that is holy and for human well being, is also present in humans in a way that is discontinuous with all other creatures as I already argued. The most profound discoveries of modern science, such as Einstein's formula, and modern ethical insights such as the need to defend universal human rights or the capacity to recognize virtues in people from all cultural and religious backgrounds, are in fact universal, and not a mere "scholastic" speculation. The idea of a Common Grace, given in creation by a Creator, offers the best account of this reality available. Christian believers can confidently argue for such concepts in public discourse with non- and other-believers.

At the same time, as already argued, at the phenomenological level "nature" — that which is based in creation but is not conscious of a Creator — is divided against itself. It can find no fuller harmony of existence. Disease corrupts, the wolf eats the lamb, parasites invade all living things, HIV/AIDS turn bodies against themselves, entropy threatens existence, and all life tends toward death. Moreover, human nature is fragmented, and is, at least in part, alienated from God even if God never gives up on humans. Thus, reason asserts its arrogance over will and affection, or is trumped by an assertive will, while our affections invite us to fall in love with powers and processes that distort common loyalties and the love of God or bind the will to degrading desires and irrational calculations. We become split selves, not differentiated souls, attacking within ourselves and in other people the very dignity God bestowed with the *imago*. Meanwhile, societies — tribes, cultures, political orders, economic interests and cultural solidarities — array themselves against their neighbors, dominate and exploit them, and bring untold suffering. Even more, one can see why the great achievements of modern,

complex societies — science and the university, legal systems and
jurisprudence, medical care and hospital networks, management
and corporate economic institutions, the media and artistic creativity — can become centers of idolatry and autonomous technique,
competing for fame and fortune in careers filled with technical excellence but without spiritual or moral substance. In noting this,
we can see why the Darwinians propose a natural, lawless and
morally purposeless struggle for existence marked by "the bloody
law of tooth and claw." We can understand why Marxists see life
as an unmitigated story of the agonistic struggle of classes and material interests. And the Christian can grasp why the Buddhists hold
that attachment to the illusory and passing "things" of the world
brings suffering and is less authentic than a detached and pure consciousness of "no-thing-ness." This level of existence, taken alone,
is enough to make one believe in total depravity in all things, in the
"Fall," and in Sin.

"Out of the Garden"

At this point I must draw attention to certain globally pertinent
themes contained in the often neglected "third creation story." After
the Priestly and Yahwistic accounts of the creation of the earth, the
creation of humanity as the most favored and endowed creature,
and the early symbolic betrayal of these endowments in Genesis
chapters 1 through 3, those archetypal figures are thrust into the
mytho-poetic portrait of the beginnings of real history. They are
pushed out of the idyllic status of primal innocence and its distortions, and angels with a flaming sword are placed at the gate to the
Garden. There is no turning back. Every attempt to romanticize or
reclaim the life of the Eden, to preserve or reenact the dreaming
innocence of a state that exists only in God's intention, every effort to establish a colony or commune or civilization where all is in
perfect harmony with nature, God and fellow humanity, and every
quest for a martyrdom that will return one to such an innocent state
that does not recognize the persistent reality of evil in the misuse of
human abilities that must be combated is doomed to failure. Here
is a profound sense of realism; an agonistic element is necessary to
society. Given the reality that the intelligence, will, and affections of
the most favored creature can be used to distort what God intended

as well as to fulfill it, there is no alternative but to build, out of the residual abilities that humanity had been given, society.

Genesis chapter 4 through most of chapter 11 deals with the fumbling and violent efforts to form a society whereby humanity can survive under conditions of disharmony and the distorted use of their capabilities. The cluster of stories that point in this direction reveal first of all the logic of conflict laden familial, political and economic relations. This is dramatically stated in the story of Cain and Abel, the first legendary generation thrust into a non-idyllic world. The brothers represent a willful primal conflict over parental affection and two alternative ways of rationalizing the use of land. One was the domestication of animals, which led to herding and semi-nomadic cattle-breeding, and the other was the cultivation of plants and the development of agriculture, which entailed a settled village or town life. The herder and the farmer were ever difficult neighbors. It was thought that herding was most primitive, and thus most favorable to God, a judgment that Cain deeply resented. But Cain's resentment is closely followed by the Lord's promise: "If you do well, will you not be accepted? And if you do not do well, sin is crouching at the door: its desire is for you, but you must master it" (Gen. 4:7). But the jealousy was unabated, and in a paradigmatic betrayal of human brotherhood, Cain kills Abel, claiming that he was not his brother's keeper. Here, we see both the principle of a division of labor in the economy, with competition, and the fact that, unregulated, it can become murderous, the denial of the dignity of those closest to us, and a willingness to sacrifice human bondedness for gain, sometimes by the use of deception. It induces an alienation from other humans and the earth.

Ironically, Cain's agriculture-based economy triumphed over the nomadic cattle-breeding one, and it is Cain's son Enoch who built the first city — a social creation that can only happen in a settled economy that produces enough surplus beyond subsistence to support more complex social and cultural functions. At this point we begin to see the flowering of the division of labor and multiple bases for societal organization. There were not only the various families, some of which continued to dwell in the traditional tents and have cattle, but others who became culturally creative. Some developed musical instruments. Others developed new technologies, such as metallurgy, which of course make agriculture, weaponry and architecture more efficient. All this creativity takes place in the context of an emerging differentiated social order with implications for a primitive political structure — various sheiks, heads of clans, or tribal leaders are celebrated as great leaders with mythically extended lives, signaling their impact beyond any normal life span, perhaps by hereditary rule, but a new urbanized civilization is on the horizon (Gen. 5).

I have summarized these stories in an effort to draw out implications for a global civil society for three reasons: The development of a complex civilization is evidently allowed by divine permission, even given the fact that the economic and political heritage that generated it is located in sinful humanity — Cain deserves to die for his murder, as his parents also deserved judgment for their mythic disobedience regarding the fruit, but they are allowed to live and it is from this line that Cain bears a son who develops the city. Civilizations are built out of the memory of a relationship with God and out of residual human abilities, but also with the full consciousness of sin, disobedience, conflict and violence. The text recognizes in these primal myths that every society requires a family structure, an economic structure, a cultural system, and a political system. These are normatively and functionally required spheres of life in every viable human society, although they may be modulated by different cultures and are episodically dysfunctional, as we have argued especially in vol. 1 of this *God and Globalization* series.

This last point leads us to the last line of the third chapter of this creational protology as it turns from physical existence to habituated life. The bio-physical universe was populated by humans with a particular dignity and ability; the distortion of these and the consequent "fall" marked the move toward the creation of new wider society. And it is here that we find the words: "At that time, the people began to call upon the name of the Lord" (Gen. 4:26b). In brief, what holds the fabric of society together is religion — itself a construction out of revealed insight and cultural creativity. In the mythic innocence and even its betrayal in Genesis chapters 1, 2, 3, and the first part of 4, God is an immediate presence, in direct communication with humanity. There was no need of prayer, of worship, and of naming the transcendent Other. But in a complex, differentiated civilization, religion becomes a crowning synthesis of meaning, an ordered reminder in the midst of many spheres of existence that they are all under an ultimately unifying reality that can be named.

There are three other great stories in this portion of scripture that demand at least brief mention due to their potential capacity to reveal universalistic themes for our globalizing age, and they point us toward less mythic, more historical understandings of spiritual and moral life. One is cryptic story of relationship of the "Nephilim" and the "sons of God," the second is the famous story of Noah, and the third is the story of Babel. The historicity of all three stories is doubtful, the ethical implications of each are profound.

The first, found in Genesis chapter 6, suggests a semi-mythical memory that the descendants of Adam and Eve were not the only humanoid creatures on earth, and that there was either another genetic line which interacted with humans, confusing human identity, or a borrowing from other mythic stories of the ancient world, in which half-divine/half-human "giants" or "great warriors" are honored. There are other references in the Hebrew scriptures, in apocalyptic and apocrypha texts and in Luke 10:18 that point in the direction of "fallen angels," divine creatures established by God to constitute the councils of heaven, but who sought to become integrated into the human world and claimed an autonomy from God's rule. These are "powers" that manifest psycho-spiritual and social potentialities in the world of humanity, but which become both dehumanizing and anti-theological, but over which it is possible to exercise spiritual and ethical control.[21] In short, the creational interpretation suggests that there are personified "spiritual" forces in the world, that are a primal part of human experience, but which can become highly demonic if they are not held under constraint and harnessed to serve creative ends.[22] Psychiatrists understand some of these powers, and the social-psychologists of mass movements and institutionalized subcultures and social pathologies can understand others of them (e.g., racism, sexism, consumerism, militarism,

---

21. The best brief treatment of this passage I have found, that has both balance and scope is in the entry by P. W. Coxon on the "Nephilim" in Karel van der Toorn et al., *Dictionary of Deities and Demons in the Bible,* 2nd ed. (Grand Rapids: Eerdmans, 1999), 618–20.

22. In many classical theological sources, and in comparative historical studies of religions and cultures, the presence of various powers are recognized and often feared or appeased by ritual means. In this series, we have recognized a social version of these powers as a matter that must be dealt with by ethical theory and theological discernment. Many Christians recognize the passage by Paul in 1 Corinthians 15:20–29 as an authentic part of the eschatological promise of the Gospel concerning the reality and ultimate destiny of these "powers."

etc.). These can come to dominate an ethos, but it is likely that a theological-ethical analysis of them is necessary for a fuller grasp of what is at stake in the formation and preservation or the decay and destruction of a civil society.

The story of the flood and the ark contain two major implications for such a global public theology. Every society has stories about the ways in which some kind of distorted human or spiritual wicked agent threatened the very existence of humanity through a supernaturally induced catastrophe, sometimes due to an evil intent, but usually as a punishment for doing wrong. This of course indicates a primal sense that human life depends on the existence of a moral ethos, and it also suggests that each people has a sense of participation in some violation of the "right order of things." In this story, humanity became so corrupt, forgetting God, distorting the bestowed dignity, betraying the capabilities and giving loving licence to the powers that we associate with fallen angels, that God decides to end this creational experiment. But, as with Adam and Eve, and with Cain, the deserved punishment is mitigated. Not only Adam and Eve, but Cain and his family and Noah and his family, and now also the creatures of the earth, are preserved. The creator God is also the one who preserves humanity and the bio-physical world. Indeed, it is in the context of this story that the first use of the term "covenant" appears, a term that we shall explore more extensively in later chapters, a term with providential and salvific significance.

The third of these stories presses us even closer to an historical understanding of life. After the basic moral and spiritual fabric of existence is articulated in the protological accounts, we find a story of warning. According to Genesis chapter 11, humanity, as represented by the descendants of Noah, taking pride in the abilities that had been given in creation and in all their technological and cultural accomplishments, however much they are disrupted by the condition of sin, desired to develop a unified culture signaled by a single language. They decided to build a monolithic civilization symbolized by a tower that could reach to heaven. Here, we see the greater proximity to historical, and not only mytho-poetic, awareness for the story is surely based on memories of the great cultural and architectural achievements of the Mesopotamian societies, especially the ancient capital, Babylon. The tower at its center, called "Babel," evidently meant "gate to the god" to its builders. Ironically, it became the symbol of arrogant idol worship, which is always self-worship of the idol makers, of precisely the wrong way to develop civilization. The construction of a homogenous, theocratic political order that can so control political, economic and technological resources that it can provide the "ladder" by which their civil cult can climb to the very center of the divine life — and legitimate the divine status of the those who built it — is an inversion of the meanings of the creation. There is no signal that they are dependent on God; they have no desire and no need to have God come to them. Such cultural arrogance, in many forms, has given the world many wonders — as we can find on every continent. But it is no way to build an enduring civilization. The many wonders fall quickly into ruins. And the people forced to pay the taxes for, or to "donate" their labor to build these magnificent towers of pretense scatter into differentiated tribes and clans, the residues of broken civilizations who want nothing to do with such arrogance. The authors of this story saw "Babel" not as a gate to god, but as an arrogant confusion of heaven and earth, as a civic religion that falsely tries to manipulate divine rule to assure political dominance. It is wrong, and it does not work. Too much centralized power fractures civilizational possibilities, it does not construct them.

What does work is the topic of the next several chapters, which will deal with the formation of those structures and practices that can providentially sustain human existence in a sinful and broken world, a sustaining grace that also points toward the grace of salvation. But these are impossible without the proximate fact that common grace is given to all humans in creation — with warnings and realistic recognition of natural and human limitations.

– *Chapter 4* –

THE SECOND GRACE

PROVIDENCE

Living with Sin

As we have seen, a Christian public theology has a protology which proposes that it is God who brought the cosmos into being, establishing an ontic basis for the existence of life, and allowing the contingencies of evolution to produce the many species of flora and fauna on earth and bestowing the capacities of human creativity to form culture and society. In a poetic sense, this was the primal globalization in the context of an entire cosmos, which theology and science both seek to understand. On this globe, one species was created with a conferred dignity, seen in the human capacities for reason, will and affection. This species was also given the duty to use these abilities to exercise stewardly dominion over the malleable and underdeveloped possibilities of the rest of creation. These creational themes imply both a constancy and a contingency in the bio-physical universe and in the fabric of human nature, with possibilities of distortion of what is good at the hands of mistaken reasoning, misdirected will and misplaced affections of human beings. These possibilities of distortion within the basic goodness of creation allow the bio-physical forces and their psycho-spiritual "powers" that are perennially present in human life and social relationships (e.g., Eros, Mammon, Mars, the Muses, Religion, etc.) to declare an independence from their Creator and their distinctive, divinely intended order and purpose, and to become preoccupied with the glories of their own potencies. As Augustine held, they curve in upon themselves. They assert an innate worth that is not bestowed, and arrogantly claim that their reason, will, and affections have no need of guidance or aid from any "external" source divine or social in discerning or doing what is right or good — which, they hold, are mere constructed conventions anyway.

These distortions coalesce into moral wrong and evil in patterns of personal and social life; they threaten the flourishing of sustained existence for they establish both lifestyles and institutions that inhibit the possibility of genuine communion and cooperation of humanity with God and between human persons and groups. Such distorted structures and dynamics refuse to gaze upon the standards for their righteousness and the ultimate good, and reflect an alienation from God. Christians identify this as "The Fall" or "original sin," which names the possibilities of undeserved suffering and destruction. These distortions also imply that God must be self-limiting. We must presume that God allows the different parts of creation to have their own limited autonomy that can issue in creative or destructive rationalizations, choices or passions. This implies that we live in an open universe where there is contingency in the bio-physical world and a degree of freedom in the psycho-socio-spiritual world. This implication is especially notable with regard to humanity. If humans are to become God's companions and agents on earth using the gifts bestowed and recognizing the dignity of all fellow creatures, and if God's righteousness and purposes are to be known, chosen and held dear in any measure by humans as agents of God, and not preprogrammed as fate, humans would surely not have been given gifts that are to be exercised without predetermination.[1] Such, Christians claim, with some variation of accent, is the prologue to history — a good and long-term ontic reality with contingent dimensions subject to both malformation and creative formation by a morally fallible but capable species.

Christian protology is conveyed by the early biblical narratives that are punctuated by pregnant claims about the ontological and ethical structure of the universe and of human life. These claims allow us to understand how moral and spiritual matters are in the world and set the necessary stage for understanding something

---

1. This, of course, raises the question of "predestination" as held by the Augustinian tradition of Catholic theology and by the leading Reformers. That doctrine is held by most Christians in regard to the question of ultimate salvation — a matter in God's hands, not in ours, as we shall discuss in the final chapter of this volume; but that ultimate matter does not determine all aspects of penultimate ethical matters of understanding, choosing and caring that bear on globalization, except as standards by which all penultimate matters may be ultimately judged.

of the drama of history, wherein we find evidence of the "second grace" — Providence.[2] In history, no one lives in a garden of innocence. Evil, wrong, tragedy, conflict, violence, disease, egoism, greed, chauvinism and death are real and recurrent in the human soul, in human relationships and in social institutions.

Yet, that is not the whole story. In history, if reasonable truth is sometimes disclosed and articulated, if right and good decisions, or at least less wrong and less evil ones are made, care can be nurtured into compassion and holy affection can be experienced and expressed — in every culture. On these bases, humans may display the fruits of "common grace" and serve God's principles and purposes in the midst of a distorted world. Indeed, on these bases, an ethos may be formed that fosters the cultivation of the gifts of creation, communities of reasoned communication, commitment and care are established and sustaining societies are built. Insofar as these "preserve" the powers of creation in spite of sin, "empower" humankind in spite of the disabilities of distortion, and "provide" for the earthly well-being of persons and communities in spite of the inevitability of death, we experience these sustaining possibilities as surprisingly gracious, largely undeserved, manifestations of the providence of God. Christians believe that God is often present in the contingencies of historical life, manifesting God's creational intent and helping humans limit the disorder, evils and wrongs that are in the "fallen" world. People find that help comes when unexpected, that a door of promise opens when the dead-end door of despair seems locked, that rescue arrives when all seems lost, that the heart finds strength to face suffering and both courage and consolation in the face of death, when all "realistic" evidence would incline the heart to bitterness.

"Miracles" do not always happen in times of distress, of course, and often the distorted powers of life seem to bear their bitter fruits with little sign of mercy; but providential miracles happen often enough that people in all cultures feel a sustaining grace that no other explanation than super-ordinate intervention satisfies. So

---

2. I am indebted to Craig G. Bartholomew and Michael W. Goheen, *The Drama of Scripture: Finding Our Place in the Biblical Story* (Grand Rapids: Baker Books, 2004), with regard to several aspects of our human misunderstanding of Providence. It is not, of course, a second grace in the sense that it is discontinuous with the first grace, but in the sense that it has some features that require distinct analysis and treatment beyond the main themes of creation.

they turn to mythic terms to express what they experience. Even secularists or anti-religious sceptics speak of chance and serendipity or accident, as if these did not imply a universe that is open to the unexpected and unexplained. Such experiences are often intensely personal and anecdotal, but all morally and spiritually awake people are at least vaguely aware of what such experiences are like, even if they are not always sympathetic to the idiosyncratic, mystical and quasi-magical ways in which they are discussed. Speaking of "Providence" signals a reasonable confidence that when life and history are taken as a whole, there is a sustaining grace at work in spite of the sin, tragedies and pain. This, Christians hold, is neither magic nor fantasy. It points toward a spiritual reality temporally engaged in a sinful world for human benefit. No account of human life or history is complete without recognition of it — including the lived experience and historical reality of globalization.

The public theological significance of the providential power of this spiritual reality can be seen in the witness of the scriptures in at least four basic ways, some of which are paralleled by other great traditions in other terms. In each of these, a divine presence is held to be involved in human affairs — each one of them is civilization forming in a way that limits or overcomes the destructive effects of sin, evil, defect and wrong. It tends to appear in four modes: Covenant and Vocation, Wisdom and Hope. These are the topics of this chapter.[3]

The Covenant Inspired

It must have been a stunning moment of inspiration when the ancient Hebrews first recognized that certain kind of relationships that are found in the histories of the Semitic peoples reflected the ways in which God relates to humanity and seeks to have humans to relate to each other. Historians tell us that the Hittite term *ishuiul* refers to a social relationship in which a powerful figure enters a relationship with a weaker one, a relationship in which each party has acknowledged duties to the other.[4] Power is a realistic factor

3. Lectures on these topics were delivered as the Mackay Lectures at the Taiwan Theological Seminary and College, in Taipei during the month of January 2006. My thanks to Dr. Chen Shang-jen, who was my primary host and translator during my time there. Portions of what follows come from these lectures.

4. The core arguments for the importance of covenantal thought in the biblical record can be found in Delbert R. Hillers, *Covenant: The History of a Biblical*

in all relationships, to be sure — after all this is real history — but the relationship is more ultimately governed by principles of mutual obligation which is also a form of power, in the long run a more powerful influence than power as force or coercion alone; they legitimate or delegitimate the use of force or coercion. That is the first revelation of providence. Real history necessitates the recognition of a divinely given or sanctioned ethical order, one that can shape the organization and exercise of power.

Similarly, the historians tell us that the Akkadian term *biritu*, related to the biblical term, involves a binding together, a voluntary agreement to a primal bonding partnership in which each party becomes a part of one another's destiny under principles of the right and the good that are to be mutually observed and that can be voided only on pain of penalty or death. Often, the specialists tell us, the two basic forms of covenant — between a sovereign and a people (as between God and Israel), or between committed parties under God (as in the holy intimacy of a joyous marriage or a sacred federation such as that between the Twelve Tribes of Israel, which anticipated the model of a constitutional republic) — were seen as quite different from the merely functional trade-offs that are sometimes required for survival amidst the hostilities of history. These were seen as a second form of divine grace, or rather the bursting into consciousness of new ways of ordering social relationships. It was an unveiling of the potential for covenantal life given in creation, the promise of God's preservative care for the whole of creation invoked after the neglect of God's ways brought destruction to the earth (symbolized by the story of Noah and the Flood) and after spiritually pretentious humanity brought about the scattering of cultures that fractured any sense of the common good (symbolized by Babel and recovered at Pentecost).

As the first grace has to do with creation, this second has to do with providence, and the giving of the covenant is one of the

Idea (Baltimore: Johns Hopkins University Press, 1969), supplemented by Patrick D. Miller, "Creation and Covenant" in *Biblical Theology: Problems and Perspectives*, ed. S. J. Kraftchick et al. (Nashville: Abingdon Press, 1995), 155–68. The best history of the impact of the idea in social and political life is Daniel Elazar, *The Covenant Tradition in Politics, Society and Religion* (New Brunswick, NJ: Transaction Publishers, 1995–98). I have offered my own interpretation of that history in *Covenant and Commitments: Faith, Family and Economic Life* (Louisville: Westminster John Knox Press, 1997). I draw much from these sources in this chapter.

major forms of providential ordering. It provided a model for the new formation of civil societies by institutionalizing models that derived from the divine/ human relationship. Moreover, the idea of covenant, which in some form may well be a part of all cultural traditions — sometimes obscured, sometimes obvious — since it was given in the possibilities of creation, was gracefully lifted up over other patterns of human relations.[5] It surpasses the herd solidarity of tribalism, racism, and classism with their subordination of the individual, the radical individualism of contractual voluntarism with its loss of community, and the various tyrannies that recur in societies on the basis of sexual, economic, political, cultural or elite professional dominations, often legitimated by religious ideologies when these spheres of life are not subjected to the principles and purposes of God's reasonable order, will and care.

Whatever its historical origins, the biblical authors recognized in covenant a basic feature of human life, one repeatedly obscured in much of historical existence, yet one central to the formation and preservation of personal identity and social morality. They applied the term to the relationship of God to Israel as a people called to be a witness to the righteous law, dynamic will and enduring care that created a people out of those who were, in the annals of history, nobodies. And they applied it to those persons called to leadership for the well-being of the common life, as we shall see shortly. They saw in the fabric of this pre-given yet freely chosen association an ordered liberty that interwove righteousness and power, stability and dynamic change, memory and promise, and, on the bases of these, formed a structured accountability that was intended to help all people to deal with one another, scarce resources and competing loyalties with equity.

The covenant, held by honored biblical scholars and intellectual giants such as Walther Eichrodt and George Mendenhall to be the governing idea of the Bible,[6] has many applications: it invokes distinctive norms for many kinds of relationships, all under basic

---

5. The old doctrinal debate as to whether God made a covenant with Adam posed a genuine issue in an awkward way. It is not an historical question. The valid point has to do with the fact that humanity prototypically has the capacity to recognize and respond by will and with passion to the promise of covenantal relationships.

6. Walther Eichrodt, *Theology of the Old Testament*, trans. J. A. Baker, 2 vols. (Philadelphia: Westminster Press, 1961, 1967); and George Mendenhall, "Covenant Forms in Israelite Tradition," *Biblical Archeology* 17 (1959): 50–76.

overarching first principles. As already suggested, it can be applied to God-human, sovereign-citizen, group-group and friend-friend relationships, and it has been applied to marriage relations by the Protestant tradition, indeed, by a host of Christian scholars as traditional family relations have been disrupted by rapid urbanization and modernization — as one can see in a number of studies.[7] In these cases, covenant took a binary, mutual form, bonding persons who were once strangers to new responsibilities and opportunities for reasonable, freely chosen affective associations. Such bondings may not ultimately save people's souls from sin and death, but they can preserve life from some of the harshest batterings of historical existence and draw life's locus away from isolation and loneliness into communities of commitment that sustain hope even if all that is familiar becomes obsolete, networks of relationships break down, and even national identities are modulated by international influences. Indeed, covenantal forms of societal and civilizational authority may be indispensable in a global environment, for they provide the moral and spiritual pattern for forming new kinds of institutions. This can be seen in a monumental study of the sociopolitical implications of the idea of covenant by Daniel Elazar.[8] Elazar points out that in many cultures already it has served as the historical inspiration for consolidating indigenous ideas of community into federated commonwealths, pluralistic civil societies and constitutional democracies, in contrast to both authoritarian or hierarchical models of domination and to purely voluntarist contractual models.

The Elements of Covenant

The most regarded of all the ancient covenants, of course, is the one made by God with Israel on the mountain through the mediation of Moses. This paradigmatic covenant served not only as the basic background for the later formation of Judaism and Christianity and, in some ways, Islam, it served as the basic pattern that was revised under new circumstances as we find in the Deuteronomic reforms. Thus, we have an archetypical example of covenantal pattern, and it

---

7. See, e.g., John Witte Jr., and Eliza Ellison, eds., *Covenant Marriage in Comparative Perspective* (Grand Rapids: Eerdmans, 2005).

8. Elazar (note 4 above) and Witte (note 7) have extensive references.

may be worthwhile to examine its main elements as they have been adapted in changing and dynamic circumstances. Although biblical scholars who study the rituals of covenant making have identified as many as six or eight elements that usually go into a covenantal rite, we are here concerned with those three basic elements that are decisive for our global era.

Moses led the people out from under slavery to an imperial power, yet the Exodus experience of freedom did not immediately teach people how to deal with their liberation. Some danced around a golden calf, some wanted to return to the security of state-guaranteed provisions, and some continually murmured that the leadership was not doing enough to assure that they would get to the ideal promised land. In that context, God offered the covenantal law to the people from the mountain, a very significant symbolic event, for it signals that the principles and purposes that were given in covenantal life were not given by a human ruler or a legislature, like the particular codes of the nations of the world. Instead, the terms of authentic covenants were more universal than any made by human edict or negotiation.

However, over the centuries, people forgot, ignored or simply violated the terms of the covenantal law as other peoples from different backgrounds became a part of the functional economic and political and social life of the Hebrew peoples, and the awareness of a new pluralism gave a comforting excuse to ignore old principles. Moreover, many of the heirs of the covenantal tradition turned its central ethical principles and purposes into routine rituals, anticipating subsequent tendencies in organized religion to substitute particular forms of piety for basic principles of justice. The consequence was a dulling and obscuring of the sense of righteousness. Some understood the covenant to entail a special privilege, not duty, or a taking pride in ethnic identity against all others. Every society is heir to these perils, and the covenant had to be renewed again and again!

The First Element: Who Is in the Covenant?

At first it was the Exodus people, but when the memory of it faded, the leaders demanded that the people come together to rearticulate and renew the covenant of Moses — to recover and reaffirm their loyalty to God and to the normative principles and purposes intended by God to providentially order their common life.[9] In this moment of covenant renewal we find these very significant words: "Not (only) with our fathers did the Lord make this covenant but with all of us here this day." In short, these principles are commended not because they are "ours" as a birthright or because they are part of "our" history, but because they have a validity that applies to all seeking the first principles of right and wrong in every period of history.

A truly universal and relevant covenant is not made only with "the fathers" of one genealogical line, but with all of the mothers, aunts or cousins whom we know and with those once foreign to us and those whom we do not know but who are present to the context in which we live — indeed, the terms of the covenant are pertinent to all. And it is pertinent to all because it is made, first of all, by the one universal God. Thus, if we follow the logic of covenant renewal as revealed in the book of Deuteronomy and seek to understand its relevance to contemporary global developments, we would have to expand, as they did, our awareness of all those who now also may shape the reception of the covenant. This means that all will have to be given a chance to test whether it can establish and preserve ethical integrity in a highly expanded and ever expanding civil society. We shall have to find out whether it now applies to the forebears of all and for all our neighbors, for its principles and purposes are not only for one people, but for all peoples in all places at all times — those deceased, those living and those not yet born.

These principles are what structures a community, orders its freedom and constrains its impulses to pretense and conquest. The first element of an authentic covenant defines the parties who are in the relevant community of social interaction, now under global conditions offered not to one people or one faith, but to the world.

There are two other decisive elements of a covenant besides the question of who is, in principle, included in it. One is the indication of the normative terms that are held to be universally valid and the other is the formation of a polity that enacts and defends them, so that life may flourish even in the midst of a world constantly tempted to sin and subject to conflict.

---

9. I refer, of course, to the renewal recounted in Deuteronomy 4ff., connected with the Josiah reforms, beyond the covenant of Exodus 20.

The Second Element:
Moral Laws and First Principles[10]

We can briefly spell out the implications of the terms of the Ten Commandments, which have been seen as the summary of God's universal moral law. The first one is the command to have no other god. But there are many gods today — not only the deities of the world religions, but the idols of the so-called "secular" worlds of politics, economics, and culture; nationalism is one, wealth is another, so is "lifestyle." None of these are necessarily wicked, for at least some of the gods people worship are actually quite inane — they harm or help nothing, even if some of the secular gods are quite influential. The question this command puts to us in a context where we are aware of religious pluralism and of a multitude of secular forces in which some place their confidence and loyalty is this: Is there a true center of all that is holy, one that created the world, one we can know, and one that can sustain life providentially, even in the midst of the sins, wrongs and evils that are inevitable in history? If we think so, we must continue to point toward this God as a central reference point to put all other aspects of life in perspective. If we are quite unsure, or even think not, we are surely required to keep the society open as we continue to search for some source or some kind of moral meaning that does not lead to nihilism. Thus, we must both respect and critically examine every claim about the source and norms of moral life.

In any case, we are not to make graven images. Under God, we may continue to create things. Indeed, we are commanded to construct cultures and the institutions of society; but what we make cannot be raised up to the level of divine truth. Today, we are besieged by images that flit across the television screens; they clutter the mind, but empty icons cannot sustain us. Neither shall we take the name of God in vain. If the making of images raises artifacts to the level of divinity, swearing and the use of sacred language for profane purposes, even the attachment of holy symbolic phrases to tedious sermons defiles and clouds the knowledge of the true center of meaning and moral discourse.

---

10. What follows here is proposed as the answer to the unsolved quest by the UNESCO for a global ethic, documented in our series by the remarkable essay by Yersu Kim in vol 1.

The fourth command instructs us to observe the Sabbath, and it links this duty to set aside time for prayer and meditation (and to be with family, friends and fellow believers) to the command to work six days a week. All who can should work, for sloth is a sin, and each has a holy obligation to be diligent in one's occupation. Yet, work can become also a compulsive manifestation of greed or pride. A disciplined attention to the center source and norm of meaning and morality puts our work in perspective and demands times for a re-creation of the spirit, body, mind and relationships.

The next command, to honor your father and mother, does not mean a lifetime of obedience to old peoples' whims, but it does imply that where there is neglect of parents, and the procreative links that made our lives possible, a failure to aid the elderly in need, a lack of respect for what previous generations have sacrificed for our good or a desecration of those patterns of life that conduce to reproduction and the nurture of the next generation, we must rectify our patterns of life, for it is a sacred regard for these relations that has allowed human life to flourish at its best.

If the command about parents has to do with the ongoing cycle of life, the command against killing demands the protection of the living. Some global developments have murderous aspects. The death penalty is a scandal for any society that has a decent prison system, and abortion should only be practiced in extreme circumstances. Torture that wounds the body to kill the spirit, by whomever and wherever practiced, is a horror before God, and when done in the name of God, a blasphemy. Some trade policies leave others starving; some ecological practices threaten generations yet unborn. These holocausts by slow degrees are as lethal as suicide bombing and unjust wars. They are morally wrong and must be condemned in a turn to the quest for a just peace within and beyond national boundaries, even if we must also have a high regard for soldiers and police who are required to use force to maintain law and order or to reestablish a just peace when it is threatened or violently disturbed.

Not only should we not murder, we should not kill the basic relationships of society. Adultery is a chief cause of marital breakup, and women and children, the most vulnerable, are often the victims with devastating financial and psychological implications all over the world. To be sure, family patterns are changing as the former patterns of extended family are declining rapidly and even newer patterns of the nuclear family are in peril. The failure to construct viable forms for responsible marriages and prepare young people for them under conditions of modernization only makes matters worse.[11]

Not only is family life to be protected, but so is economic life. It is wrong to steal, and private property is to be respected. The effort to improve the condition of humanity by abolishing private property turned out to be an economic disaster that robbed and further impoverished the poor, as now most former Communists also acknowledge. At a more personal level, the percentage of people who live directly by theft is rather low, and all countries have laws to deal with them. If development is slow and law enforcement is weak in this area, people begin to live locked-up lives and cannot trust others in even simple transactions. Equally dangerous in our global environment is commercial deception, exploitation of workers, bribery, embezzlement of company funds, swindling the public or making "sweetheart deals" with cronies that damage peoples confidence in honest business. Some behaviors steal from victims in other ways — rape and torture steal the dignity and integrity of personhood, at least temporarily and often leave enduring scars more damaging than financial loss. These crooked behaviors destroy lives, families and the common good. They rob the people in systemic ways, although the long-term trends in global economic development have brought longer lives, lower death rates for children, less sickness than our ancestors, and relatively less violent conflict over resources.[12]

So does the bearing of false witness. Lying, cheating, twisting information and evidence, especially in legal proceedings, makes what is bad look good, obscures the truth and induces mistrust and corruption. Truth and transparency light up the dark corners of human dealings in law and politics, economics and interpersonal relations. They induce trust and prevent litigation and conflict. Bearing false witness is not only perilous in these areas, it is reprehensible in academic, scientific, and religious life, for these are basic to intellectual and moral integrity.

---

11. See Don Browning, *Marriage and Modernization: How Globalization Threatens Marriage and What to Do about It* (Grand Rapids: Eerdmans, 2003).

12. See Robert William Fogel, *The Escape from Hunger and Premature Death, 1700–2100: Europe, America, and the Third World* (New York: Cambridge University Press, 2004).

Finally, covetousness is forbidden. This command, like the very first one, cuts to the heart. Most commands have to do with behavior, and they focus on what is not permitted, on what the boundaries of the moral life in society are. Such negative limits allow for wide ranges of social, cultural and professional freedom, for much is permitted. But limiting commands are framed with a first commandment that calls for a fundamental loyalty to God as the center of meaning and morality, and ends with attention to the dispositions of the heart. Life is not to be lived with the gnawing feelings of resentment or envy, or with an incessant drive to possess more and more especially if the "more" or "better" is part of the proprium of another. That corrupts the soul and the civilization and prompts us to violate all the other commands. Treating these matters in both their external and internal implications offers a sense of the second element of a viable covenant. Not only must we attend to who is included, but we must attend to the normative substance of moral law, as rehearsed in covenantal renewal and as can be restated for our global situation today.

A Comment on Moral Law[13]

Before proceeding to discuss the third element of a covenant, I want to note that I have treated these commandments as if they contained, or at least pointed to, universal absolutes. I am well aware that a great number of postmodern thinkers, including some Christians today, distrust such notions, and that many in cultures deeply stamped by other great world religions do not accent the notions of universal moral laws that can be treated as absolutes. Instead, many look to the cultivation of virtues, or of harmonious personal relationships, or of the arts of meditative awareness that removes one from the illusions of the world and of our attachments to it. These can, indeed, in some ways must, supplement a theological ethics that focuses on law. It is, after all, possible to recognize virtuous qualities in persons cross-culturally, much as it is important to deal with others harmoniously and not to be caught in webs of illusion, worldliness or undue attachment to things.

---

13. Much of this section first appeared in "Reflection on Moral Absolutes," *Journal of Law and Religion* 14, no. 1 (1999–2000): 97–117.

However, I want to argue that it is of vital importance to focus on laws of universal applicability, if we are clear about what we mean by "moral law" and "absolutes." If we define "universal" as something immediately obvious and agreed upon by all, such as "humans are bipedal mammals," moral laws would not qualify as universal. But if we say that in coming to moral judgments about human behaviors and attitudes we should both take account of their context and use the same principles as standards in similar cases, we are making a more ultimate appeal. Thus, all ought to hold that murder, stealing, rape, torture and lying are wrong, even if, in some contexts, these behaviors have variant interpretations or are only judged as wrong and evil if they are done to someone in their primary reference group, not to those outside. The claim that "all ought" to hold that these are wrong is a universalistic normative statement that applies to humanity as a species, and assumes that the common identity of humanity is more decisive at this level of abstraction than the divergent cultural definitions as to what constitutes these acts and to whom they are customarily applied. Such universalism is already implicit in a great number of international agreements, in the adoption of human rights provisions by all members of the United Nations Organization, in the criminal codes of every country with a legal system, and in the vocabularies of every language, even if they are selectively applied by police and courts.

By "absolute" is not meant that such a standard alone governs all morality. I have already acknowledged that morality may have several dimensions, such as the cultivation of virtue or the consideration of contextual circumstance. If we hold that murder is causing an illegal death, we have to ask whether the law is just — which is a moral or ethical question that stands beyond the law. If the law is just and a terror to evil, we should obey and defend the law; but if the law is unjust and a terror to good, we are obligated to oppose the law and advocate its change. Indeed, the recognition of universal and absolute moral laws that stand beyond the social conventions and codes as they stand calls us, as it did ancient Israel, to become a witness before the peoples of the world to a divine order of justice.

The notion of an absolute also means that we can seek to discern which standards are trans-cultural, and trans-national, as well as trans-legal, because at some level of consciousness we know them to be true and real. This is so even if we still have to make distinctions between accidental homicide, various degrees of guilt, and justifiable homicide (for example, in defending an innocent child against a vicious rapist who cannot be otherwise stopped, or fighting a just war to stop genocide). Such decisions depend upon a view that certain normative moral principles cannot be dissolved by the contingencies that attend them. In English, the word "absolute" comes from the Latin roots "ab" meaning away from, plus "solve" meaning an act or condition of being brought to an end, so that we do not have to deal with it anymore, or to make into another state where something is unrecognizable, as salt crystals are "soluble" in water. This term "absolute" thus implies a certain stability of moral principle that cannot be brought to an end by changing historical circumstance or conditions. If, for example, the United States is torturing prisoners, or shipping them to locations abroad where they can be tortured, such actions cannot be justified by saying that the United States was attacked by Islamic fanatics. To the nonbelieving sceptic or naturalist, such absolutes are mere projections of the human imagination; and to the *jihadi* Muslim, "righteous arms" Jew, or "Holy War" Christian, the general principles can be overridden by the perception of some overriding purpose that can justify extreme means. But to the believer in a universal creator God who gives humanity moral laws to providentially guide the behaviors of civilizations even in conflict, such "abstractions" have a home, a ground beyond the fabric of existence, and can be applied cross-culturally to all peoples at all times. For those nonbelievers who would condemn such crusading behaviors, their recognition of the injustice implies universal moral laws that they hold to be absolute even if they have no God by which to explain how and why they exist. Such laws are "written on the heart" of all.

All of this forces the question: Is it true that when the Hebrews spoke of a God-given moral law, to which they are covenantally bound to observe and witness to, they were in fact inspired to recognize that, by God's providential grace, there are universally valid, absolute moral laws that can guide people in the formation of civil societies? Jews, Christians and Muslims, and some animists Confucians, Hindus and Buddhists have come to agree, and have become activists in defending such principles as those embodied in the Ten Commandments. That can best be accounted for, I suggest, by speaking of providential grace.

The Third Element: Purposes

In addition to a definition of the parties to be included and a statement of moral laws, the core structure of a valid covenant has purpose. It is future oriented. It wants to bring things into actuality that are not presently realized. The biblical text is quite clear about this, and recognizes that the covenantal order forms a community of commitment: it makes a people who are witnesses to God's laws of righteousness out of a conglomeration of peoples who were divided by history, experience and status. Israel was called to be a "light to the nations," witnesses to all the peoples of the world to the justice of God's law — a calling that Christians also claimed for themselves.

Moreover the principles gave guidance on how to regulate the continued effects of sinfulness within the covenanted community. In the biblical record, we read in the following chapters after the one recounting Moses' delivering the paradigmatic covenantal laws, and also in the chapters after the Deuteronomic renewal, extensive casuistic guidelines on how to deal with a wide range of behaviors that violated one or another of the principles that makes human life less inhumane and civil society more possible. These case-summaries, developed further in commentaries and glosses over the centuries, became models of how sages and legal scholars, rabbis and clerics could reason their way through complex cases to solve persistent and recurrent conflicts. Indeed, Christians often used comparable methods in later centuries, and Muslims codified a comparable set of reflections and casuistic precedents on the moral laws that they see revealed in the Qur'an and in the remembered judgments made on specific cases by Mohammed — which became the basis of *Shariah* Law.

These too had a purpose. It was a promise that if these laws and precedents were followed it would go well with them as a people; but if they were not followed, all sorts of evils would befall the community. This listing of promises and woes is repeated in several forms. This was a people who knew that they were under mandates not of their own construction. They had a duty before God and before the peoples of the world to study the law, to live by it, and to exemplify a righteous community. They depended on the providential care of the creator and covenant-giving God and constantly sought to reorder their personal and community life to that end —

a monumental contribution to human history of a relatively small society in an otherwise obscure corner of the globe. They found, however, that it was not always possible to follow every detail of the moral law, both because of failures of reason, will or affection and because of external forces that they could neither conquer nor convert. Thus, in times of grave trouble, they hoped for someone able to redeem them from their distress and powerlessness. Gradually, this became the basis of the hope for a messiah, one who would come directly from God and set the world right, renew the covenant again, and point them toward a better civilization.

For our purposes what is remarkable about these developments of a future-orientation is that the hope for the Messiah rendered a fresh beginning of a theology of history, a recovenanting with renewed moral commitment. No longer would they only look back to creation or seek to remember the great covenantal events of Moses or its renewal in Deuteronomy, but they would look forward to a new beginning.[14] That attitude was fateful for subsequent religions and civilizations, and it is fateful for us in our globalizing world, as we shall see.

Vocation[15]

Some people in the biblical tradition had a vocation to defend the covenant and its laws and to continuously form and reform the community that was called to be witnesses to it. The term "vocation" comes from the Latin *vocatio*, and is related to "calling," rooted in the Greek *kale*. The Semitic root *qr'*, the biblical correlate of the old German *Ruf* (and related to the Arabic *Qur'an)*, indicates an announcement, directed to an audience and intended to evoke a response. All of these presume a "caller" and a "callee" that establishes a commanding yet potentially mutually responding relation between the parties. In the creation story, God called humanity, male and female, into existence and commissioned them to be fruitful, to til and subdue the earth, and to name the beasts. Humans, from the beginning are, in other words, called to the task of stewardly

---

14. For another rendering of how these elements fit together, see vol. 1, "The Task of Theological Ethics," in the General Introduction.

15. See my "Vocation," in *The Oxford Handbook of Theological Ethics* (New York: Oxford University Press, 2005), 189–204, from which I draw some of the following paragraphs.

dominion over the earth and given the vocation to create a culture and, as we saw, to form a complex society as history unfolded.

A decisive moment in this early narrative came, according to the scriptures, when God called Abraham to leave the ontocratic structures of his traditional pattern of life, and to enter the flow of history. He and his wife Sarah and their children "went out," seeking a city that had Godly foundations, after humanity learned to call upon the name of the Lord. What held them together in this historic quest was not a "gene-pool identity" or an attachment to a sacred homeland; but a calling from God to respond to a binding, promise-laden relationship — that is, a covenant. In this primal exodus, however, we find the paradigmatic notion that an authentic sense of personhood and, indeed, peoplehood is not to be formed on the basis of a loyalty to a tribe, tradition, ethnic identity, or even the geographical territory which it occupied, but on the basis of a call to enter a context-transcending history from a history-transcending reality.

Here is the root of the idea of a "chosen people," a people in a world of many gods and idols, of many spirits and spiritualities, of many chthonic and totemic symbolizations, who are called to be witnesses to the one God before all the world. Being chosen in the theological sense does not mean being given a privileged status over all others so that one does not have to endure the difficulties that everyone else faces; it means that some are called to certain responsibilities in the world for the sake of all in the world. The Abrahamic peoples — among whom we now number all faithful Jews, Christians and Muslims — are called to be witnesses to the reality of the one true God, even if they differ in understanding regarding the internal character of God, in identifying the most important scriptures that testify to the reality, justice and mercy of this God, and in developing the modes of worship to honor this Holy One.[16] These peoples do not always remain faithful to their calling, and their lives fall often into faithlessness and conflict, sometimes with the greatest hostility to each other; but the faithful God seeks

---

16. Bruce Feiler has written an engaging popular account of these similarities and differences in *Abraham: A Journey to the Heart of Three Faiths* (New York: HarperCollins, 2005). A more sustained, critical interpretive and comparative view is that of F. E. Peters, *The Monotheists: Jews, Christians and Muslims in Conflict and Competition*, vol. 2 (Princeton, NJ: Princeton University Press, 2003).

to renew the relationship by raising up leaders to aid the people and to expand or revitalize their witness.

In this connection, particular persons were called, or "elected," to perform specific duties for the well-being of the people and to exemplify and bear witness to this God's relationship to humanity. Of course, in every community some persons are born into, appointed or elected to, or achieve by talent or influence specific roles that are conducive to the well-being of the whole. Gender, age, connections and obvious abilities shape the results, and the internal structure of the society limits or expands the range of possibilities for these occupations or stations in life. Some of these roles are everywhere required for the functional survival of a people. Parenting, for example, and productive workers for another. Further, political authorities (chiefs and warriors or kings and councils to set common policy and maintain law and order) and cultural custodians of the lore, wisdom, language and art styles of the people are designated in every known society. In more complex societies, specialized offices are cultivated: professional teachers, healers, architects, and mechanics who know how to design and build palaces and temples, or to operate and repair devices and engines.[17]

In the biblical record, judges were appointed by Moses to administer the law when he could not do it all himself. In another time, "judges" were raised up to lead the righteous struggles of the people when they were caught in decisive battles. These uses implied someone called to bring conflict between societies or within the society to resolution. It was a theological as well as a social office. Similarly, there were scribes who had cultivated writing and reading and who kept the records of transactions and decisions, and stewards who managed other peoples' goods and properties and served as managers of the sometimes large households which were the center of production, consumption and economic life generally. There were also those who mastered certain crafts and each was to perform a service in and for the community under God's watchful eye. The

---

17. The Australian priest and scholar Gordon Preece has written imaginatively on the relationship of calling and the "work-faith nexus" to the historic changes in occupational structures of changing societies in *Changing Work Values: A Christian Response* (Brunswick, Australia: Acorn Press, 1995) in a way that has implications for our global era.

biblical record helps us to understand how complex and dynamic in occupational structure the so-called "simple" societies can be.[18]

But There Were Prophets

Although everyone had an occupation that was named a calling, as Protestant Reformers were to remind the world much later on, some people were set aside in a particular way and given special responsibilities. Among those with a special office are the Prophets who were called, often by ecstatic or visionary experience, to serve as God's messenger to humanity about truth and justice in the common life. A prophet, as the roots of the word suggest (*"pro"*=forth or fore + *"phetes"*=speak or tell), "speaks forth" for God's law or judgment or "fore-tells" what the people can expect as consequences of a wrong policy wilfully pursued or whatever they can hope for when there seems to be only doom. According to the Judeo-Christian tradition, prophets are often called to discern the meaning of the sinful conditions and visions of a likely future, and to offer an interpretation of how humans ought to be living in view of what God has called them to do in the world. They are the ones who speak out for righteous living when others are silent or silenced.

The biblical prophets differed from the founders of some of the ancient world religions such as Tao, Confucianism and Buddhism, who claimed to discover truths about the way life worked, but had a slender view of history. The prophets believed, with them, that there was a right order to life, but it was rooted in the ethical character of a righteous God, not in the innate nature of nature itself. However, they did share much with those religious founders who claimed to have been given divinely bestowed insights that they felt compelled to reveal to the public — such as Mani, Mohammed and, much later, Joseph Smith. The prophets of the biblical record, however, did not claim to be founders of a new theocratic religion, but to be voices recalling the people to the calling they were forgetting or neglecting in the face of changed historical conditions. They also shared much with the "liberal progressives" of modernity who tried

---

18. See Douglas J. Schuurman, *Vocation: Discerning our Callings in Life* (Grand Rapids: Eerdmans, 2004), especially chapter 2, "The Bible on Vocation." Cf. the older, but very valuable analysis of secular and cross-cultural views of vocation and profession, by Lee Hardy, *The Fabric of this World; Inquiries into Calling, Career Choice, and the Design of Human Work* (Grand Rapids: Eerdmans, 1990).

to invoke the prophetic tradition to confirm their belief that there was a new age on the horizon. But in contrast to the theocrats, the liberal progressives taught that new age was to be marked by the maximization of freedom in every sphere of life. Both theocrats and liberal progressives anticipate the views of current quasi-prophetic voices, but they have only part of the message right.[19]

It is true that prophets like Moses, in some ways the paradigmatic prophet, do demand liberation from oppression. They not only call others to action, but they lead them out from under the oppressions to which they have been subjected by tyrannical forces and their own complicity. But it is not on liberation alone that the great prophetic religion of the biblical tradition is formed, but on the kind of liberty that seeks to receive the law from above and on that basis to the formation of a new, called people, from all nations, who would witness to the God who ever orders history anew. This tradition recognizes that true freedom has a purpose that only comes with a new discipline under just laws for the common good. Liberation without law basically means only more wandering in the wilderness; the lack of stable principles and promising purposes leads to relativism and nihilism, to idolatry and decay. In this way true prophets were (and ever are) quite conservative. Not that they want to return to the remembered garden of innocence, or reestablish repressive policies, or defend the status quo or establish an ontocracy. Instead, they want all to remember and follow the first principles of moral law, and to subject short term gratifications to more ultimate purposes that point toward transcendent goals.

Further, they want the people to observe the right norms of worship, for they see this as the anchor of true righteousness and the refueling of a hope for the messiah who can lead them toward the city that has foundations, whose builder and maker is the creator God. They want to recall these principles and purposes to the minds of those who live only in the now, forgetting the past, and those who think that the more contemporary things are the better. Many of the prophetic oracles, thus, are like a bill of indictment before a divine court in that they appeal to absolute principles of justice. Others

---

19. See the articles on "Prophecy: An Overview" and "Prophecy, Biblical" in *The Encyclopedia of Religion*, vol. 12, ed. Mircea Eliade et al. (New York: Macmillan, 1987), 8–23; and Paul D. Hanson, *The People Called* (New York: Harper & Row, 1987), chapters 4 and 5. Together these summarize the vast body of writing on prophecy from biblical studies and related historical and social scientific points of view.

are demands for repentance and promises of a peaceful, abundant life as a possibility beyond the condemnation if they do repent. The charges in the indictment are that the people have become corrupt within and will not be able to withstand divine punishment if they do not change. Hope comes with a recovery of God's law and a dedication to God's vision of the future, which invites a clarity of reasoning, a courage to choose, and a focus for affection.

Moreover, as we see for example in the book of Amos, it is not only the people inside the community who are to be so judged, it is all the nations and peoples of other lands outside their own. The prophet does not speak for one culture's values and attempt to impose them on another culture. Rather, prophets are inspired to speak for the truth, justice and mercy that is culture-transcending; and they call all, insiders and outsiders, to account in those terms. Indeed, the blame for wrong and evil tends to fall most heavily on the prophets' culture, for it ought to know what the laws and purposes of God are. The prophet is an agent of God's moral providence for, among and to the people. Virtues such as truth, justice and mercy are the only badges of authority; these alone authenticate the calling as authentic. Without them prophecy is false, gnostic propaganda or mere demagoguery.

One of the remarkable things about prophecy is that it promises a new society beyond the condemnation of wrong and evil. It not only calls for the reform of common practices, it also generates schools of prophets and communities of conviction willing to challenge the unjust and false patterns of life that people fall into when they forget the transcendent norms over daily life. Evil becomes routine and ordinary. Prophecy requires a certain intensity of conviction, which means, of course, that the prophet is seldom a fully congenial person, easy to get along with in ordinary dealing. The charism that allows a prophet to say "Thus saith the Lord" to an ever-recalcitrant populace is irritating to many. This herald challenges the cultural habits that treasure smooth human relations above all else and constantly cover up truth-telling when it disrupts harmony; yet it takes no joy in being "radical," no pride in disturbing people; it cares for the people too much for such self-congratulatory sentiments. But the prophet knows that any culture without the ability to open itself to prophetic voices is a troubled society, probably corrupted below the surface, for it tends to deny the depth of sin and evil within it. In addition, any people unable to receive the witness of both first principles and of an ultimate vision beyond what the culture can attain by itself will eventually find itself in a fateful battle with truth and justice, without mercy, which it ultimately cannot win.

And Priests Too

Prophecy is rare historically, but it is of universal significance because of the message of truth, justice and mercy it delivers. Any attempt to form a local civil society (or to move one toward a global civilization) must be open to it, and the repression of religious freedom in any society often has to do with the fear of the truth, justice and mercy that is lacking, or even the fear of charismatic movements in general. They are quite unpredictable. Besides, profound spiritual life for most people is not experienced as prophetic. Instead, it is experienced as rite, liturgy, song, chant or prayer, and these become known through the ritual actions of the priests of the organized religious traditions who are charged with conducting worship in enculturated forms. As we saw in chapter 3, in regard to the development of differentiated economic and cultural specializations as reported in the early biblical legends of transition from primal myth to history, the text says that "at that time they began to call on the name of the Lord." This scripture reveals what we know from the comparative study of cultures: no complex civil society has long flourished or developed historically without an organized religion at its core, and every religion requires particular people set aside to cultivate and lead the practices of that religion according to ordered patterns and providential routines. These ordered patterns and routines incarnate profound spiritual insight and ethical principles in all the great cultures and guide the cultivation of the human capacities that are manifest by common grace.[20]

---

20. See the essay on "Priesthood: An Overview" with separate supplementary treatments of Jewish, Christian, Hindu, Buddhist, Shinto and Taoist traditions, by Willard G. Oxtoby et al. in *The Encyclopedia of Religion* 11:534–50; and Max Weber, *The Religion of China; Ancient Judaism; The Religion of India;* (New York: The Free Press, 1951; 1952; 1958); and his *Economy and Society,* vol. 2 ["The Sociology of Religion"] (New York: Bedminster Press, 1968), 399–634. The former summarizes current studies of the textual traditions and social functions of priesthood; the latter's works, while subject to some criticism, remains the most suggestive treatment of magic in contrast to and within religion, and of the relationships of Priest and Prophet to various strata of the world's population and to key economic, political and aesthetic aspects of social life.

In the biblical tradition, it seems to be the case that well before the Exodus event, certain people performed rituals and began to develop the lore of the religious tradition. Abraham himself, and his heirs Isaac and Jacob, built altars and offered sacrifices. It was Jethro who instructed Moses as to the lore of his people's half-forgotten traditions, before he returned to Egypt to lead his people out of slavery. Moses, himself a prophet, could not adequately speak for himself and had to depend on his elder brother Aaron, the "ancestor of all lawful priests," according to the testimony of Ezra. Aaron not only served as the first high priest, the "sons of Aaron" became the ordinary priests working among the people, supported by the Levites and, later, at the appointment by David, of other priests who were to serve in the temple at Jerusalem. Beyond that, the whole people was supposed to be a nation of priests, as Martin Luther gleaned from the Hebrew scriptures when he argued, centuries later, for the "priesthood of all believers."

This brief review of biblical accounts indicates two matters of great importance for our globalizing era. First, the formation of a faithful priesthood is an indispensable dimension of God's providential care for humanity in the midst of sinful history.[21] Some are called to be set aside from the people to be guides, mentors, and models for the people on specifically religious matters. The priests become one of the visible occupations, responsible for the sacred sites and the rituals of life's transition — birth, puberty, marriage and death — as well as for the instruction of the young or the seeker, and the comforter of those who mourn. They celebrate the holy days in the cycle of the year, and offer proper prayers for those who are suffering from disease, loss or guilt. They offer sacrifice or prayer for those wishing to atone for their sins. These and the devout laity who emulate them in families — spouses to each other, parents to their children and friends to their neighbors — minister in priestly ways as they say the caring word, stand with them in trying times, and teach generation after generation how to pray, how to think about the ultimate questions in life, and how to live responsible

---

21. While working on the *God and Globalization* series I have had the good fortune to be present in conversations, in several places and times, between Christian clergy and Islamic mullahs, Buddhist priests, Confucian scholars, and Hindu Brahmans. And while there is some awkwardness and suspicion in the dialogues, there is less hostility than unfamiliarity. Each, after a time, recognizes a certain commonality in what they are about, even if they have doubts about the primary approaches and metaphysical assumptions of the others.

and upright lives before God amidst the daily rounds of life. Like the prophets of old, priests too are called by God and spiritually anointed as God's representatives on earth to hold a sacred office.

Of course, we know that any priesthood commissioned to these tasks can go awry. Being trained in a tradition, as priests tend to be, and then anointed or ordained, does not void the possibilities and temptations of sin. Clergy all over the world and in all religions as well as parents and friends can abuse their office; they can develop cults that deceive the people; they can exploit the vulnerable sexually and the gullible financially; they can come to believe that the rites they perform have magical effects; and they can weave their religion through and through with superstition or chauvinistic ideologies of class, gender, race or national superiority. Priests often become very concerned about their status in the hierarchy of the priesthood, and jockey for influence in other centers of authority outside the priesthood. The lust for power by priests can be found on every continent, and it discredits organized religion. At the same time, the learned priests engage the best scientific, philosophical and cultural thought available to them. They help the people discern the moral aspects of issues in the local community's life, and they often advise those in positions of power. They see themselves as servant-leaders and they know the constant necessity of recovery and reform and spiritual revitalization of the faith as taught and held by the clergy themselves. Thus, although organized religion is decisive in every age for every society, the truth of the matter is what the Reformed tradition properly argues with regard to the church and its officers: "always reforming, always in need of reform."

Another reason for stressing these matters concerning the development of a priesthood in the context of reflection on resources for our globalizing era is this: priests have ambiguous relationships to prophets and to political leaders. In various periods, the prophets have been given the place of honor, with, according to many scholars, the priests being the ones who worked out the implications of the prophetic message and blended it into religious practices and sensibilities that are present in the culture.[22] In this way, the prophets were dependent on the priests for the incarnation of their message, even if prophets were sometimes as contemptuous of the

---

22. See the paradigmatic treatment of this point by Max Weber, "The Sociology of Religion," in *Economy and Society,* 439–67.

practices of the priests as they were of the policies of the political leaders.

While some of the prophets were also priests, and some of the patriarchs, matriarchs, kings and queens played priestly roles in centers of worship, and while there are several instances of the prophets and priests and political leaders anointing each other — that is, legitimating their place of authority in the leadership of society — there is also often tension between priests and prophets, between priests and politicians and between prophets and politicians. We can see such conflicts in the biblical narratives and also in the structures of the world religions, for each of the world religions has tended to order a society in a distinctive way. In those traditions without a developed sense of prophecy, the interaction and potentiality for tension between political authority and priestly authority is palpable. Thus, if we look at these traditions comparatively, we can see how the major options work. Each option offers a model of how, in the name of all that is holy, the various authorities in society are to be ordered. The model shapes the civilization. It turns out that in human history the way that the role of priest is structured, in relation to that of prophet and political ruler, is decisive.

For instance, the traditional role of the Emperor in the Confucian view, probably also influenced by ancient Taoist practices, is that the Emperor is not only the head of the political order, but also the one who performs the key rituals and issues edicts that are believed to bring harmony between heaven, the earth and society. Further, the Emperor was usually instructed in these ritual roles by learned *literati* who are not, in the ordinary Western sense, priests, but who played the role of priestly teachers with regard to the rites as well as aspired to exemplify the moral harmony and scholarly authority of the classical sage. In most dynasties the political side took precedence, aided by these quasi-priestly authorities. Prophecy was muted, except perhaps in those rites or edicts that were believed to lead to "a rectification of names," the recovery of "the right order of things."[23]

This model differs from what we find in Buddhism, which, in its Tibetan form, sees the Dalai Lama as essentially and first of all a

---

23. This paragraph and the following several on comparative religion with regard to the impact of prophet and priest on the political order are an extension of my argument in vol. 3 of the *God and Globalization* series, 40–57, in view of the particular issues raised in this volume.

priest, and only secondarily as a political leader of a nation — although his decrees are treated as political by the laity. Of course, the Tibetan form of that religion is not the whole Buddhist story and clearly not a majority report. For the most part, Buddhism saw the priest's role as subsidiary to royalty, helping the king become detached from too much preoccupation with power, physical things, fame and wealth. They thus played a spiritually supporting role to hereditary elites (as in Theravada and some forms of Mahayana Buddhism) — although in the days of warring kingdoms the monasteries became also the schools for the martial arts. In any case, the priests are often viewed a "jewels in the crown of the king," and kings often financed their monasteries and temples. Here in the religious authorities, the priests, are subordinated to kingly rule, what in Christian theology is called the "Erastian" model, although some of the "forest monks" who renounced all official sociopolitical contacts served as seers who could exemplify a prophetic alternative to the immoral behaviors of kings and commoners alike from a position of their presumed moral superiority.

These Confucian and Buddhist models differ from the Hindu model, in which the Brahminic priests are seen as the highest status people in society.[24] It is under them that we find, in official doctrine, the kings, princes, and imperial Maharajas — the Kshatriyas of the warrior caste. Below them are the landholder, trader and worker castes — and still lower, the "Outcastes," who do the dirtiest work at the bottom of the social order. In this model, the priests have the highest authority and few politicians (or, for that matter, business and professional people) would undertake any major decision or enterprise without consulting a priest. This is true although there are examples of Brahmins subordinating themselves to the Kshatriyas for the sake of position, wealth and familial influence. But structurally, the ideal is hierarchical (*heiros*=priest; *arche*=ruling figure or primary principle).

While all the societies shaped on these religious and ethical models are stratified, they are stratified on different principles and have

---

24. I offer here a brief, schematic, "standard" overview, although I have shown in *Creeds, Society and Human Rights: A Study in Three Cultures* (Grand Rapids: Eerdmans, 1984) that the actual operating system is much more complex. Cf. Luis Dumont, *Homo Hierarchicus: The Caste System and its Implication* (Chicago: University of Chicago Press, 1970), the now "classical" study that not only documents the complexity of the traditional Hindu system, but argues that it represents a reality in human societies that inevitably is the case and should be acknowledged.

differing visions of the ends for which social life is lived. For the most part, they are built on an ontocratic basis for stability, not for dynamic social change. For that reason, each of these has difficulty accepting prophecy, although there are strains in Mencius and in Chu Hsi's Neo-Confucianism that seem to have prophetic qualities, as do some notions of the Buddhist ideal of the Bodhisattva, and of course many think of Gandhi as the exemplary prophetic figure in Hinduism. None of these are primary sources of the impulses from which globalization now takes place, although cultures in all these traditions are shaped by it. Whether any of these can give shape to globalization, or whether globalization will reshape them each in a different direction because of the basic shape of the social model they developed remains an open question. But I suspect that the latter is the case, and that the adoption of prophetic motifs, the re-shaping of priestly life, and the rearrangement of political authority will be seen in the contemporary, reforming renewals of religions around the world.

Obviously, the other great non-Christian world religion is Islam, essentially based on the prophetic model, but with an overt theo-cratic emphasis. Mohammed is, above all, held to be a prophet and, like Moses, a mediator of divine law, but he was also a mili-tary and political leader of great renown — as well as one who led others in prayer, an *imam,* a fact that has given Islam a distinctive and piously militant character for much of its history. After Mo-hammed's death, however, when the traditions of clerics to staff the growing number of mosques were being developed, there were two schools of thought. One saw the prophet's political succes-sor, the Caliph and his associates, as the natural ones to lead in prayer and stand before the believers for recitation of the Qur'an, or the delivery of a sermon based on it. Later, they were the ones who appointed those learned in the Qur'an and the law to perform these functions (the Sunni, majority tradition). The largest minority school (Shi'a), however, saw the hereditary heirs of Mohammed to be the authentic line of political and clerical responsibility. When the leading heir was killed in a civil war over the matter, a prac-tice of honorific positions for learned legal scholars who were also religious leaders was developed, and these would sometimes also exercise political and religious leadership, as the Ayatollah tradi-tion exemplifies — on a temporary basis until a now-hidden heir of Mohammed would be revealed and restore the pattern of an authentic, integrated, universal Islamic leadership.[25]

The biblical tradition contains examples close to all of these models, but it did not settle on any one of them as normative. Indeed, it was only in Christianity that another kind of model was developed, one able to comprehend and put these other models into a new perspective. What Christianity shares with these traditions is that it knows that political, social and religious leadership are necessary.

The Question of Kings

There is little doubt that the reality of sin in social history means that every society needs a political system to order the potential chaos of human relationships and to bring about those mundane goods that no individual, family, clan, tribe or voluntary organization can, on its own, generate. Governments are necessary for wider human interaction and development — roads and bridges, security and defense, coinage and standard weights and measures, and the protection of those institutions and practices that foster personal and social development — families, schools, hospitals, businesses, science, technology, the arts and, above all, religion. While many of the nations or city-states of the ancient world known by Israel had emperors or kings, those who rose to power tended to exploit the people and subjugate their neighbors. They did not see themselves under a law or an authority beyond their control. But under the influence of the biblical prophets and priests, they began to see that the distinctive responsibility of political rulership is to establish and maintain a monopoly on coercive violence, symbolized in ancient lore by "Mars," so that the institutions of society and its members could flourish in at least relative peace. But because of the memory of subjection to Pharaoh, there was a suspicion of too much power in too few hands.

Still, the absence of an integrated political authority had its own perils. There was conflict with neighboring tribes and the Philistines with the religion of each people providing the legitimating model for the organization of society. Conflicts over land, the decisive means

25. See Kenneth Cragg, *The Call of the Minaret*, 2nd revised and enlarged ed. (Maryknoll, NY: Orbis, 1985); John Obert Voll, *Islam: Continuity and Change* (Boulder, CO: Westview Press, 1982); and John Esposito, *Islam: The Straight Path*, expanded ed. (New York: Oxford University Press, 1991.)

of production, were also intense, and we read the lament in the book of Judges: "In those days there was no king in Israel; everyone did what was right in his own eyes." It was not long before the prophet Samuel was inspired to anoint a king, a command he resisted at first "Lest we become like the nations of the world."

We can see several matters of universal significance in this sequence of events. For one thing, we can see a perennial tension between the need for people and institutions called to special responsibilities and given the authority to use coercive force to suppress evil and facilitate good for the people, and the fact that those in the seats of power are also tempted to use their position to serve themselves, their families, clans and retainers — who themselves take advantage of the people. The people, meanwhile, are grateful for those who protect them from criminals within and from invaders without, but they are usually simultaneously suspicious of their power. They could all too easily make biased decisions that give further advantage to the privileged, ignore the needs of the disadvantaged and award monopoly power to a handful of cronies. This tension is present in every known civilization, and if the Christian understanding of the Fall is correct, no power elite will ever be entirely exempt from these temptations. This is true even if they seek to cultivate the highest virtues of the elders' wisdom, as do tribal and Confucian ideals, if they surround the central authority with pious ascetics, as do Hindu and Buddhist traditions, if they make religious law the official law of the society, as Islamic and fundamentalist Jews and Christians have tried to do, or if they seek to establish the sovereignty of the "will the people" as a folk ("national socialism") or as a class ("proletarian socialism").

In the biblical case, that tendency is mitigated by the fact that the kings are understood to be under the judgment of divine law, signaled by the fact that they are anointed and publicly assessed by the prophets and are guided in their piety and understanding of the cosmos by the priests. That is to say, we see the providential care for political authority within the moral limits of law and justice as discerned by the prophets and the religious limits as established by the priestly leaders who cultivate social practices that are largely independent of the king. Of course, politicians can appoint court prophets and subservient priests who will legitimate anything royalty desires. But these are, sooner or later, known to be false prophets and faithless priests. If there is a sufficient pluralism built into the social fabric by the interplay of these three offices, true prophets can courageously announce judgments against a corrupt king according to the standards of the divine law, and faithful priests can nurture wise rulers who will not dishonor the covenantal tradition. This implies, of course, an early existence of a civil society distinct from the institutions of political society.[26]

True prophets, faithful priests and wise rulers can all be recognized socially by the fact that they will both represent the truth, justice and mercy of God in all they do, and foster the independent development of those spheres of the common life that sustain humane existence in the presence of sin and corruption. The most significant social lesson that we can draw from these developments is that in them, we see the deepest roots of a principled and pluralist society. The most significant theological lesson is that we can understand what is at stake when Jesus Christ is recognized as the Prophet, the Priest, and the King who brings us to the most basic and universal renewal of the covenant, one that is able to include the wisdom of the world, to inaugurate a new era of hope in the human future, and to point all who get the message toward a mission to the whole world.

A Note on Wisdom

There is, however, one other role that needs to be mentioned, that of the scholar or sage who collects, cultivates or generates wisdom — sometimes a prophet, a priest or a king, but sometimes independent of these. They were not anointed, but they played an honored role as poet, psalmist, narrator, redactor, teacher or scribe. Such a wise man or woman could be an interpreter of dreams, or one who is able to heal the sick or serve as an advisor to the anointed ones. A sage could also be, in some understandings, a magician, sorcerer, diviner or astrologer. But these were often discredited if they confronted a true prophet or a faithful priest who had little trust in displays of wondrous lore. Besides, they could also be surpassed by certain wise

---

26. I have argued this point in *Public Theology and Political Economy* (Grand Rapids: Eerdmans, 1991) on the basis of comparative and historical data, but have not connected it to the classical doctrine of vocation in the biblical record until now. This connection is one of the reasons for my interest in Dutch Neo-Calvinism. See Jonathan Chaplin, "Civil Society and the State: A Neo-Calvinist Perspective" (Toronto: Institute for Christian Studies, 2004).

kings, such as Solomon, who is reputed to have rendered justice in difficult cases, to have known much about plants and animals, and to have composed proverbs.

The "wisdom literature" of the scriptures has examples of all these possibilities, and it is widely believed by many specialists that some of the sources of, or stimulus for, these materials as we have them in the biblical record were from outside the community of faith itself. To be sure, it appears that these have been edited so that they comport well with the insights of the mythic and legendary resources as well as with the historical, legal, prophetic and priestly materials and Deuteronomic narratives; but what is amazing to many is the fact is that they can be edited to fit so easily. The recorders and transmitters of the sacred scriptures evidently believed that it was both possible, prudent and perhaps indispensable to God's providence that believers in God should also learn from nonbelievers, especially from the sages of other cultural, religious and literary traditions. Such insight not only strengthens the case for the importance of a developed sense of common grace, it makes incumbent on Christians who today encounter multiple faith traditions to be open to the possibilities that they have something to teach us, and that we can include some of their insights in our own development of doctrine and worldview.

Moreover, it suggests that the wisdom of the world's religions and cultures can be taken as authentic background, along with the culturally embedded covenantal traditions with their sense of universal moral law, and along with the insights of inspired prophets, faithful priests and wise kings of all traditions who facilitate the development of an open, pluralistic civil society. Indeed, while it may be possible for people to come to know Christ by direct converting experience or the inspiration of the Holy Spirit, it is unlikely that a personal experience of that sort can alone grasp the meaning of God's providential care with regard to globalization without being drawn into familiarity with the wider expressions of God's grace. In fact, it is only in the wake of these developments that a Messiah who is the fulfillment of these and who can transform the world is expected in history.

The Covenant and Offices Renewed

These ancient themes are adopted, adapted, developed and refined in the New Testament written in the context of a Hellenized culture, the Roman Empire and trade routes that reached from China to Spain, and from Africa to Scotland. What was once provincial and tribal became cosmopolitan, catholic and ecumenical as well as evangelical. Most importantly, Jesus was seen as the Messiah, the Christ, the anointed one — the one who was not only the Son of God and the redeeming *goel,* but the New Adam, the symbol of a new universal humanity, the renewer of the Covenant, now with an eschatological thrust, the Son of God who finally fulfilled the offices of the previous biblical record.

We can see the beginnings of this precisely in the beginning of the Gospels. The Gospel of Matthew begins with a reference to King David and presents a genealogy that leads to his legal father, Joseph. This establishes his identity as the son of David, and displaces Abraham as the primary source of identity. Indeed, a few verses later, we read that God can raise up sons of Abraham out of stones. This is a king who will not be confined to any people or nation, a king for all peoples, a King who, like Josiah, could renew the covenant and its ancient law, and would in the end commission all who get the point to go to all the world with the message of discipleship.

However, the Gospel of Mark, by contrast, begins with a reference to the prophecy of Isaiah about a messenger who shall prepare a new way. Later, Mark identifies John the Baptist as the great preacher of repentance and forgiveness and the last and greatest prophet until prophecy is fulfilled in Jesus — as the expected one who is possessed by the Holy Spirit so that he can resist temptation, gather followers and heal those possessed by disabling powers. This Gospel basically ends with the empty tomb: the powers of death and destruction are, in principle, defeated. It is a message of good news for the whole creation.

In addition, the Gospel of Luke, in still greater contrast, begins his reference to Jesus by recounting the story of a priest, Zechariah and his family. He was serving in the temple when a vision came upon him about his people's future. He was so affected that he fell silent. The routines of that priesthood had nothing to say any more, and after his term of service, he went to his home to await the birth of his son, the cousin of Jesus. When that happens, this priest receives the gift of the Holy Spirit, and is able to celebrate again, in a new way, the traditions of Israel, for he realizes that the knowledge of salvation and the forgiveness of their sins is granted to them. This Gospel ends with a reference to the law of Moses and psalms of worship, a command to stay in the city, Christ's ascension, and a return to the temple, blessing God (although according the Luke's second book, the Acts, the church is formed and replaces the temple as the center of worship).

There is still one more Gospel. John begins with the stunning announcement about the first grace, the grace of creation. "In the beginning," he starts out, "was the Word," the *Logos*, the ontological order of all reasonable discourse, the ordering power of will, the manifestation of a loving bond. All things were made by and according to this Word, and in it is life and light. This is not the folk-wisdom of the elders or the magical formulas of the wonder-worker, nor the philosophical-ethical wisdom of Confucius, nor the enlightenment for which the Hindu *sadhu* or the Buddhist *bhikku* quests, nor the insight found in the words Mohammed was inspired to recite, for this Word became flesh. It entered into the very fabric of human existence, and dwelt among humankind. This light enlightens everyone. On this basis, it becomes possible for those from all over the earth to understand the promises of God, each in their own tongue. This Word overcomes the effects of Babel and it forms a new kind of community, centered around the church, that is both a new kind of institution in civilization and a visible sign of the growing Reign of God among the peoples of the earth drawn, as Abraham had once been, into the flows of history. Here, in short, is the basis for a reconceptualization of Wisdom, one that lays a new groundwork for the new vision of prophecy, priesthood, kingship and, indeed, for covenant renewal. This Gospel ends with the assertion that there is much more than what has been reported. More can be discovered and written. Revelation and the development of doctrine is not a closed matter.

Most importantly, Jesus was recognized as the Messiah, the one who can reestablish a humanity made whole. In this global context, expectations have been, are, can be, should be transformed. The fulfillment of the promise of the offices of the previous biblical record has begun; it will reach to all peoples through direct and indirect channels. Jesus becomes not only the one foretold by the prophets, he is the truth that is prophesied. Jesus is not only the priest who offers a sacrifice to atone for the sins of the people and instructs them in true religion, he is the sacrifice and the instruction. Jesus is not only the king who has a kingdom not of this world, he is the Prince of Peace on earth with a message that can rule the world.

It is in this context that the understanding of "vocation" took on new meanings. For many centuries, it meant a calling to one or another form of Christian ministry — apostles, teachers, deacons, preachers, evangelists, etc. Gradually, as these offices in the church took on more formal structure, it came to mean a calling to "the religious life," that is, to one or another of the monastic orders or, later, to the secular priesthood. This had two providential consequences in society. On the one hand, it firmed up the formation of the church as an institution distinct from family (and thus from the tendency to identify religion with a family's extended forms — clan, tribe, or nation), and from the dominant social classes that controlled the political-economic institutions of the day (and thus from a tendency to identify religion with those who controlled the city-state, empire or feudal estates). On the other hand the sense of a vocation demanded a response — a "profession" both of faith and to an occupation that was held to be God-related, God-selected and God-blessed. Here is the womb of the development of the professions that eventually became highly developed in the West and the drivers of globalization — the professor, the jurist, the doctor, the engineer, the manager, the scientist and the exemplary statesman.[27]

In contemporary life, these specialists have largely lost their rootage in a sense of God's creation, providence, or in the theological linkage of vocation and profession. Thus, as Burton Bledstein argued some time ago, a "culture of professionalism" has developed in the West generally and in American academia particularly that has abandoned any sense of theological grounding.[28] Those who understand the long range perils of these developments and are willing to engage the issues of a creational understanding of

---

27. These are the topics covered in volume 2 of this series: *The Spirit and Modern Authorities*. See the essays by Richard Osmer, John Witte, Allen Verhey, Ronald Cole-Turner, Jürgen Moltmann and Peter Paris.

28. B. J. Bledstein, *The Culture of Professionalism: The Middle Class and the Development of Higher Education in America* (New York: W. W. Norton, 1978). Although residual effects of the deeper history can clearly be found in many of today's widely expanded professional organizations and academies, the loss or neglect of any overt spiritual and moral grounding for what today's professionals do so very well is increasingly lamented. See, e.g., William F. May, *Beleaguered Rulers* (Louisville: Westminster John Knox Press, 2001); Thomas L. Shaffer, *Faith and the Professions* (Provo, UT: Brigham Young University Press, 1987); Warren Nord, *Religion and American Education* (Chapel Hill: University of North Carolina Press, 1998); Joseph Allegretti, *The Lawyer's Calling* (New York: Paulist Press, 1996); James T. Burtchaell, *The Dying of the Light* (Grand Rapids: Eerdmans, 1998); and Nicholas Wolterstorff, *Educating for Life* (Grand Rapids: Baker Books, 2002).

human nature and the bio-physical universe, and of the providential understanding of covenant and vocation, will have much to offer a globalizing world. They will be, in all their roles in life, Christ-like, in the sense that they will be professionally given to prophetic justice in the society, priestly ministries to their neighbors, and princely ambassadors of wise policies for the world's true king, forming covenantal relationships in every institution that they can touch. Since Christ inaugurated the Kingdom of God on earth, the prophetic, royal priests who are laity will be God's agents in a history that is on the path to a redeemed humanity. Until that redemption is complete, the common grace of creation and the sustaining grace of providence will guide us; but we are also caught up in a greater grace that is developing even now and promising a fulfillment to come. There is, in the midst of sin, the space for and warrant of hope — a mark of which will be the globalization of such values.

– *Chapter 5* –

THE THIRD GRACE

SALVATION

Grace Enfleshed

I have argued in the previous chapters that the biblical record provides many resources for a public theology able to grasp and guide
our thinking and action in regard to contemporary globalization.
It offers an interpretation, in mythic form, of the basic character
of being and existence, one that points to the most comprehensive
worldview available of how and why things generally are in the cosmos. Christians can claim, with confidence, that the bio-physical
universe is a gift to humanity, which is a spiritually connected
species created by God through a process that includes evolution.
The theology of this tradition can both accept the findings of the
natural sciences and have regard for humanity as a blessed creature
with a conferred dignity. At the same time, it holds that neither naturalism nor humanism can be seen as offering the best account of
being, existence or historical development, or taken as the ultimate
point of reference socially or ethically. Although those who take
nature or humanity as ultimately normative see in part, they blind
themselves to the possibility of seeing the whole. We therefore can
grasp the significance of the public debates about the role of religion in public discourse and education and why theologically aware
people continue to resist anti-religious scientism and humanism as
well as anti-scientific creationism, and to hold that the main points
of this protology are valid. All that is can best be interpreted in a
context that includes consideration of a transcendent reality.

Moreover, Christians hold that the dignity that we humans have
derives from the fact that we are created in the image and according
to the likeness of God, and by that common grace, we have certain

capabilities that make it possible to assume the duties of the stewardly management of malleable nature. We are designed neither to simply fit into nature nor to exploit it for our own short-term benefit. Our perennial failures to properly use these gifts or respond to these duties, and the repeated tendency to declare independence from their source, mean both that the powers of malleable nature are not developed in their most fruitful directions and that a positive distortion of the malleable aspects of nature and of those capabilities compound evil. This is the true insight, articulated in a poetic myth: what we are, what we have, and what the powers of life are with which we have to deal are both good and evil — flawed and subject to deeper distortion. Therefore humanity is plunged into the crises of historical life, with its promise and perils, from which there is no retreat.

In history, institutions to constrain and guide the principalities, authorities, regencies and dominions of social life are constructed as means to cope with the "powers" of a "fallen" world. They involve the formation of differentiated spheres of life to make viable societies, simple or complex. These too are basically good, for they channel the energies of the powers and constrain their tendencies to evil. If we did not have them we would have to make them anew. However, they can also be distorted and prompt occasions of devastation and fragmentation, symbolized by the biblical legends of the Flood and Babel, the destructive power of nature and the fracturing power of self-idolatrous human creativity. Still, nature and humanity are preserved from utter destruction by God's grace and are given new possibilities precisely as we are inspired to construct, reform, or bring moral integrity into these spheres of life. Over time, they can become more complex, differentiated and universal. These possibilities are present in dramatic ways in the dynamics of contemporary globalization. These dynamics have been legitimated and accelerated by the historic impact of Christian theological ideas that have been plowed into social history and are now reaching around the world. The paradigmatic patterns of life, discerned profoundly in all their glories and tragedies by the biblical authors, are therefore indicative of what we are facing today, and what we will face in ever new historic forms in the future.

However, the contemporary theologians or church leaders and even fewer social scientists who study the structures and dynamics of life today seldom grasp the religious depths of what is at stake. They tends to read the social sciences as simply facts without spiritual or moral meaning, or as anti-religious and anti-theological ideology.[1] So also most of the social scientists read religion and theology as constitutionally anti-intellectual and anti-scientific.[2] Religious statements thus tend to be thin on data and drift toward Gnosticism, while social science tends to be thin on interpretive depth and falls into a new "flat earth" syndrome with little height or depth.

When such matters are engaged theologically, as does the biblical record in symbolic terms, we can discern the providential grace of covenant, moral law and the offices of prophecy, priesthood and political responsibility, guided by wisdom in the very fabric of history even with all its tragedies. Humanity has, in the midst of historic perils, been prompted to form organizations that sustain life and to shape their interaction in ways that constitute dynamic societies. Such societies are what functionally preserves life from the chaos and terror that the scriptures associate with demonic forces — the powers of life gone wrong, tempting others to further distortion. As we have seen all too often, the breakdown or destruction of a society unleashes these powers. Indeed, due to the denial of, resistance to or betrayal of the gifts of creational and providential grace, people find themselves in thrall and want even in many of these almost functioning societies. The principal powers of human interaction — Eros, Mammon, Mars, the Muses and Religion, plus those of the modern professional authorities and the model "lords" of the great world religions — declare their autonomy from the world's Creator and from the grace of providence. They have the potential to become a threat to the wider, longer, deeper, higher view of human history's guiding principles and purposes and to the limits of cosmic and moral boundaries. New forms of destructive influence show up socially in a variety of ways — not only in racism, classism, sexism, nationalism, militarism and imperialism, as are today widely discussed, but in learning without wisdom, legalism without justice, technical acumen without ontological respect, medical care without

---

1. The most influential of these is John Milbank, *Theology and Social Theory: Beyond Secular Reason* (Oxford: Blackwell Publishers, 1990).
2. Burton Bledstein traces the relative triumph of these attitudes in parts of the modern university in his *The Culture of Professionalism* (New York: W. W. Norton, 1976), a development which led to the alliances of some religious voices with anti-modernist and postmodern philosophies.

compassion, and ideologies of domination that serve as substitute religions. Anyone of these can lurch between an individualism with little sense of the common good and a collectivism that swallows persons into herds in the name of a common good. Even the various academic fields, as they cultivate excellence for their own tasks, tend to turn in on themselves and worship their own reductionist perception of the human condition. A temporary methodological reductionism may be necessary in some phases of research but it is fatal when taken as a worldview. Everything is reduced either to psychology, or economics, or politics, or cultural construction, or physics, etc., in the face of which distorted theologies try to generate simplified worldviews — Fundamentalism and Liberationism, for instance, in our day.

The human incapacity to overcome such multiple manifestations of temptation and arrogance without divine assistance becomes the occasion for God to offer human covenants marked by moral law and divine purposes, and to call leaders to special offices for the guidance of the people. Most of all, however, it led to a hope for a savior who could both restore the fallen fabric of creational grace, preserve the sustaining power of providential grace, constrain and channel the residual and constructed powers of chaos and destruction and thus begin a new era that points proximately to a more just, loving and merciful reign of God in history, and ultimately toward a new civilization with a new heaven and new earth. That development invites us to consider the third grace, Salvation, given according to the biblical record in Jesus Christ, God in fully human form. In Christian theological perspective, this is testified to in scripture, rightly interpreted by the power of the Holy Spirit, seen socially in the formation of the church and emerging in every sphere of society as signs of the coming Kingdom of God.

Saving Grace

In this regard, the theological tradition speaks of the special grace manifest in the birth, life, ministry, death and resurrection of Jesus Christ. The dynamics that have flowed from these historic events have, in spite of resistance from beyond Christianity, reactions from within and many detours and set-backs, moved much of social life toward a less patriarchal family structure, a postimperial political order, a constitutional fabric of law that defends religious freedom and human rights, an open economy that is productive in a way that brings affluence to more and more of the world's population and a culture that allows great creativity and diversity. These familial, political, economic and cultural developments are among the dynamics that have generated modernity and fostered globalization, although they have done so only ambiguously. These spheres have been further modulated as Christianity also accepted and enhanced the idea of vocation and thus the development of new authorities in more complex societies. This spurred the formation of the modern professions and the cultivation of new relationships to the biophysical universe and to moral universals. While the development of these authorities has promoted further specialization in society by differentiation, it has also given rise to more interdependence and the generation of new and wider areas service, such as education, law, medicine and engineering. It is true, to be sure, that each of these areas has sometimes become so self-celebrative that they have fractured the sense serving the common good, they have been partially constrained by the fact of their interdependence. Yet, their self-centered temptations to worship their own field of values will continue to plague humanity until the promise of salvation is brought to fulfillment.

Many relationships, practices and policies do not honor God or the image of God in humanity, do not use technology in a way fulfills the cultural mandate to take stewardly care of the environment, do not develop covenantal relations instead of exploitative ones, and do not seek to infuse all of the spheres of social life with moral and spiritual vitality. Instead they draw on these graced forms of spiritual, ethical and social capital for personal or group advantage without replenishing their spiritual and moral content. Globalization, theologically seen, may be faith-based and grace-full, but its very openness can allow opportunities to deplete its own best resources and it repeatedly reveals that, on its own, it does not and cannot finally overcome sin and death. The very best principalities and authorities of the emerging global civil society need salvation.

Christians await the fulfillment of that promise with open anticipation. But the waiting is not passive. Because it has already begun in the Kingdom of God, inaugurated by Jesus Christ, it is possible to cultivate an engaged personal faith and the ethical arrangement of the institutions of the increasingly common life to contain the evils and enhance the goods of life. Serious improvement is possible within the limits of history. The cultivation of personal faith, in Christianity, is based above all in the theological doctrine that in Christ's birth and ministry, God became present to human life, and that in his crucifixion and resurrection, sin and death are in principle defeated. It is not that there is no more sin or death; these are obviously real; but when Christ took on himself the sins of the world on the cross, the debilitating power of sin and of the fear of death to ultimately rule our lives was defeated. The power of sin continues, of course, and it effects our reason, our will and our affections; but it no longer so distorts their ability to function for the right and the good that we must spend all the resources of the grace of Providence constraining wrong and evil. Empowered by a dominion beyond our own capacities, we can become agents of the right and of the good. Sinfulness can be acknowledged with honesty and with the assurance that forgiveness, reconstruction, and replenishment is possible. The divine reality that knows all the pain and suffering of human experience can overcome the human incapacity to cure what ails us by our own efforts.[3] Moreover, according to the doctrine of resurrection, the nihilistic threat of death, of entropy, of total nonbeing and of meaninglessness as the inevitable human destiny is defeated. Life has the possibility of a fulfillment that stands beyond the emptiness of nonexistence, precisely in the face of the reality of death. In these two doctrines, Christianity differs from the other two most compelling world religions, Islam and Buddhism. Both hold that one can earn salvation; one by gaining a perfect if primal physical state of existence, the other by gaining a purified consciousness beyond any physical or social existence.[4]

---

3. I am indebted in this area to two former students and a former colleague. Stephen Healey, now a professor of comparative religions at Bridgeport University, has gently chided me for not previously clearly stating my view of the doctrine of atonement; and Richard Floyd, one of the leading "pastor-theologians" of the United Church of Christ, has written the important little volume, *When I Survey the Wondrous Cross* (San Jose, CA: Pickwick Press, 2000). The latter is introduced by a former colleague, Gabriel Fackre, who has been more influential in my theological reflections than he realizes.

4. One of the debates between Christianity and Islam is precisely on the nature of Christ and of his work in salvation. These matters are debated in highly symbolic terms, but they have to do with the vision of the ultimate future toward which these religions tend to take as the ultimate goal of existence. Islam views Jesus as a prophet, but not in any sense a savior; with the Christian attitude toward Islam being suspect of the presumption that humans by following Islam or, especially, by becoming martyrs can earn a salvation that returns them to a garden of innocence. And in

In the perspective of dominant Christian views, all human history, so far as we can trace it, reveals that the basic spheres of life have been ordered into a variety of relatively stable cultures centered in and spiritually guided by the various religions of the world. What is distinctive about the movement toward modern societies is that the cultures fed by the special grace of Christ have come to see that these spheres can be multiplied and, in one sense, sanctified. The Church as the "body of Christ" on earth after the resurrection, is a paradigmatic new organization. In fact, the predominant idea is that it is a divinely initiated opportunity to participate in embodied communities of conviction and spiritual nurture. Further, we can constantly reform it and the various spheres of life surrounding it by repeated "social formations" of other new dynamic spheres of life. This is a distinctive feature of Christian-influenced societies, especially those deriving from the Catholic orders, the Reformation denominations and the missionary movements of Christianity, in contrast to both primal and feudal religions which tend to protect old patterns of life from the "incursions" of new institutions. This feature has invited various kinds of specialization of function and opened the doors to more and more complex occupations and callings that, on the one hand, increase the material well-being of the people. On the other hand, this feature also demands the development of more highly differentiated personality structures that require persons to be able to interact in more complex social settings — a demand that can tear people apart if they do not have a spiritual center of loyalty and identity.

For those who allow themselves (and are graced) to be drawn into these forms of social creativity, life and its meanings tend to improve. For those who deny the process (or are unable to recognize grace), life and its meanings tend to get stuck in a static impoverishment.[5] Their traditional culture can no longer be a whole in itself;

---

its debates with Buddhism, Christianity does not view the ultimate salvific state of existence as one of the "no-thing-ness" or the bliss of pure consciousness achieved individually as discussed under the doctrine of Nirvana, with the total disappearance of material reality, but as a recognition of the reality of death and a reconstitution in and of a new city that includes and comprehends creation, as we shall see later. Whatever else we can learn from these traditions and however much we can respect believers in them, Christians see these eschatological views as unrealistic.

5. I have treated these themes in *Capitalism, Civil Society, Religion and the Poor*, written with Lawrence Stratton (Wilmington, DE: ISI Press, 2002); and "Protestantism and Poverty," *Insights* 121, no. 2 (Spring 2006): 15–40.

and if it does not become a part of the larger whole, marginality, deprivation, anomie and hopelessness are the consequences. Indeed, a nontransformed, continued unrevised trust in the old securities and sense of identity self-victimizes the community, accelerates cultural decay and further disempowers the people by preventing the cultivation of differentiated yet integral personalities. Nor are they aided by the romanticized idealization of their traditional virtues by contemporary alienated intellectuals from complex, developed societies who want to protect them from globalization or use them as a force for resistance to it. In either case their culture is redefined by the global developments — in the negative. The dominant sense of a common good of the past is simply not common enough or good enough to be a model for the global future or even to sustain them as they will inevitably have to encounter and adapt to a global society. It is not, in the theological sense intended here, sanctifying. It is in this respect that Christ and the Church become access points to cosmopolitan identity and new society organizations that also provide the moral and spiritual criteria for preserving parts of the past and resisting total capitulation to the dominant culture.

This view implies that a traditional cultural heritage is not entirely to be abandoned; but that it will have to be selectively adapted and revised so that it can keep distinctive qualities that are of interest or aid to the larger society, reconstructed so that the peoples of the world can integrate into the global dynamics, and not live in perpetual alienation. This usually happens by allowing the deepest and most valid religious values driving global dynamics to synthesize and transform the culture, and by turning to deepest principles of the faith against domineering or debilitating external pressures. To do that, we need nothing more than a revitalization of a world missionary movement, one that joins a converting "evangelism" to a reforming "social gospel."

New Directions in Missions[6]

Christianity is a missionary religion. It holds, like the healer, the prophet, the movement organizer and the revolutionary, that a basic change is needed. It comes partly by the unintended transformations

---

6. I am indebted to the United Theological College of Bangalore, India, to the Center of Theological Inquiry of Princeton, NJ, and to the colleagues from East and

that attend inspired alterations of the mind, will, and heart, partly by human response to them, and partly by the consequent reorganization of the "powers" that, over time, reorder the habits of mind, the resolve of the will, the expressions of affections and thus spiritually sustain the dynamic reordering of the common life and its culture. The objective is always the same: conversion — a deeply controversial idea in those contexts where it is believed that all religions and cultures are sovereign and equal, and in other contexts where it is suspected that missions are usually imperialistically imposed. But both the motivations and the results of the changes are related to the very complex processes of the conversion of persons, the planting of new kinds of institutions, the encounter, clash or fusion of worldviews and views of the human condition, the ethical reformation of the psycho-spiritual "powers" that grasp the loyalties of the soul, the struggles for truth and justice, and the consequent formation of a conviction-based ethos that is ever the core of a civil society or a civilization. True conversion may only be accomplished by divine intervention, as accepted by the new believer; but those who see themselves as proximate agents of that divine reality usually sense that they are commissioned to draw attention to the need for, possibility of and benefits of such a change.

Such changes are spoken of, in biblical Hebrew, as *gūr* ("to draw near to God") close to the sense of what the Greeks called either *epistrephō* ("to return or turn back from a perilous direction") or a *metanoia* ("a change of 'mentality'") on the part of a *prosēlytos* ("one who has come to a new place"). All of these were usually translated into the Latin as *conversio* ("a turning over," a pondering or examination to get a better grasp of the meaning of things). They all imply a coming to a changed state of existence that is "salvific," prevents continuing in a dead-ended direction. The English word "convert" is dependent on these previous terms and thus may imply an approach to something anticipated, a recovery of something left

South Asia, Europe and the USA, who worked with me and Lalsangkima Pachuau on the writing and coordination of some twenty-four substantive, inter-religious and cross-cultural essays, *News of Boundless Riches: Interrogating Missions in a Globalizing World* (New Delhi: ISPCK Press, forthcoming). I am also indebted to Kang Phee Seng of Hong Kong Baptist University, and the other contributors, who is now editing the essays on *Religious Values and the Public Forum*, based on the 2006 Conference he organized. The forthcoming book will take up some parallel issues with regard to East Asia.

behind, a change of mind, or a turn to something new, and various missions may seek any or all of these.

The whole idea of conversion is usually thought of as a highly individual phenomenon, although multiple agents are usually involved. And, indeed, there is no substitute for the conversion of persons. No one is a born Christian; a new identity and social matrix is necessary. Neither will any religion or transformational social project get rooted or thrive without convicted persons. Even those religions or social movements that resist the notion of "proselytism" also observe rituals of transition or initiation. They may speak of the "twice born," thereby reflecting an awareness of experiences that are believed to alter the consciousness, identity and behavior, and thus the life-orientation of the individual. Conversion to a new basic life-orientation and a new, dynamic social fabric is thus always a controversial matter, but is probably unavoidable in human history. Indeed, Christianity holds that it is necessary, for no life-orientation or social fabric has yet been revealed, discovered or invented that has also been so intrinsically present or so widely shared that it satisfies or fulfills persons permanently without transformation. Even Christ sought baptism, was tempted in the desert and agonized over his destiny before his arrest.

Moreover, we cannot number the variety of felt needs and sociopsychological promptings that bring persons to accept a new faith, or even to renew a commitment to the one in which the person is nurtured, for the combination of promptings is experienced as particular and unique by each person. Still, it is not infrequent that a new or renewed believer confesses that a gift, an insight, a new perspective has been received — one that is more intellectually coherent, more ethically compelling, more emotionally satisfying and more socially just and advantageous than what was known before. To grasp the prospects for mission in pluralistic, globalizing societies, it is important to attempt to understand how change takes place in human historical existence. The key reference points in understanding this change are Christ and his Church. They lead us toward a constructive view of missions today.[7]

---

7. For historical examples of these dynamics in the West, see Rodney Stark, *The Rise of Christianity* (Princeton, NJ: Princeton University Press, 1996). For an analysis of cross-religious dynamics, see my "Missions/Missionary Activity," *Encyclopedia of Religion*, ed. Mircea Eliade et al. (New York: Macmillan, 1986), 9:563–70; revised edition forthcoming, 2007.

It could very well be the case that the capacity for conversion and the inclination to undertake a mission is one of the most distinctive marks of what it means to be human. We may be, as creatures, largely driven by the interaction of our genetic makeup, our medical history, and the social groups into which we are born, as these interact with the environmental options, ecological and cultural, to which we are exposed. And we may have instincts to act in particular ways and can be trained to respond to certain stimuli. In this, we are little different than the beasts of the earth. Moreover, we are each like humans in general in being gifted with the capabilities of reason, will and affection. But in conversion, persons are inspired to step beyond the confines of these factors of existence. People discover a new objective spiritual reality to which they become related. They find that genetics is not destiny, that healing can take place, that those previously viewed as "others" become brothers and sisters, that accepted conventional beliefs and actions suddenly seem empty or futile or that exposure to something new offers a new reason for living. When any of these happen, many find a new ability to become agents in their own lives beyond instinct, habituated responses, and common capabilities, and they find a deepened, widened implications in the capacity for thought, for will, for love. Together these bring a dramatic sense of discipline, freedom and a radiance that is in, behind, and beyond the mere factuality of the world — and they find it even in the lingering midst of tragedy, alienation, oppression, and ugliness.

However, it is also true that persons are almost never converted in isolation. Not only is it the usual case that some persons (the missionary, the reformer, etc.) discuss, preach, teach or write something that attracts the mind, will, or affections of another, but the one attracted is often linked by a thousand bonds to others. Some persons who are drawn to convert by these means are often "representative persons" — the head of a village, clan, caste, or a ruler, or even a gifted youth, a spouse, a friend, or a "bad actor" who becomes a "transformed person." They become the agents who lead other members of the family or group into the new ways of thinking and living. When such a leader of a traditional society is converted, often the entire community whose identity these persons represent also is converted. The reasons for their conversion may well be that they are exposed to a better "metaphysical-moral vision" of reality than the one they knew, or a personal experience of a salvific presence. It may also be a quite practical matter: they discover a higher standard of justice than the one in operation, they find themselves healed of some physical, moral, or social disability, or they sense an option for a better life for the people for whom they are responsible. After a communal or mass conversion, other individual persons in the group are gradually converted in the more personal sense. Through nurture, habit, practice, catechesis and socialization individuals are initiated into the faith, usually bringing much of their cultural background, previous communal beliefs and social practices with them. More often than not, they tend to interpret the new faith in the old terms — and to reinterpret the old traditions in new terms. In short, they tend to "baptize," in a way that modulates, many of the existing patterns of life and their presuppositions, thereby generating a fresh synthesis of new faith and old ways. This synthesis must be tested and revised over the years, with the old selectively approved and the new given a fresh inculturated expression, even if the new religion is, in principle, "exclusionary."

When persons are converted, it often involves a decline in exclusive loyalty to their "home" tradition and a turn to a "trans-local" metaphysical-moral and social frame of reference. A generation ago, Robin Horton identified a difference between a "microcosmic" frame of reference — one focused on the spirits of a people's ancestors, on a geographical territory, or on distinctive and visible natural phenomena (a volcano, a mountain, the forest, etc.) — and a "macrocosmic" one — one which has an account of the universe and the supreme divine power(s) that order the whole of existence, as do the great world religions. He argues that the primal religions are largely microcosmic but often have a thin macrocosmic dimension that is invigorated and redefined by contact with one or another of the world religions. The new framework provides a new range of possibilities for understanding and new reference points for one's personal and social self-identity.[8]

The inclination that leads to this kind of conversion may be triggered by a dramatic healing of some wound in their lives or because

---

8. R. Horton, "On the Rationality of Conversion, Part One" *Africa* 45, no. 1 (1975): 219–35; and "On the Rationality of Conversion, Part Two," *Africa* 45, no. 2 (1975): 373–79. I am grateful to Pangernungba Kechu, my student, for drawing these materials to my attention.

of a growing suspicion of or alienation from their previous society or its leaders — parental, religious, cultural, economic, or political — when they encounter a more complex civilization. Something in the way life is lived and legitimated simply does not make sense anymore, or does not provide for physical, economic, social or spiritual opportunity or well-being in the way that the alternative does. Integrity requires a shift, and an act of freedom — in fact, quite possibly the most important freedom possible to humans.

The consciousness that a decision can be made, that we humans can "become what we are not" (as Paul said), or cope with a major disruption in our accepted meaning system, or respond to an act of grace toward us that alters our relationship to others, entails an experience that is more formative of identity than most other life experiences.[9] No longer are we victims of the pre-given "powers," the "principalities, authorities, thrones, and dominions" of life. Personal conversion is a decisive opportunity by which humans may discover the possibility of transcendence over and thus the reorganization of the psycho-spiritual forces that have become embedded in the material, social and cultural patters that define most of life for most people most of the time. To deny this opportunity to others — or to force them to pretend to accept this change by a conquest that imposes a new religious order — is to deny the very humanity of the other. In conversion we and they can come to know a reality other than the given conditions of life in a way that allows us with them to transform the given conditions of existence.[10]

In the midst of and, even more, after a conversion, however, the individual ordinarily does not remain a free, isolated, and autonomous person. The new convert feels a duty to convert other individuals, and together they inevitably seek to found a new community or to reform the old one by generating a sect, a cell, a fellowship, an institution such as school, or as in the Christian case, as already emphasized, the church — a community of commitment

9. See Sebastian C. H. Kim, *In Search of Identity: Debates on Religious Conversion in India* (New Delhi: Oxford University Press, 2003). This is one of the most important new studies of the psychological and social implications of conversion and the context in which it occurs in recent years.

10. Some of these themes are identified in my "Deciding for God: The Right to Convert in Protestant Perspectives," written with the help of Deirdre Hainsworth, *Sharing the Book: Religious Perspectives on the Rights and Wrongs of Proselytism*, ed. John Witte Jr. and R. C. Martin (Maryknoll, NY: Orbis Books, 1999), 201–30.

that shares the new macrocosmic vision and becomes a part of a missiological movement. If this development does not happen, the experience quickly falls into the category of an odd psychic occurrence subject to psychiatric or sociopathic analysis, and may become the source of cultic tribal, class, or national idolatry. The high significance of the formation of a new identity in Christ and a distinct institution in the society is that a new social fabric is woven that reconstitutes civil society itself, incarnating the prospects of chosen communities of conviction — a voluntary association that opens the door to a more complex social and personality structure. The prospect appears that each person may be related to multiple kinds of institutions, now by choice, not by pre-given ascription. If the act of conversion may well be an exodus from the old station in life, the formation of a new kind of association, one that relates persons as brothers and sisters outside one's inherited community, we have identified the seed-bed of a reformation of the whole of society, the social incarnation of true pluralism and freedom with a new order of discipline. This is a second, a social conversion, often a manifestation of the grace that is unintended.

This should not mean that the past is to be utterly abandoned or repressed. People cannot avoid bringing their pasts with them, as mentioned earlier. That is part of what it means "to honor your father and mother." In all known cases, aspects of the previous understandings of life and its meaning, its patterns of relationship and its loyalty inevitably survive; but they are brought under standards and critical judgements that did not operate previously. In the new faith-based associations of life, all aspects of the society and culture, and their legitimating presuppositions, become subject to redefinition and reconstruction. New convenants and vocations and offices are constructed. The founding and formation of a new community not only reflects the conversion of persons, but the conversion of social relationships usually in one of three directions. One is to withdraw from the dominant society and to form an enclave of alternative piety and morality. We can call this the Qumran strategy, adopted in various ways in Christian history by monastic movements, communitarian sects, and sometimes by converted clans, tribes or castes who must defend themselves from persecution by a dominant religion or ideological politics. A second, which we may call the Philemon strategy, is to form an open and affirming

attitude to other people on religious grounds within the given institutions of society, and thus to accept the ethnic, linguistic, class,
gender-based, or caste subcultures as they are, leaving unchallenged
the dominant political and economic fabric as a part of one's national cultural identity, but promoting a parallel set of relationships
on other terms. These strategies do understand freedom by gaining
a liberated attitude, but they do not grasp the mandate to reform
society by new covenantal formation.

The third, which we can call the Kingdom approach, sees in the
principles and purposes of the newly adopted movement centered
in Christ the resources to move toward the reconstruction of the
whole society: political, economic, familial, cultural professional
and religious. This approach to the immanence of the Kingdom
(as expressed in the New Testament phrase, "The Kingdom of God
is within you," which is also properly translated "among you") entails the presumption that the power of God inaugurated by Christ
is in fact already at work within and among the persons and processes of social history, transforming them toward God's ends. Thus,
one of the tasks of converted people is to discern where, in the
midst of life, that power is at work, and to become agents of it
so far as possible. In this context, traditional identity and many
cultural patterns remain, for it is seen that God has also worked
through them; but they become much less determinative for life
and more of a background factor, with the recognition that they,
like all existing institutions, are subject to reformation. This direction is simultaneously culture affirming and culture transforming,
both on a selective basis.

Of course, there is a peril in each option. The new community
can become spiritually arrogant, a "saints' church" that recognizes
no integrity beyond itself. It denies the sovereignty of God except as
negative judgment over "the establishment." Or it can become a social club, full of fellowship within but structurally indistinguishable
from the surrounding class or racial or political subculture. It denies the persistence of original sin in institutional arrangements that
seem so natural, and it denies a need for repentance, rectification
and sanctification. Or it can become a militantly aggressive society
of reformers seeking to subject the world to its own view of life by
coercion and legal control — a temptation found in the Christian
"crusaders," in tribal war-lords, in Islamic *jihadis,* in Confucian

"legalists," in "Hindutva" nationalists, in Buddhist *ninjas,* and in militant secular revolutionaries.[11]

But for those who are converted to Christ, the marks are clear. They have a sense of calling, one which not only invites them to find those activities of life where they are, or can become, equipped to act professionally in the work they do, but which prompts them to become prophetic advocates of righteous law, priestly practitioners of caring ministries in leading worship and sacrificial service, and "princely" statesmanlike participants in the governance system of every institution with which they are associated in civil society. In these roles, they help form, reform or sustain many covenantal communities of commitment and see that they play a responsible and wise role in shaping the common good. That good is understood in terms of the proximate actualization of God's Kingdom in history, so far as that is possible, and in terms of the more ultimate vision that God, "with whom all things are possible," will bring a New Jerusalem in its redeemed, perfected state as a complex society, beyond history. That more ultimate view prevents utopian thinking and heaven-striving action in history, yet it allows us to get our view of the direction toward the common good right. Such a view recognizes that what is ultimately good and what is to be made truly common cannot be fully accomplished by us in history, but it can orient our lives toward a transcendental end.

Social Conversions

As we shall see, except at one point, the decisive pluralism of modern life is not a clash of cultures, nor an awareness of ethnic or sexual or class differences, although these are real enough as contemporary debates over multi-culturalism suggest. However, more important is a certain kind of pluralism in the organization of social institutions, and thus in the human personality, as these are

---

11. I am, in this matter, indebted to revisionist versions of the tradition of religiously shaped social theory that derives from the social theorist Max Weber, the social ethicist Ernst Troeltsch and the public theologian Abraham Kuyper. Troeltsch wrote of the "withdrawing" and the "aggressive" sects in Christianity in contrast to the "church-type" directions of Catholicism and the Reformation, while Weber saw parallels in other religions. And Kuyper saw similar patterns in political parties. These three, a "religiously unmusical" social scientist, a liberal Lutheran ethicist and a conservative Calvinist theologian, were all political and social activists who held that faith shapes ecclesiology and that shapes the social polity.

shaped by three key influences. We shall briefly glance at the first two before turning to the third. One is the debate among the world religions about the normative vision for the ordering of society as it reflects competing senses of eschatology as was discussed in Volume 3 (and to which we shall return). The second is a declared or functional atheism, which implies a freedom from any such considerations. Each unit in society — each person, institution, sphere of life, society or state — is able to pursue its own end with no necessary sense of a metaphysical, religious or ethical overarching vision of the common good. This can be seen as a chosen kind of spiritual and moral anarchy

Particularly decisive in the latter case is the sphere of politics which, for centuries, in many parts of the world, sought to use the instrument of an established religion to order, indeed to dominate, both the persons and the other institutions and spheres of life within a specific territory for its own purposes. Only a few of the great world religions self-consciously set forth normative alternatives. The reaction against the political domination of religion took place in those parts of Europe where religious movements, counter-intuitively, backed the attempt to desacralize the state, a development that has not taken place yet in many parts of the world. It did take place where churches (and later political parties) claimed the spirit of Christ or the example of Jesus to gain the right of free association and placed their loyalty to God above loyalty to the state or its rulers. This challenged both the idea of a Holy Roman Empire and the idea of the Divine Right of Kings.[12] Under the impact, however, of the French Revolution, the drive to desacralize the state became not only secular but atheist, which meant not only that the state was subject to society but that the society was no longer seen as subordinate to a more ultimate sense of truth and justice than its own will. Under these conditions, whoever could gain ideological dominance became the highest authority — as we see with regard to national chauvinism in the Napoleonic wars, in the racial ideologies of American slavery or German Fascism or in the class interests

---

12. This is one of the chief findings of two of my honored teachers, George Huntston Williams, *The Radical Reformation*, rev. ed. (Philadelphia: Westminster Press, 1982) and James Luther Adams. See D. B. Robertson, ed., *Voluntary Associations: A Study of Groups in Free Societies: Essays in Honor of James Luther Adams* (Richmond, VA: John Knox Press, 1966); and James Luther Adams, *Voluntary Associations*, ed. Ron Engle (Chicago: Exploration Press, 1986).

in mercantilist capitalism and Proletarian Socialism. None of these has proven to be morally, socially, politically or economically viable. Still, these developments not only perpetuated the avoidance of an inclusive concern for the common good by focusing on the good of only a part of humanity, they did this because they denied the transcendental reference that pointed to a divine concern for the whole of creation, world history and all humanity.

Any realistic analysis of the various institutions of the common life would reveal that none of these arrangements of the institutional spheres of life is capable of manifesting a concern for the common good. What is required is one formed into an interdependent system of systems wherein each seeks not only its own good, but seeks the good of the whole by subjecting itself to a transcendent law and purpose that it seeks to serve. This means recognizing that various efforts to seek the good of the whole may have other distinctive purposes that can best be actualized by forming a federated set of cooperative linkages with other institutional clusters. Thus, it helps to form a network of associated spheres subject to a common sense of justice, one that allows for the relative freedom of other spheres and institutions to cultivate their own good under God in accord with a complementary vision of the common good.

Certain strands of the Christian theological tradition have an account of these matters that Christians may affirm are decisive for the future. This is the third option which is based on the third influence, the salvific application of the doctrine of covenant, extending its creational and providential meanings. Those who hold this view also hold that our fallen nature inclines us to pursue a competitive advantage over other persons and groups. A cluster of institutions constituted by collective selfishness haunts every effort to cultivate the common good. But they also hold that, in spite of our human sinfulness, the residual effect of common grace is "written on our hearts" with its awareness that there are standards and purposes that stand over and before us all. Due to the character of God and, as argued in the last chapters, the fact that we humans can know, choose and adore that character since we have the residual presence of the image of God in each of us, in spite of sin, we can recognize the renewal of the covenant that not only preserves humanity, but points us toward salvation. Further evidence is due to the discernable presence of God's providence in social history, and by the presence of Christ in personal experience. These allow us to recognize that it is right and good to be called into covenanted communities of discipline, entrustment, excellence, and responsibility, and that in federated dialogue and debate about these standards and purposes, we can recognize a "higher law" able to order our various pursuits of various goods in ways that our own efforts could not accomplish.[13]

The implications of this evidence can be spelled out in some detail. As already suggested in previous chapters, one of the two Christian models is hierarchical. Formed by both natural law and divine will, its power is limited by subsidiarity and administered through sacrament to enhance the realization of the perfected society of heavenly, sanctified life. This view recognizes that most civilizations are highly stratified, and that the elite of every such society argues that it is necessary for the well-being of the people and the best approximation to holy living. Such was the dominant Orthodox and Catholic position for several centuries, with some parallels to the structure of Hindu and Confucian social ethics. However, it is possible to see this view as it took shape in the West under the influence of Catholicism as too Roman in character and not fully catholic in its potential reach, as Eastern Orthodox and the Reformation authors argued.

In spite of the fact that socially alert contemporary Protestant Christians recognize their continuities with the magnificent legacy of the Roman Catholic traditions, and particularly applaud the extended development of the doctrine of subsidiarity as a manifestation of divine law, Protestants tend to continue to argue for a federated "principled pluralism" of covenanted social bodies, and a greater openness to the inbreaking of the future into the present. It is one of the chief insights of this understanding of the biblical tradition that a confederation of covenantal spheres and institutions with a recognition of the variety of ways these are formed among the multiple settings in life enhances patterns of life that can pragmatically generate a plethora of ends and goods and theologically be more faithful to the biblical forms of common, providential, and the special grace of salvation. Each one of the spheres or institutions of a society will likely have within itself hierarchical and subsidiary

---

13. For a fine study of the covenantal fabric of relationship and responsibility, see Joseph L. Allen, *Love and Conflict: A Covenantal Model of Christian Ethics* (Nashville: Abingdon Press, 1984).

elements, and each will have its own calling to fulfill certain mandates for the whole of civilization; but even these will have to be subject to a more universal law and a more ultimate purpose than it can generate, manifest or fully mediate — a sensibility that requires an acceptance of the fact that we are bound by God to disciplines, purposes and people we do not chose and cannot construct or deconstruct. Our minds can be reasonable but easily rationalized. Our wills can make choices and exercise resolve but can be easily bent. Our affections are powerful but easily misplaced. This can only be overcome in history by those covenantal possibilities that are given in creation and providence and as renewed in Christ and infused by the Spirit of Christ. These are God-initiated and God-sustained; they invite us to concrete embodiments of the laws, ends, and mercies that allow life to flourish in a horizontally organized community of communities. Insofar as they are "natural," they are "creational," insofar as they are preservative they are providential, and insofar as they are salvific they are "re-created" in the Spirit of Christ, for they point both to the Creator beyond what is empirically ordinary in social behavior, and toward an ultimate future that is the most uncommon common good.[14]

Moreover, insofar as there are human agreements that work to establish peace and enhance life's possibilities, they depend upon a "graced" consent to a partially common, but also distinctively particular, institutionalized sphere of committed communities. The covenantal possibilities point to a more ultimate good that transcends what is possible in ordinary life. As this tradition claims, it was inaugurated by Christ, who renewed the divine covenant for all humanity and pointed life toward a new more holy destiny.

The goods of these pluralistic centers of principle, purpose, and practice do not easily converge and cannot be forced into any single model of the good in history without risking an increased centralization of coercive power, which previous hierarchical, imperial and theocratic ages have manifested and shown to be the source of great social and ethical disaster. At the same time, each institution within

---

14. See the discussion of these matters in Nanch Rosenblum and Robert Post, *Civil Society and Government* (Princeton, NJ: Princeton University Press, 2002), especially 223–64. See also the collection of historical documents that represent these debates by James Skillen and R. M. McCarthy, eds., *Political Order and the Plural Structure of Society* (Atlanta: Scholars Press, 1991). Also valuable is William Johnson Everett, *God's Federal Republic: Reconstructing our Governing Symbol* (New York: Paulist Press, 1988).

a sphere, and each person within each institution, must acknowledge that all parts and persons in the social system are tainted with the temptation to self-aggrandizement and rebellion against others. Thus, every civil society is pluralistic, and it requires an ordered, but limited, political government to secure the relative peace possible in history. However, no political order is ever competent enough to control the whole complex of activities that must be managed by individuals, families, associations, independent institutions, corporations, and federated spheres below and beyond the government itself. None of these modules of human commonality and potential good, including every local and regional political unit, lasts forever or can achieve the perfection of the good. Like persons, they become unstable, less focused, and less productive over time unless they are sustained and renewed again and again by a moral and spiritual power beyond themselves. Like cells in an organism, or parts in a machine, they die, break down, or wear out. With spiritually and ethically renewed principles and purposes, however, they can reconstitute the patterns needed to form new covenants, renew older ones, generate new units, including combining or separating into new varieties of institutions and spheres. Our participation in a quest of a just law to order these involves an ever-changing interaction that invites us to cultivate an ever richer array of personal and group potentiality. It points to a larger hope given by God for an expanded integrity and fulfillment beyond history, even if they are not able, together or individually, to bring the fullness of the common good within history.

This view, deeply associated with theories of a principled, pluralistic and a free civil society, does not presume that the goods of the various spheres of life all point in an obvious single direction. Nor is it so that they should incline us to a solidarity of purpose in all areas of life. In fact, the failure to recognize the pluralism of spheres in society, and the attempts to establish a society dedicated to a single definition of the common good, sometimes religiously blessed, but usually based in naturalistic or humanistic grounded orientations, has been the chief source of those authoritarian and totalitarian efforts that have brought so much misery and suffering in recent centuries. They have not only damaged hopes for a common good, they have destroyed many of the common's goods, as the rubble found in ecological and archeological ruins shows.

We should surely take into account the fact that historic attempts to define the common good are most active in two processes. One is when a people's old traditions and social order break down, usually because the influences of more complex civilizations are threatening their ways of life, and they cannot adjust to the new ones. The definitions of common good then are calls to retreat to the wondrous ways of the romanticized elders or to renegotiate the old definition of what is common and what good. The other is during the formation of a new collectivity, when new models are unclear. Historic examples include the transition from a hearth culture to the ancient *polis*, the transition from local city-states to the imperial city, the transition from collapsed imperialism to a feudal society, and from that to the system of modern nation-states that we call the "international community."

Where Is the Kingdom Hope?

We should recognize that premature identification of the locus of the Kingdom of God has prompted many crises in Christian history. We are warned in the New Testament not to identify it with any particular "here" or "there," for it has no specific geographical locus. Yet, the temptation of "misplaced concretion" has overwhelmed far too many. It also has no predictable temporal identity. "No one knows the time," as Jesus said. It also has been seen in the establishment of a Christian empire at the time of Constantine. In fact, that event probably preserved the church from further intense persecution. Later the end time was identified with millennial dreams as the year one thousand approached when the church of the "high middle ages" were beginning new chapters in development — chapters which led to mobilization of the forces to stop the expansion of Islam, which gave rise to the Crusades, but also to the advances of scholarship, architecture, trade, agricultural production, etc., of the late middle ages. Some five hundred years later the Kingdom was identified by some with the Renaissance or the Reformation. But these gave rise to both Christian nationalism and the reaction against it in the Enlightenment, including its hopes for a "perfect classless society." These too proved to be examples of the failed Paradise — the arrival of the fulfilled Kingdom that did not come.

I should interject here that one of the difficulties of both the contemporary "ecumenical movement," for all its contributions, and of the neo-Pentecostal and neo-Evangelical movements, for all their vibrant energy, is that their members remain wedded to a model of the modern nation-state. This is certainly true of the Eastern Orthodox community which is historically and contemporaneously organized on the basis of a series of national patriarchs — the Greek, Russian, Romanian, etc., Orthodox churches. Although they have inter-national Orthodox convocations and conferences, religious identity remains largely nationalistic, and certain key doctrines of the whole ecumenical church are interpreted in such a way to reinforce that fact. And it is largely true that many of the Reformation-based Protestant Churches are organized by national identity. One thinks not only of German, Danish, Swedish, etc., Lutherans, of the Scottish, Hungarian, American, etc., Reformed and Presbyterian churches, or of the British, Canadian, Australian, etc., Anglican churches; but also of various Baptist, Quaker, Mennonite, etc., denominations. All of these, to be sure, have international bodies and most participate in ecumenical councils of churches that reach across national boundaries; but these are often quite feeble, and some of them are deeply stamped by the late twentieth century decolonializing movements for liberation, which reinforced neonationalism in the previously colonialized nations. The developments in the Orthodox and Protestant churches and more recently the "newer churches" which joined the ecumenical movement when nationalism was on the rise, and the legitimation of the rising nationalism by these various bodies, remain a problem for the witness of the churches in a globalizing era. Each of these nationalist movements strengthened the power and authority of nation-states even as they, like the medieval church before them, developed the church as another center of power in familist and statist dominated societies. There is, of course, a proper place for a guarded patriotism and for the witness of a national church within the modern nation-state, especially if the nation-state is threatened with subjugation by an imperial or theocratic colonialism. But there are dangers as well, some of them signaled by new bursts of apocalyptic hopes and fears.

These transitions in the past are now being surpassed by a more encompassing and simultaneously more diversified civil society that is not yet, but could become a worldwide and enormously complex and differentiated civilization, as I have repeatedly suggested. Thus, amidst considerable turmoil and suffering, these historic models are being superseded by the prospects of an interdependence more encompassing than previously imagined — powered by modes of technological, communication, and economic organization and new forms of consultative, regulative or service agencies — the United Nations, of course; but also the World Bank, the World Trade Organization, the IMF, and a host of nongovernmental relief, development and advocacy organizations. For these there is no overarching, centralized governmental center nor is there any known comprehending vision, although as we noted in the Introduction to this volume, Michael Mandelbaum has persuasively argued that, in some respects at least, the United States acts as a hegemonic world government, largely with the acquiescence and quiet approval (if also the overt resentment) of other nations.[15] Whether America is doing well at this is a matter of hot dispute; still, in such a context, every effort to identify and actualize the common good of some nation or class, some profession or independent sphere of human activity, without reference to the global state of affairs, will tend to render an intolerable self-idolatry. Even if we try to organize the whole politically, we may well end up with but another arrogant hierarchical, imperial or theocratic system — if it is so in the future as it has been in the past. None of these portend the Kingdom of God in history, or the end of history.

Decisive in constructing an alternative is the reality of religion. As argued earlier the great world religions have historically supplied the metaphysical-moral visions that have woven the diversity of spheres present in complex cultures, plus the hopes of persons, into comprehending visions of what is common and what is good for humanity, even if they recognize that their vision cannot be fully attained in this life. The great syntheses not only offered a portrait of the transcending reality, they formed the inner moral architecture of the historic civilizations. These religions have, in other words, generated profound and guiding senses of what the righteous order of things ought to be, and what the good ends to be pursued should be. All these visions are now being tested to see if they can cope with globalizing forces, and all the options are brought to every part of the world by migration flows, media, travel, cross-cultural studies and missionary work. While it is clear that the religions and the cultures stamped by the great faiths have many things in common, they seldom have the same ultimate vision of the common good.

---

15. See Mandelbaum, *The Case for Goliath.*

Thus, we must find ways of engaging in the comparative evaluation of the world religions, for that is where the issue of the common good in relationship to multiple definitions of what is common and what is good will find its knottiest problems. In short, this is the area where the quest for a public theology is most urgent, for a satisfactory one must be able to operate in a much wider public than has been the case before.

We have already seen that there are some areas of philosophically and theologically discerned ethics, especially deontological ones, where there are prospects of relative agreement. And there are others areas, essentially ethological ones, which allow us to recognize comparative similarities and differences in regard to ways that complex societies are characteristically organized. On these points there is the possibility of an overlapping consensus and of the ability to assess pragmatically those in need of expanded possibilities. And there are still others, primarily teleological ones, that prompt us to point out differences that are not in any foreseeable period of history resolvable. Yet precisely these differences will force us to make choices between our proximate ends because they are variously shaped by visions of the ultimate end — eschatology.

It is in interaction with other world faiths on the issue of eschatological thought that the most difficult issues of the Kingdom as it points to the common good come to focus. I take this to be necessary because of the way in which we live in a much expanded understanding of what is common, and because the world faiths have distinctive views of what is ultimately good and how that ultimate good is to be anticipated by or related to life in the here and now. If the theologies of these world faiths are articulate, they will state in one way or another the implications of the goods or good of their unique, uncommon eschatology not only for persons, but also for the institutions and spheres of society, which partially overlap with those of other traditions, and for the ways their faith is inclined to interpret and apply their sense of the universal moral law which they share with other traditions.

When Christians think about the good toward which all should aim, however, we think first of all the messianic expectation that is present in the prophetic visions of the Hebrew scriptures, and of the Christian conviction that the messianic age has begun in the life, death, and resurrection of Christ. In these events, the Kingdom of God was inaugurated as an earthly reality that points to

the New Jerusalem, which comes to us from the other side of the
end of history. To hold such views is to deny the contemporary
claim that there is no universal meta-narrative that can be known
by humans. In fact, the eyes of faith see, and theology reasonably
discusses, willingly chooses to believe and passionately holds that all
discerning humans can recognize that each one of these motifs has
special meaning for understanding the nature and character of the
common good. The messianic expectation continues to be a theme
that Christians share with Jews in the sense that a final coming is
expected. Christians, of course, hold that the messiah has come in
Jesus Christ, yet the expectation is not completely fulfilled. Thus,
when Christians speak about Christ coming again, they continue,
as do the Jews, to be people of hope. Christians cannot turn to any
particular moment in the past — Creation, Exodus, Sinai, even the
Incarnation, the Atonement or the Resurrection — and say that all
truth, knowledge and justice has been given, everything is settled,
and the rest is simply a cleaning-up operation. We live always in
history with the utopia- and illusion-shattering recognition that all
that we have that is good is but prologue and that only in the ultimate future will we know final truth, and with it, the grace of true
justice with its judgment and mercy.[16]

The motif of the Kingdom of God, the dominating idea of
Jesus' ministry and preaching before the eschatological moment, as
reported in the New Testament, has three fundamental social dimensions, as H. Richard Niebuhr pointed out two generations ago.[17]
Each dimension points beyond itself. Indeed, not only many biblical images of this idea, but every compelling philosophy of world
history could be sorted according to which one or which combination of these ideas is being used at particular points. The first

---

16. One of the most compelling analyses of the similarities and differences of
Christianity and Judaism on this point remains as a telling portion of Reinhold
Niebuhr's masterwork, *The Nature and Destiny of Man* (New York: Charles Scribner's Sons, 1943), vol. 2, chapters 1 and 2. The similarities and contrast of both with
secular utopianism and theocratic apocalypticism and mystical spiritualism are also
explicit, but it is only implicit with regard to Islamic and Buddhist eschatologies.

17. See H. Richard Niebuhr, *The Kingdom of God in America* (Chicago: Willett,
Clark, 1937). Like his brother's work (ibid.) this was written in the midst of conflicts
with Nazism and Communism, and meets these challenges by a turn to basic biblical
and theological terms. While he applied them to the social questions facing America, the resources on which he draws and the implications for public theology are
pertinent to our more universal context. I adapt and refine his typology to address
the issues also raised in regard to globalization.

is the Sovereign Reign of God over the public affairs of humanity, which bears the implication that there is a universal moral order which can be well enough known to write constitutions of relative justice for the ordering of the common life. With the renewal of the primal covenant in Jesus Christ, Christians become more aware of this Sovereignty of God, and the wider world acknowledges that this was a turning point in universal history every time they refer to A.D. or C.E. The God who is creator of, law-giver for and providential sustainer of the world can be known more clearly when the Messiah is manifest. As the classical tradition says, the *lex Christi* clarifies the inner meaning of the *lex Moysis* and the *lex naturae*, refines the *lex gentium* (and serves as a foil, supplement and occasion for reasonable debate with regard to the Confucian concept of *li,* the Hindu view of *dharma,* the Buddhist *dhammapada* and the Islamic *shar'ia).*

The second motif is the quite personal Reign of Christ in the heart of the believer, which brings with it a renewed capacity to find faith and hope, to love the neighbor and to recognize that novelty is introduced as a factor in historical existence. The meaning of life cannot be found only in the constancy of order, although it remains an inevitable and perennial reality at a very profound level, in spite of disruption and distortion at the less fundamental levels of existence. Without that constancy, neither being or science or a human wide morality would be possible. But the meaning of life cannot be found in the cycles of nature, although they do recur; nor can it be found in a singular logic of history that infinitely repeats the dynamic interaction of factors. It can be found in the recognition that new realities can and have been introduced into time, and that one of these novelties is of both world-historical significance and repeatedly capable of renewing the inner personal life of persons.

The Kingdom Is Still Coming

Third, and most pertinent to our present discussion, is the expectation of the Coming Kingdom, a dynamic that breaks into time from beyond time and presses prophetically toward the overcoming of the meaninglessness that besets our understanding of everything that is threatened with death, including the passing temporality of an entropic creation. Niebuhr is weakest on his interpretation of the Kingdom at this point, for he does not see how it is at work socio-spiritually as a counterweight to the implicit nihilism of the nontheological or anti-theological philosophies or political theories that seemed to be determining the future in his context. Nor did he affirm, as classic doctrine teaches, that the Kingdom is ever at work within and among us, pointing history toward a New Jerusalem in spite of the temporary threats of misery and defeat. That coming Kingdom ever points us toward a fulfilled and transformed city of the nations that is not yet visible except as promise. Still, it invites us to live toward it. This vision and pending reality is given by grace; it cannot be imagined or attained without grace by even the best human act. Yet, those who grasp it see that this is the best vision morally, spiritually, personally and socially for the ultimate end; it is most uncommon, but ultimately the only truly common good.

Christians believe that the Kingdom in its first two dimensions is made possible by creational and providential grace, and made specially present in the life, death, and resurrection of Christ, although we do not know with much precision what life in the resurrected state of being would be. It is a hope-full assurance that decay, dust and ashes are not the final chapter of human existence, and rubbish is not the final end of civilization. Although these are indisputably real, and these are the ends to which all come, they are not the ultimate *telos* of life. Moreover, the motif of the Kingdom indicates that under the triune God's reign, neither the church nor the many spheres of civilized life wherein the Kingdom has become active are empty of promise. However bleak the social situation looks at any given point in history, God saves through Christ fragile reeds of social and personal potentiality to bear the weight of promising possibilities in the midst of disconfirming evidence. Everyone dies but heaven is populated, marriages may fail but families continue, governments fall but new ones develop, economic systems collapse but alternatives emerge, cultures are subjugated but the creativity of their existence leaves indelible traces, schools teach badly but students learn, hospitals do not cure but compassionate attention heals the heart and gives comfort and courage. Indeed, religions rise and fall, and many have faded into oblivion, but elements of those traditions are carried into renewed faiths. And insofar as a constant reconstructive dynamic is directed toward the discovery or recovery of a God-oriented sense of principle and purpose, traces of the Kingdom of God can be, more or less, discerned in the midst of the actual, fragile structure of being and in the sinful, distorted events of history. Those able to discern them are called to be its agents in this life, in every sphere. Yet neither the personal trust in the Atonement and the Resurrection, nor the discernment of the Kingdom, acted upon with humility, courage and wisdom, can bring the ultimate good end.

One of the distinctive characteristics of Christianity is that it does not hold that getting personal faith right, or doing things right in the social contexts of this life, can guarantee for us the fulfillment of either our own best hopes for immediate goods or the most ultimate common good — or even of establishing the proximate common good of any given institution, sphere or system of spheres in history. While the eschatological mythic portrait completes the protological myth of creation and reveals its divine ultimate purpose, a critical discontinuity, an apocalyptic gap, an eschatological break stands between the very best we humans can imagine or attain on the one hand, and the fulfillment of the divine purpose for all on the other. Such things can only be grasped in symbolic terms; they are beyond the scope of ordinary personal efforts or social programs and projections. And, in this regard, all the projects for personal or social betterment, captured by concerns for the common good, are put into another perspective by salvific grace.

Thus, we hold that the vision of the ultimate end, signaled in an anticipatory way by the appearances after the Resurrection, and glimpsed in the gains that can be made in history as we discern and seek to actuate the Kingdom of God in our common life, depends on something that is radically and uncommonly good, the gift of grace that changes all our ethics by directing all potentialities toward perfection. That is what allows us to live toward death without despair and that is what empowers us to celebrate the modest gains possible as we seek to actuate a little more justice in our civil societies and a little more love in our hearts. It is also what demands that we do not overestimate our own heroism in facing difficult situations and do not hold that our societies, even the very best of them, can form the common good by good living and wise policies, by habituating people into virtue and certainly not by forcing others to follow our lead. Should we face the prospect of death personally with the confidence that asks "Death, where is thy sting?" Certainly, but we cannot do it without graced faith. Should we be active in seeking to restrain evil and establish more justice in the institutions of the civilizations of which we are a part? Of course, but we dare not think that we can accomplish the common good by political, economic, cultural or military mobilization; and we must guard against temptation to self-celebration — wanting to live forever or making our society the center of human civilization.

The final good is deeper and more ultimate than any personal immortality or any enduring civic arrangement. Consider, for example, the words of the final chorus of the classic requiem mass as a summary of the elements of the ultimate good. After judgment and remorseful tears of repentance, we hear:

> May angels lead you to paradise,
> may the martyrs greet you at your coming and
> lead you to the holy city, Jerusalem.
> May the angelic choir receive you and,
> with Lazarus, once a beggar,
> may you find eternal peace.

This compressed version of the last few chapters of the Book of Revelation, with echoes of promise that this is also the fulfillment of the inbreaking of a promised future begun in Jesus, draws our attention to each particular person, for each one is of worth, although each will know defeat and death, with their inevitably loneliness. It points beyond the collapse of the hope that all that one wanted to be and do on earth are brought to the void. Still, persons are lovingly led by unseen powers — the powers that portend good news that did not fall or become self-centered psycho-spiritual forces that reject God — to another kind of realm and welcomed into a communion of saints by those who have been persecuted for their faithfulness and righteousness. Another kind of companionship than any communal identity, national purpose, or progressive program is envisaged, a kind of companionship that fulfills what the other purposes and programs inevitably failed to deliver.

Moreover, this paradise is not a return to Eden, and neither a recovery of some idyllic primal oasis of innocence, nor an attained bliss of "no-thing-ness." It is not the absorption of the personal soul into a cosmic "Over-soul," nor is it rejoining of spirits with the departed ancestral elders, nor is it a perpetually enduring harmonious society in tune with nature and heaven. There is no sense of a tiny remnant of a select few who have proven their moral and spiritual merit, and gained their rapture. Indeed there is no temple, no church, no family except the brothers and sisters in Christ, and no politics except "the lamb who was slain on the throne." Rather it is a gifted destiny that comes to us from another dimension as a complex civilization into which all the nations may bring their gifts, a city where marvelously engineered and artistically formed structures invite joyous exaltation in the participatory cultural activity of singing, and even the laws of nature are transformed so that trees bear fruit and healing leaves each month, and where an exuberant spirit of holiness welcomes the least — even the most neglected beggar finds a just peace. It is the most uncommon, greatest good that has ever been presented to humanity. To speak of it requires a theological imagination, one able to invite the global public to its portals.

What Difference Does It Make?

The question, of course, can be asked as to what difference this eschatological vision makes to the question of how we organize the common life in a global era. The answer is: all the difference in the world. The way we envision the ultimate and salvific possibilities for ourselves, humanity in general, and the bio-physical universe impinges on our present and shapes our orientation to each sphere of life. The eschatological definition of redemption anticipated in the hopes for a messiah and inaugurated by Christ brings all that is given in the graces of creation, providence and salvation to fulfillment. It trumps and transforms every naturalist teleology or humanist contract or every counter-cultural claim of realized perfectionism, and thus it reorders the decisive concept of what is common and what is good. And if we hold, as the classic tradition of Christianity does, that the eschatological promise has already broken into the present and is both objectively as well as subjectively operating in the depths of history and consciousness, we find that every believer is enabled to discern hints and glimmers of the fruits of the Kingdom of God that is within and among us. That very discernment enables humanity to live toward the future with confidence in spite of the continued presence of sin and death, terror and failure, and to accept a vocation to work in ways that point toward the New Jerusalem with neither an utopian optimism nor debilitating despair, since wrong and evil continue to beguile the powers. The principalities, authorities, thrones, and dominions fail when they seek to lead humanity and history in directions that ignore God. In fact, faith allows us to seek to draw these powers too into covenantally bonded relationships that they may serve the whole and that plenitude becomes fulfilled and fulfilling of each. It is the perennial function of government to establish just law and keep the peace; and it best does this in a way that also foments institutions beyond itself able to preach, teach and exemplify the truth, justice and mercy that points to the global Holy City. It is also the task of economic institutions to create wealth; and those do it best which allow the support of families, educational, cultural, and charitable organizations without destroying the ecological order, and thus offer hints of the New Jerusalem. The responsibilities of families, schools, hospitals, and especially religious organizations all differ, but they all pursue their own particular ends best if they too think of themselves as Kingdom agents, pointing beyond themselves toward the more ultimate end of life that also comprehends and perfect the ends of other spheres of the common life.

Of course, all this theological sense of promise, with its inevitable use of symbol and poetic image, does not quite depend on "knowledge" in the sense in which either the academic or the political community has confidence. To many, the kinds of assurance that come from other kinds of evidence and insight seem much more secure, for to live toward an eschatological end is to live by hope, even by faith alone. That is, in part, because the evidence of what will ultimately happen in the future is not fully available yet, and a proper indeterminacy is required in our efforts to point toward the most promising possibilities. Yet, intellectual, social, and political movements toward the common good have within them presumptions of what the good ends ought to be which are also laden with elements of love, hope, and faith, and are extremely difficult to prove by conventional means. Moreover, other religions with which we now live have other senses of what the chief problem is and what the ultimate end might be.

We can, I think, argue with confidence and good warrants that the Christian tradition, when it has been faithful and dependent on this ultimate view helped generate attitudes in life that we deem to be essential to the common good, and that other traditions have functionally adopted, are adopting or want to adopt or adapt them. But that is not a foregone argument, and some eschatological views are in fact strongly resistant to the Christian motifs set forth here.

In any case, the "proof" that this vision and its fruits is or should be the vision of the common good for all is very difficult to offer, although its practical fruits are desired by many. For that reason, other major aspects of moral discourse must be brought into play as we think about keeping an open prospect for such an ultimate vision to be discussed, to find new loci of operational promise in human affairs, or to be modified by new exposure to alternative perspectives.

Those other aspects of moral discourse are precisely a deontological understanding of moral law, embodied functionally today in such institutions as the international covenants of human rights; and an ethological analysis of dynamic social pluralism found in theories of sphere sovereignty and of subsidiarity as these bear on civil society. In brief, a serious discussion of the common good, from a theological-ethical point of view in our globalizing world, demands a recognition of the eschatological nature of the vision of the good for humanity, a demand for universal standards of right and wrong and an operational pluralism to sustain dynamic openness to those possibilities. This is what, I propose, a Christian theologically based perspective has to offer to the world more than anything else. It is the final grace, inconceivable without a sense of common, providential and the special grace of Christ. These alone are deep enough, wide enough and long enough to guide global developments.

Toward Sanctification?

The Kingdom at work in human hearts and social history is not the New Jerusalem. It points toward that perfected possibility, and, rightly discerned, it renders promises that the heavenly city will come, although it has not yet done so. That is why the Apostle can say that the world's salvation is "already but not yet." We live still only in the anticipation, but with a new assurance that the promises of old have begun to be discernable in the concrete experiences of human existence. Still, the New Jerusalem, the cosmopolitan city of God, stands before us as promise and lure, especially in an age of global development. In continuity with those hopes engendered by the recognition of the grace of Creation and the grace of Providence, with those renewed hopes of salvation fueled by the coming of the Messiah, and with those great movements that have already begun to transform civilizations in Christ's name — the Orthodox,

Catholic, and Reformed traditions — the current Evangelical and Pentecostal traditions are bringing new spiritual and moral energy into the family of movements that both manifest the power of the Kingdom inaugurated by Christ and point toward the Second Coming of Christ with its reawakening of the expectation that the New Jerusalem is humanity's final destiny.

But it is not yet realized, and a fundamental question confronts us, one that has perplexed earlier generations of Christians. Since the Kingdom has not yet been fulfilled as some of the biblical authors apparently expected to be immanent in their lifetime, since Christ has not come again, and since the New Jerusalem has not appeared on the horizon, shall we say that the expectation is false, that the biblical vision of eschatology failed, and that any transformational teleology based on it is a pipedream? Or shall we say that all this expectation that there will be evidence of the Kingdom is based on a false understanding of the nature of the Kingdom? In fact, an alternative view holds, it has nothing to do with the visible dynamics of a common social history. Instead, the Kingdom is present visibly in time, but the locus of its presence is within and among the saints of the true, counter-cultural church, in the enclaves of those who have been justified, redeemed and sanctified and live an alternative life style outside of and mostly against the dominant patterns and dynamics of "real" social history.

The classical Christian view is neither of these as stated, but each has something to add to our understanding. The one overestimates what can be known about the time line for the fulfillment of the Kingdom, in spite of Christ's warning about no one knowing what it is. Still, this view presumes that the Kingdom inaugurated by Christ is coming, even if we do not know when, in the common life of humanity. Christ is not only Lord of the gathered community under the steeple among those conscious of Jesus as the Christ; Christ is Lord of Lords, King of Kings, and thus has to do with all dimensions of life, whether they know it or not. The Kingdom is not fulfilled, but it is growing. As belief in Christ spreads it becomes more operative in people's lives, but it is also growing in the development of more and more covenantal relationships in human experience, in the spread of principles of universal moral law, in the cultivation of the professions with a sense of calling, and in the expectation of social improvement in all the spheres of life. This can best be discerned by the spread of a public theology of history that points our attempts to discern purpose in social life in the right direction. In these ways the indirect effects of Christ's offer of salvation are being manifest in discernable traces of the Kingdom.

Those holding the second view overestimate the difference between the church community and the wider society by pretending to be more righteous than they are and reading the social context to be more wicked than it is. Still, they recognize that those in the church have a special role in advancing consciousness of the Kingdom reality and they can sometimes be corrected by identifying it not only with justification, redemption, and the sanctification of souls, but also with the redemption of the institutions of society from their temptations to declare autonomy from God's Reign by infusing them with a consciousness that they are under a higher law and dedicated to a more ultimate end.

Globalization is neither the Kingdom of God nor the New Jerusalem, but the dynamics and patterns of globalization that manifest the effects of Christ's inauguration of the Kingdom and that depend on the historic influences on social history by movements that structured institutions able to channel life toward a future of a complex, inclusive cosmopolitan civilization are present in globalization. Christians know not the time it will be fulfilled nor can they claim a special virtue by reason of their faith. The church is more like the other institutions in society than they often recognize, but it bears a capacity to discern the presence of the sanctification in society as well as in exemplary persons. The various spheres of life that engendered modern globalization may have had their basic reason for being obscured by a quest for autonomy, by secularization, by self-idolatry, by the loss of a sense of living under any universal moral laws or for a more ultimate purpose, and they may have traded in the form-giving ideas of subsidiarity and covenant for ideas of hierarchy and contract. In all or any of these ways they may well have unleashed the powers the were designed to guide and constrain, but by the power of Christ and the Kingdom they can be redeemed and justified — indeed, they can be instruments of sanctification. They can be renewed and reformed precisely because they bear within them elements of Creational grace and Providential grace so that, in Christ, by the power of the Kingdom and for the sake of all nations who shall be welcomed into the New Jerusalem, they can approximate holy living. Under these influences they can make the common graces found in Creation and in Providence capable not only of sustaining life, but of actually improving its patterns and dynamics.

This means that an appropriate social ethic must be developed for the times in which we live, a new version of an "interim ethic" that builds on those themes bearing on a social ethic present in the New Testament, and extends the monumental efforts to work out the implications present in the patristic period of the church, and most extensively honored by the Orthodox traditions, in the classic Catholic traditions, especially from Augustine to Aquinas, in the Reformers, from Luther and Calvin to Wesley and Edwards, in the efforts to confront the pathologies of modernization, from the Social Gospel to Christian Realism and now in the new world missions manifest in the Evangelical and Pentecostal mission movements, especially as they appear in Asian, African and Latin American contexts. In short, since Christ inaugurated the Kingdom of God not only as a creational grace and a preserving grace but as a salvific grace, the global mission of the faith has been under construction, reaching and yearning for the final grace. It has brought us to the present promise of globalization, with all its ambiguities, faults and gaps, and it will require a temporal, interim ethic to respond to the challenges we face if it is to bring us a bit closer to the New Jerusalem. In the meantime, the Kingdom is extending its influence among peoples and in persons whom it has not previously reached.

– *Chapter 6* –

A SUMMARY WITH CONCLUSIONS AND IMPLICATIONS

Globalizing Christian Ethics[1]

There is no single doctrinal attitude or programmatic statement that articulates *the* Christian approach to globalization, or, for that matter, to global trends in ethics and society. Yet, all the multiple dynamics in family life and economics, politics and culture, education and law, technology or politics, are dependent on and often the carriers of religiously rooted ethical principles and ends, as well as on their own functional requirements. And many of these principles and ends have been emphasized by Christians, but accented in different ways. Still, the lack of a single view is due in part to the fact that there are competing definitions of what globalization is, its sources, range, and effects, and in part because there are several alternative understandings of what the most important features of Christian Ethics are. Neither the biblical resources nor the classical traditions present Christians with a monolithic perspective. Although there is one Christ, Jesus is portrayed with different accents in the Gospels by many authors. Similarly, although there is one God, that unity is held to be constituted by a Trinitarian set of "persons" in interactive relationship with each other and with the world. Further, the one Holy Spirit who is part of that Trinity has a mobility that can show up in many places, including in non-Christian cultures and religions. In Ethics as well as Theology (or other comparably comprehensive worldviews), which is always a necessary companion to Ethics, acknowledged or not, several key

---

1. Portions of this chapter have appeared in a collection of essays written for an Ethikon Conference, namely, "Globalization and Christian Ethics," in *The Globalization of Ethics: Religious and Secular Perspectives,* ed. William M. Sullivan and Will Kymlicka (New York: Cambridge University Press, 2007), 53–74.

modes of normative discourse have been joined in various ways in various parts of the tradition. Thus, I briefly repeat the dominant motifs that I think are important for a Christian Public Theological Ethic for a globalizing world.

As discussed in the Introduction to volume one of this series, ethics has three modes of discourse, each corresponding to the tasks of ethics.[2] The first task is to define the operating values and norms that dominate a social or cultural ethos (analytically and ethologically); the second is to determine what values and norms are right or wrong (deontologically) or good or evil (teleologically). And the third is prescriptive and activist, calling upon people to enter into the reconstruction of the social or cultural ethos as needed to make them more right and good, or to defend its valid parts when it is substantively right and good and under threat. A variation of these three focuses on contextual, deontological and teleological analyses, but one that sees the context in terms of various individual virtues cultivated by particular practices, and one that sees the reconstructive efforts as based on the formation of an alternative context, are opposed to that of the dominant society or culture, which it therefore seeks to avoid or revolutionize.

The argument of the four volumes in this series has several parts. First is the claim that any analysis of the context or of the ethos must include an analysis of the religious patterns of thought and belief that have shaped it, and that theology provides necessary resources for this analysis.[3] In this regard, theology is seen as a mode of public discourse, and that much of social, academic and political debate is impoverished by a failure to be candid about the reality, the socially and culturally forming influence of theology. This view of theology stands in tension with those who claim either that theology is a privileged mode of discourse known and knowable only to the insiders of a particular faith, or that when it goes public it does so as

---

2. "General Introduction" in vol. 1 of the *God and Globalization* series, 9–18.

3. This fact has been increasingly recognized in Development Economics and in International Relations and Diplomacy, as can be seen in the newest book of Scott Thomas, *The Global Resurgence of Religion and the Transformation of International Relations: The Struggle for the Soul of the 21st Century* (New York: Palgrave Macmillan, 2005). Thomas is also a contributor to vol. 3 of the *God and Globalization* series. See also former Secretary of State Madeleine Albright, *The Mighty and the Almighty: Reflections on America, God and World Affairs* (New York: HarperCollins, 2006).

a party platform trying to impose its irrational presuppositions on an uncomprehending public.

Second is the claim that at the level of deontology, most of the world's religions, in fact, share a great deal about what is right and what is wrong.[4] At the same time, there is an enormous difference in the teleological ends pursued by the various spheres of society and especially in the ends pursued by the great religions of the world. The different purposes that the various professions pursue are quite remarkable, but have overlapping qualities, primarily because the great traditions of modernity that so deeply influenced the development of the professions and thus the dynamics of globalization and the newer global institutions were all informed by a Christian theological ethic, as we saw in volume 2 of the *God and Globalization* series. These are now being adopted and adapted into other cultures and societies and are modulating the value systems of these other traditions. They are also producing new syntheses that Christian theology must take into account in its own self-understanding, although the theological themes behind these changes are not always overt and conscious by those who advocate the changes and those who adopt them. But the differences of eschatologies of the world religions, as discussed in volume three of this series, and echoed in this final volume, are quite remarkable and finally incompatible. In both cases, however, theology and theological ethics are required to understand what is going on in the world, how the various spheres of complex society justify or legitimate their social organization and policies, and how to assess their relative validity — the latter point having to take place in a prolonged discussion that is likely to be punctuated by debate if not conflict.

To speak of the various spheres of life points us to the third major argument of this series of books — the fact that all debates about globalization must recognize that it is a complex process

---

4. See, e.g., Paul G. Kuntz, *The Ten Commandments in History: Mosaic Paradigms for a Well-Ordered Society* (Grand Rapids: Eerdmans, 2004); Jean Porter, *Natural and Divine Law: Reclaiming the Tradition for Christian Ethics* (Grand Rapids: Eerdmans, 1995); and Walter Harrison, *The Ten Commandments and Human Rights,* rev. ed. (Atlanta: Mercer University Press, 1997). See also Hans Küng, primary author of the "Declaration Toward a Global Ethic," passed by the Parliament of the World's Religions in 1993. The core of this Declaration rather obviously echoes the Ten Commandments, and the subscription to these principles by many signatories suggests that some religious particularities may in fact bear within them universalistic principles that can be affirmed by all. See *A Global Ethic,* ed. H. Küng and K.-J. Kuschel (New York: Continuum, 1995).

driven by many "powers," with many institutions, spheres of life, social classes, ethnic groups, regions, societies and cultures interacting in increasingly complex ways. A key implication is that any view of globalization that isolates one of these and pretends to explain globalization with reference to it alone is reductionistic and inconsequential. How then are we to understand this complexity? The third argument is that there are psycho-social forces at work in human history that have spiritual and moral dimensions and implications and that theology can best unpack. Thus, religious analysis is required even at this level.

I have proposed to the contributors of these volumes, and most have structured their arguments around the theme from the Christian scriptures that much of life is influenced by the "powers" — the principalities, authorities, regencies (thrones) and dominions — that demand institutional ordering and constraint. In the biblical world, as in almost all historic cultures, life was seen as populated by spiritual powers that brought relatedness or alienation, sickness or health, wealth or poverty, war or peace, and life or death. They held that physical, biological, political and economic forces are bent by psycho-somatic, spiritual and moral causes. Serious theology today does not believe in little spiritual beasties that flit around the skies or our lives, tempting us to do evil or prompting us to do good. But it is hard to deny that there are psycho-socio-spiritual forces of human relational and institutional life in which people believe and that sometimes go out of control, become self-idolatrous so attractively that we too put our trust in them, thus make the contexts in which we live unfit for human habitation.[5]

Yet, Christians view history in a way that sees God's providential reformation of those flawed relationships and institutions in such a way that "the powers" can, in some measure, be drawn into disciplined associations of moral service under God's laws and for God's intended purposes and thereby better serve rather than only disrupt human flourishing.[6] The "spirit" or "mentality" or "ethos" of a community can be transformed and renewed by the agency of those

---

5. See G. B. Caird, *Principalities and Powers* (Oxford: Oxford University Press, 1956), now a classic on these terms; and my earlier references to Walter Wink's interpretations in the previous volumes.

6. For this reason, Christians often debate with great intensity the moral shape of family life, of polity in church and society, of rights and duties in politics, of economic systems, and of the procedures of decision making in all the professional areas of life. These issues are central to a Christian ethic of and for the world.

who have a calling and work with others covenantally, by coming to know Christ personally and by the influence of the Holy Spirit in communities of commitment that reach toward holiness. Thus, a social theology of history, publicly debatable, enables us to read the dynamics of a social ethos through the resources of an articulated faith, even as the ethos undergoes rapid social change, to see what possibilities there are for restraining a plunge toward destruction or for cultivating new potentialities.

Beyond this, Christian theology holds the belief that there is a master narrative lurking at the depths of human history. Every social development can be seen as under "the powers" (such as Mammon or Mars) in various degrees, or more or less constrained or guided by common, providential and ultimately a saving grace. This is a theme traceable not only in biblical history, but in theological reflection on it in various contexts of life where it has been accepted. One can see it in thinkers from Augustine (in his *City of God*) to the great historic reformers of the church, but others from the Dutch neo-Calvinist Abraham Kuyper, to the German Lutheran martyr Dietrich Bonhoeffer and the American "Christian Realist" Reinhold Niebuhr, to the remarkable "Social Encyclicals" of the twentieth-century Roman Catholic popes, to the activist Baptist Martin Luther King Jr. to the new generation of Pentecostal and Evangelical Christians arising among developing peoples. This series is intended to be in continuity with such traditions.

Today, the most disputed area of ethics has to do with competing attempts to discern what is going on morally and spiritually in globalization, and how to relate that dramatic development to the first principles or ultimate ends that Christians endorse. Clearly the contexts of life in which increasing percentages of the world's population live are undergoing transformations, and these changes are creating a wider context that comprehends and modifies all local social and cultural contexts. These dynamic changes have many implications for the world as a bio-physical planet, for the world as an interdependent cluster of societies now interacting in dramatically new ways, and the world as a philosophical-theological and ethical concept. While Christianity and other religions have had world-comprehending perspectives for centuries, the extent and rapidity of current change demands a reassessment of those influences that have contributed to the expansive ethos that is now disrupting and changing every cultural, political, and economic order, but also potentially leading humanity toward a new encompassing world civilization, one of greater complexity, pluralism, diversity, and inclusiveness than the world has yet seen — although it also brings crisis and sometimes at least partial fragmentation to traditional and closed cultures.

To many in closed cultures, to others trapped in anti-cultural dogmas, and even to many in "modernized" societies from which they are alienated because they cannot discern the faith foundations in many contemporary developments, "globalization" has little to do with theology or ethics except the threatening of the folkways and beliefs by which they used to live. They do not know how to resist it, control it, or to join it. They simply view it as the actions of some powerful "them" disrupting their traditions and imposing "secular" or "materialistic" or alien forms of corrupted morality. The perspective of this volume and of most of the essays in the previous three stands in contrast to this view, for it tends to see globalization as "another fall" and appeals to a hostile and defensive form of piety — often by reasserting (or reinventing) local traditions. They resist the contemporary globalization of the ethics born by many global trends.

Globalization as "Another Fall"

This perspective sees social history in terms of political economy and its succession of lapses from the kind and quality of life that God intended, Christ called for, the Holy Spirit could inspire and the Kingdom is bringing. The first fall, of course, is portrayed in a mythic story of the generic human departure from a primal harmony that God presumably intended for humanity and nature. In postmythic history, humanity lives in a world of tempting desires, distorting deception, bloody competition, and pretentious arrogance, and in tension with the forces of the ecosphere. Judgment was rendered against human civilization by paradigmatic events — natural disaster (Noah), cultural division (Babel), and social enslavement (Pharaoh). God, to be sure, raised up figures such as Abraham and later Moses to lead the peoples to a city that has foundations, and to a mountain where a divine law was disclosed. But the people and their kings kept wandering after false gods, and forsaking the ways of justice, in spite of the warnings of prophets, priests, and sages, who faithfully kept alive the hope for a coming messiah who would fulfill the law and inaugurate a new age.

Christians hold that the good news of the Gospel is that the Messiah has come in Jesus Christ and formed a new kind of community, based in faith, love, and hope made present in him. In the "another fall" view, however, this cluster of commitments is essentially alien to the institutions of the common life. They demand a counter-cultural form of discipleship and organization. In the Roman Catholic and Eastern Orthodox churches, this impulse took shape in the great monastic traditions, emblems in a sinful and broken world of an entirely other order of reality, demanding an alternative lifestyle that eventually became articulate in the vows of poverty, chastity, and obedience (to this alternative reality as manifest in the discipline of their order, and thus not to any earthly social order). Laity were expected to be economically engaged, to be married, and to serve an earthly "lord" in battle as necessary; but this involvement with wealth, sex, and power entailed a lower spiritual status. The echoes of this tradition can still be heard among those who are deeply suspicious of technologically and corporation produced affluence, love-celebrating sexuality and power politics that uses coercion.

However, over the centuries, the church became wedded to imperial power when Constantine not only demanded toleration for but also supported the establishment of the faith. This brought with it, over many centuries, economic privileges, and a changed attitude toward the use of force, with teachings (later known as the "Just War Doctrine") that made distinctions between just and unjust use of coercive power.[7] In the perspective of this first view as it took root over the centuries, this Constantinian development was seen as evidence of this other "fall," now of the "official" churches insofar as their embrace of and by political power led, as some say, directly to crusades, inquisitions, religious wars, colonialism, and

---

7. This is one of the key doctrinal developments in the early Catholic tradition, one that now informs most of the Christian traditions. Although a minority defend pacifism, and it is presumed by all that we should ordinarily live with our neighbors in peace, it is also recognized that Christian participation in politics depends on the view that ethical principles can apply to all areas of life, including the use of military and police forces to ensure the defense of the neighbor, to prevent the disruption of civility, and to contribute to a just society. The Peace, Catholic, and Main-line Protestant churches generally agree, however, that Just War criteria have not always been used by Christian leaders, and that some wars, even if they were justifiable, might well have been differently conducted had they done so.

the holocaust. Against this captivity of the established churches to the idol of Mars, we need, so say the advocates of this view, a recovery of the Gospel for a faithful, confessing church, standing as an alternative witness to the powers of the world and against a faith that has compromised both the law of love and the peaceful purposes of God reign.

This "confessing" sectarian type of Christianity is not the only example of the notion of an alternative believing community. Other Christians, often tied with populist movements, are more "radical" in their sense of Christian alienation from the structures and powers of society, and they have taken their convictions in a more militant direction. They have seen it to be a sacred duty to confront "the powers" that are, in reality, the artifices of power elites. To set things right, they are willing to use force, for instance, in "just revolutions." Thus, they chart a Christian way of open dissent, opposition, and in some cases, revolt willingly accepting the role of martyr at the hands of established power. A famous hymn by James Russell Lowell states this mood in poetic terms:

> Though the cause of evil prosper, Yet 'tis truth alone is strong;
> Though her portion be the scaffold, And upon the throne is wrong.
> Yet that scaffold sways the future, And behind the dim unknown,
> Standeth God within the shadow, Keeping watch above his own.

Here too is a counter-cultural vision, in continuity in some ways with the early Manichaeans, the Peasant revolts of the late Middle Ages, the Diggers and the Levellers of the Puritan period, and some slave uprisings. The vision persists into the present among some liberation theologies: to be faithful means to be in radical solidarity with people's revolutions when they arise, for they experience the violation of first principles in society most directly and they see the promise of a redemptive reversal of good and evil most clearly. Christian socialism comes from such roots.

However, for many in these two wings of the Christian tradition, a further fall is lurking, if not already here. During the period which we now call the Enlightenment, many intellectuals turned to humanistic philosophies and scientific methods in efforts to overcome the dogmas that, they said, had caused violence and wars.

Their project, however, had unintended consequences. Out of their repudiation of theology as a mode of public discourse and resource for ethics, a hyper-modernist set of secular ideologies developed that accepted the techno-scientific view of nature with its utilitarian view of reason, fomented the industrial revolution that displaced millions of people (and is doing so still in developing countries), fostered "Manchesterism" (now called "Neo-liberalism"), and unleashed human greed. This generated a capitalist economic system which has little regard for faith, the moral law "written on the heart," an eschatological vision that portrays another dimension of reality, the character of traditional communities, or the intrinsic worth of the earth. Everything becomes a commodity, marketed for gain, and "the good" is reduced to "more." In globalization we face the consequences of these developments, terrors of imperialism again, now less from the geo-politics of iron and blood than from the geo-economics of markets and profit.[8]

This view was aided in many respects by the rise of the modern nation-state and its tendency to dominate all of society and later by the trenchant criticism of free-market capitalism by Karl Marx, even if the political prescriptions of his disciple, Lenin, turned out to be disastrous. It was possible for a time to regulate the emerging power of the technocratic corporation, in this view. However, the development of the corporation in its multi-national or transnational forms made it possible for the capitalist system to escape the control of political and legal constraints. Thus Mammon became the functional deity of postmodernity — the driving force of a globalization that chews up all in its rationalized, calculating, neo-colonial path. This is the primary reality of the globalization that is engulfing the world and impoverishing the peoples of the world while those in command of the new world economy, the corporate and hidden financial elites, are served not only by the armies of

---

8. I draw this typological sketch from one of its leading theological advocates, Ulrich Duchrow mentioned in the introduction. See his *Global Economy: A Confessional Issue for the Churches* (Geneva: World Council of Churches, 1987); and his *Alternatives to Global Capitalism* (Kairos Europa: Heidelberg, 1995) as well as from parallel sources, some of which he cites: R. H. Tawney, *Religion and the Rise of Capitalism* (New York: Harcourt, Brace, 1926); Karl Polanyi, *The Great Transformation* (Boston: Beacon Press, 1944); David Korten, *When Corporations Rule the World* (W. Hartford, CT: Kumarian Press, 1995); F. J. Hinkelammert, *The Ideological Weapons of Death: A Theological Critique of Capitalism* (Maryknoll, NY: Orbis Books, 1986); and, in some ways, Walter Wink, *Naming the Powers; Unmasking the Powers; Engaging the Powers.* See the Introduction to this volume.

the great powers, but also by their new international inventions, the IMF, World Bank, and WTO.[9] These together are crucifying the weaker peoples of the world and destroying the ecological systems which make life possible.[10] Against this, many say, believers must raise their voice in prophetic protest by becoming again a confessing or a radical church. They must again reassert that God is Lord, support solidarity with various people's movements, seek to overcome the rampant individualism and materialism of modern life, and oppose those who are engaged with Mammon as well as Mars.

The "Providential Grace" View

A second theology of history is held, also in various versions, by a large percentage of the world's Christians who believe that the dynamics of the common life, personal and social, can only be grasped and interpreted at its deeper levels theologically — although it has only rarely, so far, been so articulated in regard to contemporary globalization.[11] This second view of the globalizing ethos also recognizes the centrality of Creation, Fall, and Redemption, but it sees

---

9. In fact, the creation of these new international institutions, like that of the United Nations in politics, can be seen as the nascent, if still weak and underdeveloped, efforts to bring world economic interactions under agreed upon principles of just law after the end of colonialism, with its imposition of national laws on many regions, and for purposes such as aiding poorer countries and aiding development.

10. Columbia University economist Jagdish Bhagwati takes up these charges one by one and summarizes the data of the many studies that have (some reluctantly, others enthusiastically) refuted them. See his *In Defense of Globalization* (New York: Oxford University Press, 2004). In brief, where the dynamics of globalization are embraced, as in China, India, Brazil, Peru, etc., they dramatically raise the standards of living more pervasively and rapidly than at any other time in history. Further, they create new middle classes at astounding rates, the most remarkable economic result of globalization, although it is also true that they create (at least temporarily) greater ranges of inequality between those who benefit greatly and those who do less. Those parts of the world that remain in poverty usually do not have the kind of ethos that fosters change, the formation of a civil society distinct from kinship and one-party political institutions. The ethical issue this data raises is whether the reduction of poverty can and should override the ethical ideal of local communal or national identity and thus whether agents of globalization should continue to introduce those religious, ethical, and material options that bring with them transformation, the prospect of participation in the global community, and increased opportunity for many even if not for all.

11. This view is more often held by believing laity than by clergy, but a few theologians have seriously grappled with these issues in a systematic way. Among the new, creative works in this area, see especially: David Hollenbach, S.J., *The Global Face of Public Faith: Politics, Human Rights, and Christian Ethics* (Washington, DC: Georgetown University Press, 2003), who is in dialogue with official Catholic and Ecumenical statements; William Schweiker, *Theological Ethics and Global*

them in another aspect. This view is alert to the fact that humans inevitably distort the gifts that God gives humanity. Thus, it recognizes globalization's obvious ambiguities. Yet it sees the chief forms of sin not in the use of legitimate coercive power by political authority, nor in the development of instrumental reason in advanced modern technology, nor in the operations of a market-oriented economic system, nor in the organization of corporations. Rather, they are found in the wanton violence, ignorance, scarcity, poverty, and mistrust that occurs when these spheres of life are not present or are not guided by a religiously and ethically shaped civil society, a regulated system of just law, and a hope for a better world beyond the wrongs and evils of history.

In spite of the fact that politics, technology, and economy are sometimes distorted and misused, this view sees society and history as also influenced by moral and spiritual realities so that we can rejoice when the frequency and severity of wrong is reduced, some persistent evils are at least partly overcome, and some measure of good is done. Further, while believing that in Christ, a new age has begun that points toward Redemption, most of social life is lived in the midst of conditions that remain sinful, broken, and distorted, from which neither confessing churches nor radical movements are exempt. Thus, most of Christian Ethics has to do with how to live in the "in-between" times, where providential grace sustains civilized life in ways that reduce drudgery, want, pain, suffering, injustice, and premature death, and points toward the possibility of a fulfilled salvific grace already begun yet still to come to fruition.[12] In the meantime, one of the tasks of theology is to work with philosophy, science, and social analysis to form and sustain the moral architecture of civil society.

Dynamics (London: Blackwell Publishing, 2004), who is in dialogue with contemporary philosophy and hermeneutics; Amos Yong and P. G. Heltzel, *Theology in a Global Context* (London: T & T Clark, 2004), which is in dialogue with the philosophy or religion; and Leonardo Boff, *Global Civilization: Challenges to Society and Christianity* (London: Equinox Publishers, 2005), who is in dialogue with the Liberationist movements of Latin America. My own perspective is also influenced by dialogue with the sociology of religion.

12. This view is often called "Christian Realism" and was articulated by Reinhold Niebuhr in the crisis of the mid-twentieth century when both the neopagan Nazis and the militantly secular Communists threatened the world and neither confessional nor radical Christian stances were unable to challenge them effectively on the ground. See especially his *The Nature and Destiny of Man*, 2 vols. (New York: Chas. Scribner's Sons, 1939–41). There is a current revival of his thought today.

The ever-present evils are mitigated when humans are enabled to use the gifts they are given: the story of creation, as we saw in chapter 3, tells us that humanity is stamped with the divine image, commanded to have dominion over the earth, and given the capabilities that allow the cultivation of its incomplete possibilities. The residual capacities to reason, choose, and care (*intellectus, voluntas*, and *caritas*) remain part of each person's potential and can be nurtured by a sound faith and an open, flourishing civil society, so as to make the quest for truth, the principles of freedom, and the relative possibilities of justice more actual in the common life. Moreover, this view holds that God, the source and object of that faith, is ultimately the Lord of history, and God's expansive, providential grace anchors human existence in covenanted communities and vocational commitments. The church particularly is called to preach, teach, and cultivate this grace, so that all can live in a viable ethos able to sustain a viable civilization and foment the possibilities of a more abundant and just society. Although it recognizes that some modernizers repudiate religion or theology, it views them as a modern form of "flat earth" thinking, plagued by an incapacity to imagine the heights and depths of mind, heart, and affection.[13]

This view draws on the Bible and religiously sympathetic social theory to identify those paradigmatic events and developments that allow us to interpret contemporary history.[14] When applied to an understanding of globalization, this view reminds us that when Greek cultural influence, Roman political rule, and vast networks of trade connected Europe to both Asia and Africa, the first proto-globalized civilization was formed. In God's providence, that is when the Christian movement was formed and began to expand,

---

13. See William F. Storrar et al., eds., *Public Theology for the 21st Century* (London: T & T Clark, 2004).

14. This view tends to draw more from Max Weber than from Karl Marx. It does so because Weber took religion seriously as a causative factor in social, political, and economic ethics, and not only as a product of social forces, magic, myth, or interests. Moreover, he studied the major religions and ideologies on a comparative basis and held that they were, more or less, rational systems. Yet, he held that different ones had differing effects on social life because the assumptions behind their rationality and the constituencies to which they appealed shaped the way reason was deployed. It is true that he thought the modernity toward which Protestantism led inclined us to secularism, but he also foresaw the possible resurgence of religion — as now seems to be the case around the world. In one sense it can be said that many theologians and Christian ethicists studying globalization take key elements from Weber much in the same way as earlier parts of the tradition selectively adopted and baptized Aristotle.

extending once-tribal boundaries of covenantal bonding, renewing the understanding of the universal moral law and offering a new vision of God's salvific purposes, now open to all the peoples of the world. The life, teaching, death, and resurrection of Jesus were taken as evidence that God's Kingdom was inaugurated, providentially working in the hearts of persons and in the very fabric of social history. It oriented then and it orients now all who would attend to the vision of a complex, comprehending and holy civilization, a New Jerusalem on the far side of history to which all nations could bring their gifts — the divinely intended end for humanity to which all may contribute.[15] Christianity formed on this basis not only affirms a universal moral law, it transforms the inner structure of every person and society it encounters and orients all of life toward a new, trans-natural *telos*. Until that ultimate promise is fulfilled, personal meaning and human society are sustained by providential grace, even in the face of wrong and evil.

In such a view of history, it is possible to see the impetus for several ethical dynamics that became decisive in forming the moral and spiritual bases of today's globalization. For one thing, these developments substantively shaped other parts of the world — the early Greek church shaped all of Eastern Orthodoxy, and through it Slavic civilization, as the Roman tradition shaped Catholic Europe and Latin America, and as the Reformation did much of Northern Europe and America. Beyond the West, various missionary movements not only converted souls and planted churches, but also spread modern educational systems, medical care, ideas of the equality of men and women and all races before God (and gradually also in church and society),[16] and the notion of inalienable rights (which also entailed the freedom of religion, the rights of speech, assembly, and association), constitutional democracy, a

---

15. Bob Goudzwaard et al., *Globalization and the Kingdom of God* (Grand Rapids: Baker Books, 2001).

16. See, in terms of the contemporary implications of these movements in global developments, e.g., Robert W. Hefner, *Conversion to Christianity* (Berkeley: University of California Press, 1995) (with special focus on the Islamic world in Malaysia/Indonesia). Cf. David Martin, *Tongues of Fire: The Explosion of Protestantism in Latin America* (Oxford: Blackwell, 1990); Philip Jenkins, *The Next Christendom: The Coming of Global Christianity* (New York: Oxford University Press, 2002), regarding Africa; and David Aikman, *Jesus in Beijing: How Christianity is Transforming China and Changing the Balance of Power in the World* (New York: Regnery, 2003).

culture conditioned by open use of the media and communication systems, technological innovation, and economic opportunity — all taken by those who hold to this theology of history as signs of God's continuing and expansive grace.[17] These, after many centuries of slow and widely resisted development, formed a new ethos by providing the moral and spiritual architecture for the complex and dynamic civilizational transformations now on the horizon.[18] Some leaders of other religions (some Muslims, Buddhists, Hindus and tribalists, for example) who are hostile to the effects of modernization and globalization on their own society are not entirely wrong when they blame it on Christianity and its ethics. The implication of this brief sketch of Christianity's influence on societies, often unintentional, is that once we become aware of unintended consequences of the faith, that faith may have to take upon itself the responsibility of forming and informing an emergent global civilization ethically in an intentional way with a new consciousness of its encounter with other religions and cultures.

The deeper historical evidence suggests that the classic Roman Catholic, Reformation, and, now, the newer Evangelical and Pentecostal traditions tend to generate an ethos that foments modernization, a fact that is arguably traceable to a basic attitude toward the duty to convert souls, societies, and gain stewardly dominion over the ecosphere in a fallen world. However, for this to take place, people must be free to change or modify their religion, their culture, their society, and their environment. To insist that one must

---

17. I traced the historical background of many of these developments in my *Creeds, Society, and Human Rights, A Study in Three Cultures* (Grand Rapids: Eerdmans, 1984) in comparison with developments in Eastern Europe and South Asia. For a new, compelling study of how direct the influence of Christian ideas were see John Nurser, *For all Peoples and All Nations: The Ecumenical Church and Human Rights* (Washington, DC: Georgetown University Press, 2005), which traces in great detail the ways in which the development of the United Nations Declaration of Human Rights was essentially driven by Christian thinkers with Jewish support, drawing on deep traditions, supported by para-church NGOs working behind the scenes from the 1930s on. And recently, with Lawrence Stratton, I have written a bibliographical essay calling attention to the growing body of research that challenges the conventional secular views of these developments and documents the theological influences on them: *Capitalism, Civil Society, Religion and the Poor* (Wilmington, DE: ISI, 2002).

18. See John Witte Jr. et al., *Sharing the Book: Religious Perspectives on the Rights and Wrongs of Proselytism* (Maryknoll, NY: Orbis Books, 1999). Cf. Lalsangkima Pachuau et al., *News of Boundless Riches: Interrogating and Reconstructing Missions in a Global Era* (Delhi: ISPCK, forthcoming).

remain in the context of the ethnic group into which one is born, or be obedient to fixed social ontocracy, or to a pre-given cultural, political, or racial pattern of life leads to a lie in the soul, a repression of the capacities to reason, choose, and form affectional bonds, and often to the formation of new fundamentalist movements to secure local and static identity.[19] If conversion is successful, it forms new associations and creates the social space for a civil society wherein people develop their own institutions and leadership, seek to influence the hearts of others, reform the ethics of public institutions, and openly debate the truth and relevance of the first principles of justice and the ultimate ends of life.

The development of a pluralist civil society was aided in the West by the little-known history behind the development of the modern corporation. The formation of ecclesiastical organizations that fought for and eventually won the rights to hold property and engage in production and trade outside the control of the patriarchs of the family and the grasp of the princes established the precedents for both nonprofit and business corporations.[20] In a long history, these have became the primary organizational home of complex social and economic activities in modern and now global life. They took root first in the European cities of the middle ages and the Renaissance/Reformation periods, as a wide variety of autocephalous bodies were formed.[21] Some became universities or hospitals, some took the form of proto-democratic organizations (elected town governments and populist lay movements), and some evolved into limited liability, trustee-guided, for-profit economic organizations.[22] These supported concepts of basic rights, governance under law, and the cultivation of civic virtues. They evoked wider

---

19. See the multi-volumed series edited by Martin Marty and Scott Appleby, as a part of the cross-cultural studies "The Fundamentalism Project." The overview volume is *Fundamentalism Comprehended* (Chicago: University of Chicago Press, 2004). It is argued that Fundamentalism is much the same in all the world's religions and frequently forms itself in resistance to historical change and cultural or ethnic pluralism.

20. See, especially, H. J. Berman, *Law and Revolution* 2 vols. (Cambridge, MA: Harvard University Press, 1983, 2003).

21. This development was earlier (c. 1914) charted by Max Weber in "The City," the last section of his massive *Economy and Society,* trans. G. Roth and C. Wittich (New York: Bendminster Press, 1968), in a way that Berman thinks needs revision.

22. See my "The Moral Roots of the Corporation," *Theology and Public Policy* 5, no. 1 (1993): 29–39.

reflections on the doctrines of covenant and vocation, and applied them to daily life.[23]

Moreover, the impetus to change the world by the use of the "mechanical arts" gave rise to modern technology. That impetus came from the doctrines of protology and eschatology, but became a part of providential thought. Nature was interpreted as fallen, needing repair and development to be what God intended it to be. The intention in religiously cultivating these arts was, however, not only the restoration of the basic "original design," corrupted in the fall, but it became also (especially under the influence of the Joachite movement) the formation of a more just and abundant society, one that reduced the drudgery of the many and pointed toward, even if it could not attain, the hoped-for vision of the New Jerusalem.[24] While every civilization has had its scientists and philosophers of nature, it is essentially in a Christian environment, driven by these concerns, that technology in its modern forms was theologically driven, and that it not only shaped the Industrial Revolution, but altered communications, medicine, production, education, transportation, and produced, more recently, bio-engineering and geo-engineering.[25] The ethical consequence of these developments is that many in Christian-influenced cultures see it as a moral mandate to form pluralistic societies with many kinds of institutional spheres, to establish and defend constitutional democracies with guarantees of human rights, and to develop open market economies and the technological capacity to produce wealth and manage the ecosphere.

There have been frighteningly ambiguous effects of each one of these developments, all of which, cumulatively, are the progenitors of globalization. The frightening possibilities appear, many Christians say, when humans begin to think that they are sovereign

---

23. For the historic impact of the biblical concept of covenant over the centuries, see Elazar, *The Covenant Tradition in Politics, Society and Religion.*

24. On this see note 11, above, and especially David Noble, *The Religion of Technology: The Divinity of Man and the Spirit of Invention* (New York: Penguin, 1999). Some of his interpretations are controverted, but the work contains a suggestive review of historic sources on this thesis. For a similar argument from a cross-cultural point of view, see Toby Huff, *The Rise of Early Modern Science: Islam, China, and the West* (New York: Cambridge University Press, 1993).

25. These themes are artfully summarized in Brad Allenby, *Observations on the Philosophic Implications of Earth Systems Engineering and Management* (Charlottesville, VA: Batten Institute, University of Virginia, 2002). See also David Landes, *Revolution in Time* (Cambridge, MA: Belknap Press, 1983).

over life and do not see the capacities to develop these possibilities as under God's laws and for Godly purposes. While reforms, constraints, and limits must be put on a number of them, they are, at base, seen in this view as a manifestation of the expansive, providential grace that needs to be shared with those presently left out, helping them become prepared for these dynamic changes and inviting them to bring resources from their own traditions and cultures to enrich and refine them. Constitutional democracy, human rights, the corporation as part of civil society, and technology are among the contemporary worldly carriers of the secondary, often unintended, effects of the Christian ethical vision, socially incarnated.[26]

Thus, Globalization as Mission

Indeed, globalization fed by these developments may well be the new form of missions, a mandate for our time to invite all the peoples of the world to become participants in a global civil society that is marked by the empowerment of the people in these ways. The church and its leadership will probably have to recover its memory in these areas, critically evaluate where these developments have gone wrong due to distorted theological and ethical influences or the arrogant denial of them, and take responsibility for the consequences of its own doctrines and actions in so far as this is so. It may have to consciously prepare the people in the pews to face and become partners in the moral guidance of new developments in these areas. These are all basically consistent with the expectation that there can be, in these areas, under God's providence, degrees of progress in humanity's increasingly common history. The fact that globalizing developments have been shaped by Christian theological roots means that they probably cannot be understood, modified, resisted, or ethically extended on a global scale without seeing them as in need of continuous theological and ethical critique and guidance.[27]

26. One of the pioneering arguments along this line was made by Arend T. Van Leewen (in contrast to the anti-modern works of Jacques Ellul) in his *Christianity in World History* (London: Edinburgh House, 1964).

27. See John Atherton, *Public Theology for Changing Times* (London: SPCK, 2000).

This is not to say that Christianity is without political implications. While it has at times adapted itself to Caesar, to feudal lords, to "Holy Roman Emperors" and to modern nationalism, its deeper theological impetus is toward a constitutional republic with a separation of church and state, a defense of the freedom of religion, guarantees of human rights, and both an economy and government under just laws.[28] We can see this in ancient but decisive battles between rulers and bishops, the formation of ecumenical councils and representative synods able to challenge popes and emperors, the development of constitutional government out of canon law, and the formation of congregations, orders and denominations that gradually won the right to exist, to elect their own leaders, and to advocate their own ideas. Religion, in other words, fomented social movements in which convinced people began to take independent actions in all spheres of life, including politics and economics, to shape the common ethos and to filter out both imperialism and sectarianism. This is what has built the inner foundations of democracy from the center out, from the bottom up, and around the world, and not from the top down. This view of the indirect but highly influential political implications of the faith is supported by the fact that theories of "subsidiarity" have modulated hierarchy, and "federations" of particular groups have linked once-exclusive "covenantal" societies. Indeed, over the centuries, these two models of social order — hierarchical/subsidiary and federal/covenantal — have become the two major Christian forms of social theory with deep roots and long-range implications.[29]

---

28. The current state of the discussion on this matter can be found in John Witte Jr., ed., *Christianity and Democracy in Global Context* (Boulder, CO: Westview Press, 1993); Daniel Philpott, *Revolutions in Sovereignty* (Princeton, NJ: Princeton University Press, 2001); and J. D. Carlson and E. C. Owens, eds., *The Sacred and the Sovereign* (Washington, DC: Georgetown University Press, 2003). For the most part, the understanding of Christianity as fomenting a democratic republic stands in partial conflict with the French revolutionary (and Russian and Chinese revolutionary) understanding of democracy, which repudiates the influence of religion.

29. This, I think, has become a part of Catholic teaching in the Social Encyclicals of the twentieth century, and is in many documents of Vatican II and the teachings of Pope John Paul II's encyclicals on faith and social issues that bear on globalization. In *Centesimus Annus* and *Veritatis Splendor,* as well as in shorter statements and letters, such as his "Address to the United Nations General Assembly" (1982), he embraces democracy and capitalism in ways that fit the emerging doctrine of "subsidiary" view of society. Further, he gives "unconditional" support to ideas of human rights as parts of the Christian approach to society and the quest for peace, while clearly holding that these must be guided by a profound theological rootage that is shaped

On the whole, I think the weight of evidence presses us to see the Providential Grace view as the most realistic and most faithful theology of history, although those of us who hold it have not abolished sin, and need the constant reminders of the perils and difficulties that attend great civilizational shifts. Those who hold the view of "Another Fall," thus, can be seen as specialized vocational "orders" in the whole catholic faith, warning lest the faith in its engagement with culture lose itself in enculturated loyalties. They remind the core, ecumenical faith that the burden of change often falls on the weaker segments of the population, and that the bearers of a transformative ethic must attend to the damage done among them. Further, it contributes the institutional insight that there must be a separation between church and state (and, for that matter, mosque and state, temple and state, Caesar and God), even if precisely that institutional separation allows ethical influence to flow from religious community into the fabric of civil society and from there into public polity and policy. In this regard, the Another Fall view stands as a resident critic, issuing warnings that must be taken seriously, but not embraced as the whole picture, since it has no reconstructive theory of society as a whole.

There is no reversing the tides of history at its deepest levels, if one believes that God's providential grace is more powerful and significant than the human sinful betrayals of that grace that rightly demand repentance and reform at the level of managing the arks of social life on the surface of the tides. Political democracy, human rights, an open economy, a nurturing family system, a vibrant culture and deeply committed professionalism cannot save humanity ultimately; and their presence does not mean that the New Jerusalem is at hand; but if they are ordered in a subsidiary or covenantal way, they are likely to give a grace filled life in a way that points toward salvation. This view suggests that it may be possible to influence and channel the energy of this massive civilizational shift called globalization so that it more nearly corresponds to the ultimately redemptive tides of history God intends, and not only critique or to resist it hopelessly. If so, we must all recover and reinvigorate

by grace. Protestant theologies of society that include accents on human rights and a transforming ecumenical vision more often draw on the federal/covenantal perspective than the hierarchical/subsidiary one, but there are increasing areas of overlap. See, for example, James Skillen et al., *Political Order and the Plural Structure of Society* (Atlanta: Scholars Press, 1991).

the attention to first principles of right and wrong that we all, more or less, know, engage and debate about what the ultimate ends are that we should seek, and consciously seek to plow these into the flow and structures of history. The agenda is before us. May God give us the insight and grace to know and do what we can as good stewards of what possibilities lie before us.

In short, a Christian Public Theology has several motifs that indicate the globalization of ethics:

1. The created world is good, although creation and all in it has become distorted and broken.

2. History is lived in the tension between the way things are, and both the first principles of right and the ultimate ends that God intends for humanity and the world which we can come to know.

3. In that context, Christians interpret historical developments and civilizational shifts in terms of repeated "falls" into error and sin, but more profoundly in terms of God's providential grace.

4. Living in this condition, we can understand how it is that the Messiah, the New Adam, the one who actualizes prophethood, priesthood, and kingship, has come and renewed the covenant that promises salvation. On the cross and by resurrection he defeated the power of death and put all the rebellious powers under the power of God, although they writhe in their bonds.

5. We can understand that globalization involves error, destruction, and sin, but it also rests on and evolves good, reconstructing and transforming Grace — and thus it invites a vision that it anticipates in serious measure: an ultimate destiny symbolized as an inclusive heavenly city, the image of a complex and holy civilization which comes to us by grace.

6. Globalization is, thus, a form of creational and providential grace coming to a catholic and ecumenical partial fulfillment that points us toward a salvific vision for humanity and the world.

Those who grasp this vision may be called to become agents of God's Reign in all areas of the common life, and channel all the powers of life toward the new possibilities, which are even now breaking into time, by drawing them into covenanted communities of commitment. A dynamic Christian Ethics, inevitably synthetic and in need of reformation, is being globalized in manifest ways. Such a vision is part of the faith and a manifestation of God's love for the world.

Index